Surviving the Baby Boomer Exodus

Capturing Knowledge for Gen X and Gen Y Employees

Ken Ball and Gina Gotsill

Course Technology PTR
A part of Cengage Learning

COURSE TECHNOLOGY
CENGAGE Learning™

Australia, Brazil, Japan, Korea, Mexico, Singapore, Spain, United Kingdom, United States

COURSE TECHNOLOGY
CENGAGE Learning™

Surviving the Baby Boomer Exodus
Ken Ball and Gina Gotsill

Publisher and General Manager, Course Technology PTR: Stacy L. Hiquet

Associate Director of Marketing: Sarah Panella

Manager of Editorial Services: Heather Talbot

Marketing Manager: Mark Hughes

Acquisitions Editor: Mitzi Koontz

Project and Copy Editor: Marta Justak

Interior Layout: Shawn Morningstar

Cover Designer: Luke Fletcher

Indexer: Kelly Talbot

Proofreader: Melba Hopper

Printed in the United States of America
1 2 3 4 5 6 7 12 11 10

For product information and technology assistance, contact us at
**Cengage Learning Customer & Sales Support,
1-800-354-9706.**

For permission to use material from this text or product, submit all requests online at
cengage.com/permissions.

Further permissions questions can be e-mailed to **permissionrequest@cengage.com**.

All trademarks are the property of their respective owners.

All images © Cengage Learning unless otherwise noted.

Library of Congress Control Number: 2010922085
ISBN-13: 978-1-4354-5512-2
ISBN-10: 1-4354-5512-6

Course Technology, a part of Cengage Learning
20 Channel Center Street
Boston, MA 02210
USA

Cengage Learning is a leading provider of customized learning solutions with office locations around the globe, including Singapore, the United Kingdom, Australia, Mexico, Brazil, and Japan. Locate your local office at: **international.cengage.com/region**.

Cengage Learning products are represented in Canada by Nelson Education, Ltd. For your lifelong learning solutions, visit **courseptr.com**. Visit our corporate Web site at **cengage.com**.

For my parents, my most loyal readers.
And for my husband Chris, my favorite editor.

—GINA

For Sharon, my precious partner in life and
Chief Encouragement Officer. It's a good day when I get
a little of her goodness and honesty on me.

—KEN

Gina Gotsill's Acknowledgments

Special thanks to the taxpayers for funding the Census Bureau, the Bureau of Labor Statistics, and other organizations that study and document who we are and what we do, and to all the people across the United States who shared their stories with us. I would also like to thank the Texas Department of Information Resources, the County of Fairfax, Virginia Department of Human Resources, the South Carolina Office of Human Resources, and The Conference Board for their generous contributions to our research and work.

Endless gratitude to Vic Passion, whose insight and friendship during the writing process gave me energy and always sparked new ideas. Thanks also to Steven Laine, Meryl Natchez, Shari McAneney, and the TechProse team for supporting this effort.

Love and thanks to my husband Chris and my parents Esther and Aldo, Jim and Sharon, and Joe and Patricia; my Nana, aunts, uncles, cousins, and friends Pam, Shannon, Matty, Janet, Joanne, Leslie, Lorena, Michele, and Cris. You all took time to listen; some of you even sat around the kitchen table with me and helped me find my way. Thank you!

Of course, this book would not have been possible without our editors Mitzi Koontz and Marta Justak. Thank you for your gracious support and guidance throughout the process. Thanks also to my teachers at San Francisco State, UC Berkeley, and the Poynter Institute for sharing your knowledge (and preferences and quirks) with me.

KEN BALL'S ACKNOWLEDGMENTS

Gratitude is something I've been learning about recently. There's a Japanese psychology that explores the illusion that we somehow live independently of others. The reality is otherwise—we are completely dependent on others. To realize how totally we are supported by others is to begin living a life based on being grateful to most anyone we interact with.

Bringing this book to fruition has been a matter of relying on the support of the genuine leaders in the fields of generational studies and knowledge retention who provided early encouragement. And we are grateful to all the creative, engaged practitioners of knowledge sharing we interviewed at the organizations where there is deep thinking about knowledge retention and where they are doing something, even small *somethings*, about it.

Thanks to Martine Edwards, a colleague and friend from our IDG Books days when we enjoyed the sweet ride of success of the ... *For Dummies* books. It was Martine to whom I sent a magazine article about Boomers and business continuity. She graciously sent it on to a colleague at Cengage Learning who acquires business books; one has to acknowledge that Martine had a very direct hand in making this book a reality.

Larry Wilson at Knowledge Harvesting challenges us with his extraordinary ability to unravel the mysteries of tacit knowledge. He has been greatly helpful in our understanding of the distinctions among explicit, implicit, and tacit types of knowledge.

Mary Young of the Conference Board and Denise Lee of Johns Hopkins University were generously there, each and every time we emailed or called to ask for help or to get answers to puzzling questions. Their patience has been appreciated.

Gail Trugman-Nikol, Jerry Landon, and Frank Tortorici were generous, too. Each helped by cheerfully sending reports, questionnaires, and articles with uncanny timing for those occasions when we really needed material to support our discussion topic.

Thanks to Larry Prusak, one of the giants in the knowledge field. Learned, wise, a successful author, and a guy who kept reminding us, in such a disarming and straightforward way, that knowledge sharing is just about people getting together to talk and listen to each other.

Steven Laine, president of TechProse, has been yet another generous contributor to our effort. He gave Gina and me the gift of time and space to judiciously get the interviews and writing done, all the while performing our day jobs.

And Marta Justak, our editor, whose trenchant analysis challenged us chapter by chapter to make each one better than what we already thought was pretty darned good. There's nothing quite like an editor when it comes to handing out reality sandwiches. Thanks to Mitzi Koontz, our acquisitions editor, who generously suffered our never-ending questions about contracts, deadlines, and permissions, and was so helpful in pulling us to the finish line.

So you may have noticed a theme: the generosity of others. Lest we express it too lightly, a warm hug of thanks and gratitude.

ABOUT THE AUTHORS

Ken Ball is a Baby Boomer and has been closely following aging in the workplace with curiosity for several years. At TechProse, the consulting firm where he does business development, Ken tracks knowledge and content management, including training and documentation, for major U.S. clients. He has more than 30 years of experience in corporate sales and marketing, including years in the book publishing business, working for IDG Books, publishers of the ...*For Dummies* computer and general reference books. Ken's most recent publication was an article in the Nov.–Dec. 2008 edition of *Continuity Insights* magazine called "Prepping Your Company for the Baby Boomer Exodus." He has a B.S. in Marketing–Speech Communications from Bradley University.

Gina Gotsill is a Gen X writer with degrees in journalism from San Francisco State University and University of California, Berkeley. She is also a fellow of the Poynter Institute, a journalism think tank based in St. Petersburg, Florida. Gina has covered a wide range of business topics that include keeping Boomer skills in the workplace, teaching finance to non-finance professionals, and growth and change in urban and suburban business districts.

TABLE OF CONTENTS

Chapter 3
Knowledge in the Workplace   41

Chapter 4
Trouble on the Horizon as Boomers Step Away 69

Chapter 5
Boarding the Knowledge Train   87

Chapter 6
Knowledge Retention by Design   137

Chapter 7
Ready, Set, Develop!   197

Chapter 8
Rolling Out Your Knowledge
Transfer Program   205

Chapter 9
A Long View of Evaluation   223

Chapter 10
Nurturing a Knowledge Culture   241

Bibliography   255

Index   259

INTRODUCTION

For some managers, the thought of losing a valued, longtime worker to retirement is enough to keep them up at night. When you research Baby Boomers and their impact on the workplace, you begin to hear stories about sleepless nights and hand-wringing. You also hear about managers who have had to pick up the phone, call a recent retiree, and essentially ask them what they need to do to keep their business running. In many organizations, longtime workers are critical to business continuity—they know the business and clientele so well that when they leave, things just aren't the same.

News stories published over the last few years have underscored how even one key employee's departure can create a headache for managers. The coverage highlighted what was really walking out the door: not just a longtime worker, but years of experience and knowledge. In many cases, skilled workers who left had unique, singular knowledge of a job, role, or function. This book took shape as we immersed ourselves in the Baby Boomer phenomenon, and asked ourselves and others how this generation's numbers could have an effect on the workplace as they move toward retirement.

A Common Sense Approach to a Complex Problem

The Boomer phenomenon fascinated us but so did Knowledge Management. We knew that KM has had a history of failure for a garden basket full of reasons. We also knew that Boomers, Gen X, and Gen Y bring distinct styles and influences to the workplace, and that these differences play an important role in how knowledge is captured and transferred. We knew about these generational differences because we, the authors, were born in different eras. Ken is a Boomer and Gina is a Gen Xer. The two of us have distinct working and learning styles, and we attribute at least some of those differences to the era we were born in and the way we learned and received knowledge in our early lives.

This book merges these three concepts: the Boomer phenomenon, generational distinctions and learning preferences, and the way these workplace trends influence knowledge capture and transfer. This is not an academic book; rather, it's a practical guide that provides a common sense approach to capturing and transferring Boomer knowledge in a multigenerational workplace, while forging a collaborative knowledge culture in the process.

Our approach focuses on five basic steps:

- Analysis
- Design
- Development
- Implementation
- Evaluation

We leveraged the knowledge and expertise of our employer, TechProse, to write much of this book. Founded by Meryl Natchez, TechProse has provided training, change management, communications, project management, and technical writing services to major U.S. companies for nearly 30 years. We also looked outside our organization and spoke to real-world companies and leaders about how they made knowledge capture and transfer work in their organizations. Each organization we spoke to had its own reasons for implementing a knowledge retention program. For some, Boomer retirements posed a tremendous threat to business continuity. For others, building an inclusive knowledge culture, where everyone freely shared their knowledge, connected teams in a new way. Regardless of their reasons, we can all learn from how these organizations mobilized to hang on to valuable knowledge.

What We Learned

Sure there are managers who can't bear the thought of losing key, longtime workers. But despite the media coverage of Boomers and how a tidal wave of retirements could impact business, many senior managers are kicking the can down the road and putting off the job of creating a system and process for capturing knowledge. We also found that many organizations don't have a culture that values the knowledge that veteran workers have cultivated over their long careers. For the past hundred years in American industry, some managers have held that older workers need to be moved out so that younger troops can be brought in. Managers throw the retiree a going away party, hand that person a gold watch, and get on about the business of bringing the replacement up to speed. This approach could lead to a great deal of deep, tacit knowledge being lost. And if it's not lost for good, it will take money and effort to recover it. Managers can avoid this by taking some steps to prepare for the day when key workers step away. We lay out these steps in the pages that follow.

Our Message

George Santayana, the Spanish American philosopher, famously said: "Those who cannot remember the past are condemned to repeat it." And, of course, that's one of the problems in not ensuring that valuable knowledge is captured. There are many effective, easy-to-use tools today that can be used to capture knowledge and share what is important with those that follow. But is all knowledge valuable? You know, without reading this book, that the answer is no. But we submit that business continuity depends on transferring knowledge that is valuable, even critical, to your organization. In fact, we believe that effective knowledge transfer can provide a competitive advantage for companies that invest in even a modest effort to bring people of different ages and experiences together to share what they know.

Who This Book Is For

We wrote this book for leaders, managers, and supervisors who may not have knowledge retention prominent on their radar screens now, but who have the nagging feeling they should start focusing on ways to retain knowledge. We'd like to believe that executives would be curious enough to pick up this book, perhaps for some of the same reasons as managers. Media coverage about Boomer worker demographics is too prevalent to ignore, and many executives have already expressed concern about what retirements could mean to their organizations.

Of course, we all know people who had to postpone their retirements because of the economic crisis that began in 2007. By the time you read this book, the economy may be in an upswing, and your most experienced workers may be getting ready to leave. Now is the perfect time for managers and leaders to launch their knowledge retention efforts. If you have a few years, all the better. Some of the methods we cover, especially those methods around capturing and transferring implicit and tacit knowledge, take time. Success depends on developing deeper connections between people, and these connections can't be forged in a two-day training course or by reading an instructional manual.

Companion Web Site Downloads

This book contains abbreviated versions of a Sample Collective Knowledge Analysis Survey (created by Robbins-Gioia) and of the Project Charter Template (designed by the Texas Department of Information Resources). The complete versions of these documents can be found at www.courseptr.com/downloads.

For more information about TechProse, go to www.techprose.com.

1

When Boomer Brains Walk

The Baby Boomers have been shaking up U.S. culture since they started to arrive in 1946, just months after the final battles of World War II in 1945. Finally home after a long war, servicemen and their families—and others who had put off having children during the Great Depression[1]—began having babies. Lots of babies.

"Everybody was having babies," Lola Weixel recalled in Connie Field's documentary *The Life and Times of Rosie the Riveter*.[2] "After the war, my God, it was like a deluge of babies. When I went to have my first baby, there wasn't even room…people were doing labor in the halls. It was unbelievable. Oh yes, everybody—and her sister—was having a baby."

Between 1946 and 1964, 76 million babies were born. An unprecedented explosion in the U.S. population, the Boomer phenomenon has fascinated analysts, historians, and Boomers themselves for more than 60 years. And there is plenty to be fascinated about. As they entered the world, the sheer number of Boomers overwhelmed hospitals and birthing units, and later schools and colleges. As they grew up, the Boomers challenged traditional mores and social ills, and earned themselves a reputation for being restless, rebellious, and, as time went on, charismatic and influential.

As Boomers grew up and moved into the labor force, they became major players in every industry from hospitality to high-technology (see Figure 1.1).

---

1 This concept represented here: Croker, Richard. *Boomer Century*, Springboard Press, New York. 2007.

2 www.clarityfilms.org.

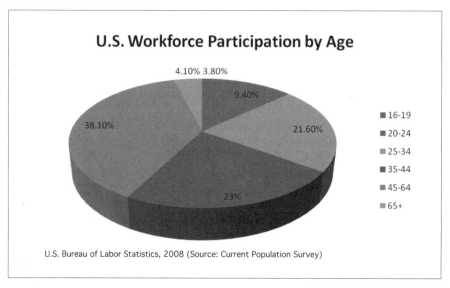

U.S. Workforce Participation by Age

4.10% 3.80%

9.40%

38.10%

21.60%

23%

- 16-19
- 20-24
- 25-34
- 35-44
- 45-64
- 65+

U.S. Bureau of Labor Statistics, 2008 (Source: Current Population Survey)

Figure 1.1   *There are more Boomers in the workforce than any other age group.*

Impending Retirements Raise Tough Questions

Now, as this highly experienced group begins to move toward traditional retirement age, many business leaders are beginning to ask some tough questions. Who will replace Boomers when they leave? And will younger workers have the knowledge and skills to run these organizations when they do? While the economic crisis has kept some Boomers in the workforce longer than they planned, retirement is still just a few years off for many U.S. workers, both in the public and private sectors.

"The economy has definitely had an effect on retirements," said David Kail, who worked in manufacturing for 30 years before becoming a director of a community college program. "People are waiting, but I don't think they'll wait until they are 65, at least not in the manufacturing industry. I think the wave of retirements we heard would happen a few years ago will be compressed—we're likely to see a sharp rise in retirements and not a wave spread over five years."

When retirements do happen, companies in many industries stand to lose what experts say could be significant numbers of highly skilled, tenured workers. But that's not all they'll lose. After years on the job, Boomers have developed valuable, institutional knowledge that many companies depend on—knowledge that would be lost as they step away from the workforce.

Organizations can stem the flow by putting in place initiatives to capture Boomer knowledge and transfer it to the next generations of workers, which would be Generation X and Millennials. Many companies have gone down that road, hoping to hang on to the intellectual capital that Boomers have contributed to organizations over the last several decades. Some have succeeded. Others have failed spectacularly. The reasons for these failures range from technology plans gone awry to half-baked planning to lack of executive buy-in and budget shortfalls.

Help is on the way. In this book, we'll discuss a step-by-step approach to retaining the knowledge that Boomers have developed over their long careers. Leaders will also discover methods for nurturing a knowledge culture where all employees freely share what they know with colleagues—a shift that promotes collaboration and helps ensure that organizations don't face a brain drain in the future.

Think About Your Approach to Transferring Knowledge

The methods companies use to package Boomer knowledge are often poorly conceived. For example, we've all heard of companies that spend thousands of dollars on documentation projects that yield dusty stacks of binders that no one ever uses. Companies must make it easier for younger workers to tap Boomers for knowledge, rather than have Boomers "pontificate down to Gen X and Gen Y," said generational expert and author Tammy Erickson.

"I generally think the model that says Boomers are going to package their wisdom and bestow it on younger generations is doomed out of the gate," Erickson said. "On the other hand, I've done some research that shows Ys, in particular, are thrilled if they can tap Boomer expertise around problems that are important to them. So, it's not a situation where the Boomer lays down the law and says, 'Here's how a job needs to be done.' Instead, younger workers can go to Boomers if they run into problems and need help."

Companies face major challenges as Boomers inch closer to retirement. First, how do you capture the knowledge in someone's head? And, once you succeed, how do you package it for Generations X and Y, two groups who aren't comfortable learning the same way that Boomers did during the 1950s, 60s, and 70s? Here's the other elephant in the room that makes finding the right approach even more critical: Once you have captured Boomers' knowledge, is their any guarantee the next generation will want it?

Why Act Now?

As Boomers move toward retirement, managers are finding a few parallel issues that require their attention. First, many, if not most, organizations employ three or more generations of workers. While exceptions apply, each generation has its own way of communicating, learning, and working (involving styles and preferences), all issues that keep human resources and training departments on their toes. Technology also plays a huge role in the workforce, as the use of technology increasingly influences how people communicate, learn, and work. All of these factors shape the knowledge retention efforts of organizations.

Second, organizations have learned that transferring knowledge from one person to another, especially when each has a different learning style and technological ability, takes time.

Pratt & Whitney Rocketdyne, a rocket engine provider, is a good example of an organization that has put in the time necessary to create a long-term knowledge transfer plan that will carry the company into the future. Like many organizations, Pratt & Whitney Rocketdyne faces losing valuable knowledge as its Boomer workforce inches toward retirement. And, like others, the company is looking for new ways to transfer this knowledge to the next generation of workers.

Pratt & Whitney Rocketdyne knew it had a problem in the late 1990s when leaders looked at workforce statistics and noted that the average age of scientists and engineers was 55. An organization with little turnover, many of these highly skilled workers had 25 to 30 years of experience working with the company's rocket component systems. These were the professionals who developed the main engines for the U.S. Space Shuttle, NASA's vehicle for space exploration, and the amount of knowledge they had amassed during their careers was irreplaceable. And, while the company recruited promising new hires from top colleges each year, these new workers lacked the experience of more seasoned professionals. Soon company leaders made another discovery: These new workers wanted to learn in a whole new way and weren't interested in receiving knowledge and information in classroom settings the way their Boomer colleagues had. They wanted a more interactive learning environment, a request that caught company leaders off guard.

The subject matter also posed challenges, according to Chief Knowledge Officer Kiho Sohn. Obviously, rocket engines were complicated systems with many components, and new hires simply didn't have a good grasp of how the engine worked as a whole. They understood the small pieces they were working on, but they didn't have a feel for the fit of the components in the larger scheme of the engine. That did nothing to ensure the retention of the longtime employees' valuable knowledge.

Knowledge management and human resources staff mobilized, and they created a multifaceted knowledge capture and transfer program that retained and shared Boomer knowledge and provided a dynamic and inclusive learning environment for new hires. The program started with a series of lunchtime seminars where longtime employees shared their expertise with colleagues. The company recorded each of the seminars and put them in their knowledge library. But the series went beyond sharing knowledge.

"When newcomers start here, they are often reluctant to knock on the office door of a more senior employee and ask questions," Sohn said. "Having the lunchtime seminars opens up the communication channels and gives newcomers the opportunity to meet and talk with these employees. After the seminars, they are much more comfortable walking up and asking questions or visiting them in their offices."

Knowledge management department leaders also launched mentoring programs and a Knowledge Management Share Fair where employees put up booths and share information about everything from engineering to social networking.

Pratt & Whitney Rocketdyne's program entered its tenth year in 2009 and has given the company a positive way to retain critical, expert knowledge and technical information, which is now available to the next generation of aerospace workers.

Taking Time to Transfer Knowledge

Other companies put in the time at the beginning of a knowledge transfer initiative and then slowly phase it out.

For example, Meryl Natchez, the founder and CEO of TechProse, a small, profitable consulting firm, wanted to retire. After nearly 30 years of running the business, she announced she would be leaving within a year. Her staff, many of whom she had worked with for more than a decade, were surprised by her announcement and said they couldn't imagine the company running without her. After all, she knew more about the business and the industries her company served than anyone else. She also had a long history with many of the company's best clients, and she understood their quirks and changing needs.

Natchez's knowledge was critical to the company's survival, and everybody knew it. Salespeople and recruiters asked for her insight before they spoke to new clients, and marketing staff often turned to her for advice and context. New hires with little experience in the field also vied for her time and attention.

The staff didn't waste any time. For the next year, they worked hard to capture the knowledge that Natchez had in her head. They interviewed her in the car on the way to meetings and in the office when she was available, asking her detailed questions about the company's history and past projects. They saved her comments and insights on the company server, Web site, and database, and they also created maps that helped their staff find critical information. They created a job shadowing plan and paired Natchez with a new hire who could take on some of her responsibilities after she left. The new hire, a Gen Xer who preferred face-to-face interaction with her mentors, took advantage of the time she had with Natchez, and even accompanied her on visits to clients when it was appropriate. After a year on the job, the new hire absorbed a great deal of knowledge on processes and clients. She reached out to Natchez when she needed assistance or guidance, but over time, her contact with Natchez became less frequent.

When all these pieces were in place, the company negotiated a consulting contract that gave them access to Natchez for a few hours a month for the foreseeable future. Then everyone relaxed a bit and looked forward to a prosperous future. Over the next several years, Natchez stepped in as needed and helped the company build its client base in ways that might not have been possible without her knowledge and style.

Seeing Opportunity in a Slumping Economy

The CEO of the consulting firm (detailed in the previous section) is a clear example of a Boomer with unwavering retirement plans. Other Boomers, set back by the economic crisis that began in 2007, have waited to make any big steps toward retirement. Their hesitation caused many managers, who were sweating over upcoming retirements before the crisis, to postpone any big plans to retain Boomer knowledge. As recovery from the financial meltdown continues, some Boomers are planning to stay in their jobs longer, or they're looking for ways to get back into the workforce. The weak economy, high unemployment, and withering job prospects have also kept many young job-hoppers from searching for new work.

The economic meltdown has given leaders and managers a reprieve and an opportunity to craft a knowledge capture and transfer plan that makes sense. Creating a successful knowledge retention plan is similar to making a great meal—both require the right ingredients, time, and a person or group that owns the process. Essential ingredients include executive buy-in and methods for assessing and identifying the kinds of knowledge that exist in the workplace and what the best methods for transferring that knowledge are. Leaders and managers assess which employees have the most critical knowledge and learn about their plans for stepping away.

Another critical ingredient is having a two-sided desire. The knower must be willing to share what he or she has, and the receiver must take the time to absorb and process what is being communicated. The catch is that knowledge, by its very nature, is complex, deeply personal, and in some cases, closely guarded. All these factors create a workforce planning issue that should motivate managers and leaders to begin knowledge retention work now, rather than waiting for the exodus to begin.

Why Should Organizations Transfer Knowledge?

Every manager knows how difficult it can be to replace a longtime employee. Employer surveys have shown that older employees rank higher in their commitment to doing quality work, are loyal to the company, have good basic skills in reading, writing, and arithmetic, can be counted on in a crisis, and have reliable performance records and experience.[3]

Janet Michael, a human resources director for a Northern California insurance company, recalled a meeting with executives regarding longtime salespeople who were considering retirement. The executives told Michael that the company needed a human resources strategy to keep these sales leaders close because they didn't want to risk losing them to retirement.

"I asked them why they were so worried," Michael said. "I told them, 'If they retire, then we'll just find new salespeople. It can't be that hard to replace them.'"

Not so, company executives told the manager. These salespeople had been with the company for years and had close relationships with customers—relationships a new hire couldn't forge without help. Retaining these relationships and transferring them to new hires over time through mentorship programs was crucial to the company's future. Convinced, Michael developed a knowledge transfer and mentoring program to keep valued employees' expertise in the company. She also worked with executives and the company's legal counsel to devise a consulting contract that would keep these employees engaged on a part-time basis once they decided to retire.

Other executives have expressed similar concerns. In 2008, Robert Half International, a staffing services firm, surveyed 150 senior executives with the nation's largest companies and asked them to rate the trends that would most significantly alter the workforce over the next decade.[4]

---

3 AARP, Cummins, Rachelle. "Putting Aging Workforce on Employment Planning Radar: Results from an AARP/Florida Trend Survey." October, 2005.

4 Robert Half International. (Press Release) Baby Boomers Stand Alone. Executives: Baby Boomer Retirements Most Significant Workforce Trend in Next 10 Years. Retrieved January 29, 2009.

Their responses follow:

Baby boomer retirements	47%
Global business interactions	31%
Outsourcing	11%
Remote work arrangements	5%
Other	5%
Don't know	1%

"The looming retirement of baby boomers has captured the attention of business leaders who are concerned about retaining the expertise of their most tenured employees," Max Messmer, chairman and CEO of Robert Half International said in January 2008 when the results of the survey were announced. "Fortunately, many baby boomers are considering working past the traditional retirement age to stay active and continue earning."

Playing the Numbers Game

Demographic trends balance out the anecdotal conversations about Boomers leaving and provide a quantitative wake-up call.

In 2000, BLS economist Arlene Dohm wrote that as the oldest Boomers begin to retire, the implications to the workforce could be enormous.[5] The oldest Boomers turn 65 in 2011; the youngest in 2029. Services in the health care and education sectors are expected to suffer "unless older workers can be retained or other sources of workers can be found," Dohm wrote. And, in some industries, such as manufacturing, where learning curves are often steep, "new workers need to enter these occupations soon, so they can become proficient in the necessary skills" before Boomers leave the workforce.

As the population ages, and as the youngest Boomers reach retirement age, the impact of their exit could be significant. Some industries, especially those where Boomers make up more than 40 percent of the workforce, are expected to suffer more than others (see Figure 1.2). Statistics show that Education and Health Services, Manufacturing, Transportation and Utilities, Public Administration, and Agriculture employ large numbers of Boomer workers. The aerospace industry is also concerned about its aging workforce. In 2008, about 26 percent of aerospace workers became eligible for retirement.[6]

5 Dohm, Arlene. "Gauging the labor force effects of retiring baby-boomers." Bureau of Labor Statistics, *Monthly Labor Review*. July, 2000. pp. 17-25.

6 America's Aerospace Industry: Identifying and Addressing Workforce Challenges. Report of findings and recommendations for the President's High Growth Job Training Initiative in the Aerospace Industry. May, 2005. p. 4.

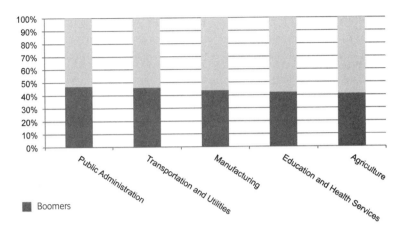

Figure 1.2 *Boomer workers are a stronger force in many industries.*

"Capturing Boomer knowledge is a pressing need in many industries," said Dr. Debby McNichols, an aerospace industry professional who has focused on knowledge transfer between Boomers and Generation X. "Perhaps the economic situation is going to give us a second chance. We really haven't taken advantage of the time we've had so far."

When Will They Retire?

Over the last few years, experts, analysts, and managers have been engaged in a vigorous dialogue over what the workforce will look like when Boomers leave. Some have predicted labor shortages, while others have denied this scenario is possible. Peter Cappelli is one of those voices. A management professor at the Wharton School, Cappelli wrote in a 2003 paper[7] that "studies that foresee labor shortages in the future assume that retirement patterns will be unchanged going forward, that is, that people will retire at the same age even as life expectancy and the ability to work longer go up."

For Cappelli, this is unrealistic, "if for no other reason than financial resources for retirement may not allow it."

The Social Security system anticipates that Boomers will work longer, Cappelli's paper asserts; for example, benefits eligibility age will likely rise to 67 by 2027. Even a small increase in Boomer retirement age, which would keep them in the workforce longer, will affect the labor supply because the

---

7 Cappelli, Peter. "Will There Really Be a Labor Shortage?" *Organizational Dynamics*, Vol. 32, No. 3 2003. pp. 221-233.

group is so large, he said. And the "baby busters," or Generation X, a much smaller group, has already been in the workforce for more than a decade. Generation Y, the "baby boom echo," is following right behind.

"The workforce will be slightly older on average, and that may raise new challenges," Cappelli wrote. "But that is by no means a bad development overall."

Other groups have also questioned that Boomer retirements will rock the boat. In its 2008 report, the Coyne Partnership, Inc. wrote that the "classic retiree," someone who has worked full time and ceases to work entirely, is a shrinking minority of the older population, forming less than 20 percent of the population of 60 year olds.[8]

Indeed, studies have shown that Boomers plan to work past typical retirement age, even if they switch jobs or careers, or demand more flexible hours. There are many reasons for this trend, including boredom with retirement, a desire to remain productive and involved, and longer life expectancies. Forward-thinking organizations are taking advantage of this time and are finding ways to retain these workers' knowledge, rather than waiting until Boomers begin to head out the door, as they inevitably will.

Many Boomers also may not have saved enough money to retire and keep the lifestyle they enjoyed while working. The perfect storm of the housing bust, the weakened economy, and a turbulent stock market led many Boomers to postpone their well-made plans, since their planned investments for retirement were changed.

Beginning in 2007, Boomers—and everyone else—watched their net worth drop as stocks and home values crashed. In 2008, Hewitt Associates, a human resources and outsourcing consulting firm, found that fewer than one in five employees studied will be able to meet 100 percent of their estimated financial needs in retirement.[9] In October 2008, an AARP study survey found that 70 percent of mature workers planned to work into what they viewed as their retirement years. The need for money was the most common reason cited. Then, in the first quarter of 2009, Americans' net worth plunged by $1.3 trillion, according to Federal Reserve data[10]. These economic and social factors suggest that Boomers will not follow the path of some of their predecessors and call it quits at 65.

---

8 The Coyne Partnership, Inc (Media Overview) Smaller Than You Thought: Estimates of the Future Size and Growth Rate of the Retirement Market in the United States. May, 2008.

9 Hewitt Associates. (Press Release) Hewitt Study Reveals Widening Gap Between Retirement Needs and Employee Saving Behaviors. www.hewittassociates.com. Retrieved August 18, 2009.

10 Federal Reserve Statistical Release dated June 11, 2009. Retrieved July 28, 2009.

Economy Is a Major Game Changer

Media coverage of the recession has been relentless. Everywhere people have been talking about lost retirement savings and how many years the crisis has set them back. Economic changes have forced many older workers to rethink retirement and continue to work full time until the economy once again finds its footing. So the popular consensus seems set: Older workers aren't going anywhere, at least for now.

Or are they?

In 2009, the Social Security Administration reported that applications for retired worker benefits from October 2008 to September 2009 had gone up 21 percent over the number of applications for the same period in 2008, about 5 percent more than the administration had expected. An earlier statement by Stephen Goss, chief actuary of the Social Security Administration, attributed the rise in retirement claims to more workers reaching the ages of 62 to 70 and to the economic recession. Goss also reported that there had been a 2.5 percent rise in the number of individuals aged 60 to 69 who were seeking employment than had been expected without a recession. He suggested that this rise might have been a reflection of some older workers seeking to rebuild their personal retirement assets.

The effects of the financial and economic crises on retirement are far from clear, economists Courtney Coile and Phillip Levine wrote in a 2009 report that examined the increase in retirements.[11] They suggested that while many experts would expect losses in equity and home value to keep people in the workforce longer, the weak labor market was forcing some people into retirement.

Coile and Levine's analysis showed that workers with more education between the ages of 62 and 69 make retirement decisions based on long-run fluctuations in the stock market. They also found that labor market conditions play a major role in people's retirement decisions as a whole. When the unemployment rate rises, as it did in June 2009 to 9.7 percent, more workers between the ages of 62 and 69, particularly those with less education, retire. Coile and Levine predicted that the increase in retirement brought about by the rise in unemployment would be almost 50 percent larger than the decrease in retirement brought about by the stock market crash.

---

11 Coile, Courtney C and Levine, Phillip B. The Market Crash and Mass Layoffs: How the Current Economic Crisis May Affect Retirement. National Bureau of Economic Research working paper. June, 2009.

Long before the recession hit, AARP research[12] showed that eight in ten Boomers planned to work at least part time during their retirement; a mere 16 percent said they wouldn't work at all. AARP research also found that in 1999, seven in ten said they could count on IRAs and 401(k)s during retirement; six in ten were counting on savings and investments for retirement income.

There Is No Crystal Ball

Studies, news articles, and data on Boomers' varying behaviors remind us that it will be difficult, if not impossible, to predict with certainty how such a large group will react as they reach retirement age.

"Although commonly viewed as a monolith, the idea of the Baby Boomers as a homogeneous group is more myth than reality," AARP reported in a 1999 analysis[13]. "With its members spanning nearly 20 years of life, Baby Boomers are represented by a wide range of life stages, life experiences, and life values. The temptation to generalize about this generation is likely driven by a compelling need to understand how this huge segment of society will shape the future. Yet, one of the key characteristics of the Baby Boom cohort is its diversity."

Still, Boomers will eventually leave the workforce, and as some companies have already learned, when Boomers retire, they take their expertise, skills, and knowledge with them. Often, older workers accumulate knowledge during many years with the same employer. Statistics show that older workers tend to stay with the same employer longer than their younger counterparts. For example, in 2008, the BLS found that the median tenure for employees aged 55 to 64 years was nearly 10 years, almost four times the tenure (2.7 years) of workers aged 25 to 34.[14] And, as seen in Figure 1.3, substantial percentages of employers feel that older workers bring valuable knowledge, skills, and client and colleague relationships to the workplace.[15]

---

12 AARP and Roper Starch Worldwide Inc. Baby Boomers Envision Their Retirement, an AARP Segmentation Analysis. 1999.

13 AARP and Roper Starch Worldwide Inc. Baby Boomers Envision Their Retirement, an AARP Segmentation Analysis. 1999.

14 United States Department of Labor, Bureau of Labor Statistics. News. Sept. 26, 2008. p. 1.

15 The Center on Aging & Work. 21st Century Age Demographics: Opportunities for Visionary State Leadership. March, 2008. p. 5.

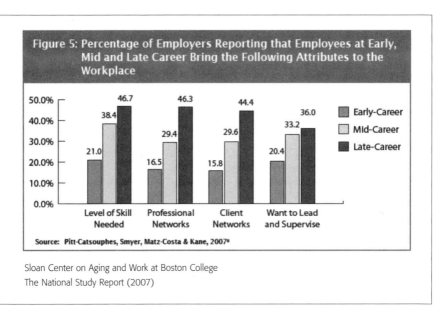

Figure 1.3   *Employers have responded favorably to surveys regarding Boomers' contribution to organizations.*

Taking the First Step

The transit agency's solution (see following sidebar) provides an example of how to refocus the lens through which companies view knowledge capture and transfer. Here, the program was not just about asking Boomers to do a brain dump for the benefit of the next generation. Instead, the program provided opportunities for workers to seek the information they needed, when they needed it.

For the transit industry, it's a high-tech solution to a problem that's not going away.

"People are just beginning to take their pensions in this industry," said Georges Primeau, a transit project manager with more than 20 years in the industry. "Transit is one of the first industries to suffer in this way, and the authorities are expressing a need to share what the old-timers know. These workers do the job the way it should be done—safely and quickly. But one of the problems is that the transit industry tends not to be an up-and-coming contender or very quick to take up new technologies. For the last eight or nine years, everyone has seen this coming. But nobody has really reacted."

Making the Transition

Essentially, some Boomers will leave as planned and some will stay longer than they anticipated. When they will leave and how long they will stay remains a crucial question. Savvy companies are finding the answers to these questions and preparing for the future. Now. They're also considering how younger workers want to receive knowledge, and they are leveraging wikis, blogs, and other Web 2.0 forums to provide just-in-time answers to questions.

Some companies are even moving Boomer knowledge to hand-held devices, a sort of mentor-in-a-pocket, a format that appeals to younger workers. An East Coast transit agency plagued by high turnover and looming retirements found an innovative way to capture senior technicians' knowledge and transfer it to new hires. The agency hired a videographer and an e-learning developer to create digitized video instruction that provided step-by-step examples of how experienced technicians approached maintenance and infrastructure problems. The e-learning developer converted the videos to training modules accessible via hand-held devices. New hires referred to the device when out on repairs. An instructional designer also created printed job aids that were designed to fit in maintenance tool kits and served as reference materials. The solution codified the practices of the agency's most experienced mechanics *and* acknowledged the value these individuals brought to the agency. It also provided new hires with knowledge in a format they were comfortable using.

While many organizations believe that knowledge loss is a real risk to operations, some experts say leaders may be too caught up in day-to-day operations to focus on this issue. The difficult economy may have also contributed to the delayed reaction of organizations, prompting leaders to hold back funding for knowledge transfer projects. And some organizations don't react to national or industry-wide aging trends—rather, they need specific data on their own workforce before they feel compelled to make a move.[16] We will cover ways to analyze the workforce in later chapters, but for now, let's look at the different generations that make up today's workforce.

---

16 This concept represented here: Young, Mary B. with Piktialis, Diane and Rappaport, Anna. The Conference Board. Gray Skies, Silver Linings: How Companies Are Forecasting, Recruiting, and Managing a Mature Workforce. 2007.

2

Defining the Generations

Before we dive in to how companies capture Boomer knowledge for future generations, let's look at the various groups of people who work, what's distinct about them, and what they have in common. We'll also look at how the economic crisis that began in 2007 has changed the way these groups view the workplace—and each other.

Today, there are four generations vying for jobs in the workplace: Matures, Boomers, Generation X, and Generation Y. This is not necessarily a new phenomenon—various generations have come together under the same workplace roof before. So what's different this time? There are many answers to this question, but perhaps the most obvious is technology and the speed in which it evolves in our fast-paced world. Rapidly changing technology has given us instant access to information and knowledge we would have previously struggled to find, if it was available to us at all. Because of this, many of us have come to accept that we live in a world where we must be ready to learn about new technologies and topics—essentially, we must be willing to adapt.

The emphasis on constant learning and change brings with it some interesting workforce challenges. Generally speaking, each generation has its own preferences about how it wants to work and receive information and knowledge.

With three, sometimes four generations in the workplace, this means businesses must be prepared to:

- Consider the societal and generational trends that make people who they are.
- Understand how these trends shape work and learning styles.
- Help workers see the value that each group brings to the table.
- Facilitate the transfer of knowledge in ways that are meaningful to subject matter experts *and* recipients.

In some organizations, keeping knowledge flowing through the organization means creating a more inclusive environment than may have existed in the past. This takes time and preparation.

Michael Frost, who has worked in law enforcement since 1981, sums up the multigenerational dynamics he sees in his industry and why it takes time to change an organization. Others may report the same.

"The Matures trained us," Frost, an assistant superintendant for the Essex County Sheriff's Department in Middleton, Massachusetts, said of his experience as a Boomer. "They didn't talk about things. They approached us in a command-and-control kind of way; they didn't ask for our opinion. We became very accustomed to military-style leadership. Generation X came along and they said, 'We're not having any of it.' They said, 'If you want us to stay, you need to listen to us and include us.' They were the bridge for Millennials. Now, Millennials come in and want to know everything the boss knows. And it's incumbent on leaders to work with these groups."

Some background on each of these groups—Generation Y, Generation X, Boomers, and Matures—helps leaders better understand where everyone is coming from. In this chapter, we'll also touch on how the different generations learn best, and then we'll cover the various types of knowledge in Chapter 3, "Knowledge in the Workplace."

Keep an Open Mind

These definitions are based on research, conversations, interviews, and our own observations. None are infallible. We are all individuals with our own unique attributes. It is not uncommon to find differences among those in the same generation.

Table 2.1   Generation Timeline

1922 to 1945	1946 to 1964	1965 to 1979	1980 to 1995[1]
Matures	Baby Boomers	Generation X	Generation Y (also known as Millennials)

What's Behind a Generation's Name?

Matures. Baby Boomers. Gen X and Y. How did these generations get their names? Let's start with the most senior group, known as Matures, Veterans, or, as Tom Brokaw called them, The Greatest Generation.[2] This is the group that gained their various names based on their harrowing experiences during the Great Depression and World War II. They were the parents of the Baby Boomers, the generation that received its moniker after writers and others began to describe the post-war "baby boom" that started in 1946. Thus, anyone born during that period became known as a Baby Boomer, or Boomer.

The generation following the Boomers came to be known as Generation X following Douglas Coupland's 1991 novel[3] that chronicled the lives and dreams of three restless, irreverent, twenty-somethings working dead-end jobs in the California desert. The group born in the late 1960s and 1970s saw their own plight and attitudes reflected in Coupland's pages, and embraced the term. William Strauss and Neil Howe in their book *Generations,*[4] which also came out in 1991, labeled the group following the Boomers the "13th Generation," as it was the "thirteenth to know the American nation and flag." But Generation X is the name that stuck.

Generation Y followed Generation X. Some call the group *Millennials,* as they were the first to come of age around 2000[5]. Others have used the term "Echo Boomers" to reflect the uptick in births from the late 1970s through the early 1990s. Which generational name do you answer to?

---

1 There has been some debate over the period of time this generation encompasses. This is the time span for Generation Y that we will use.

2 Brokaw, Tom, *The Greatest Generation*. Random House. 2004.

3 Coupland, Douglas. *Generation X: Tales for an Accelerated Culture*. St. Martin's Press. 1991.

4 Strauss, William and Howe, Neil. *Generations: The History of America's Future 1584 to 2069*. William Morrow & Company. 1991.

5 Ibid. p. 31.

Who Are the Boomers?

From the day they started arriving during the mid-1940s, the Boomer generation has represented change. There was no way around it—the size of the group demanded it.

Change brewed behind the scenes during the late 1930s when a pediatrician named Dr. Benjamin Spock began forming new ideas about children's psychological needs and family dynamics. Said to be the first pediatrician with a background in psychoanalysis, Spock rejected prevailing child-rearing attitudes of the day that suggested parents remain rigid and emotionally distant from their children.[6] In 1946, just as Boomer babies were coming into the world, Pocket Books published Dr. Spock's book, *The Common Sense Book of Baby and Child Care*, which sold for 25 cents.[7] The book was an immediate hit with parents, who appreciated Spock's advice to trust their own parental instincts and show their children love and affection.

In his lifetime, Dr. Spock's book would be translated into 39 languages and sell 50 million copies.[8] In fact, it has been widely reported that *The Common Sense Book of Baby and Child Care* was second in sales only to the Bible. While some dismissed Spock as "the father of permissiveness," there is little doubt that his book had a profound effect on Boomers' formative years and perhaps the rest of their lives.[9] His idea that parents should treat their children as individuals was groundbreaking and helped shape a generation that would buck tradition and work hard to make a difference.

Of course, not every Boomer-era parent raised their children according to Spock's methods. Still, as a group, Boomers are known for their self-assured, optimistic, get-ahead attitude, which reflects traits that experts attribute to attentive, 1950s-era parenting.[10] As they grew up, their confidence also grew, and their sheer numbers all but guaranteed their voices would be heard.

"Part of the Boomer experience has been seeing life through the lens of television," said Jackie James, co-director for research at the Center on Aging and Work at Boston College. "They were the first generation to grow up with television, and they have great expectations. There has also been a lot of talk about Boomers' experience with social crowding, which may be why they need to be distinct. When they were born, hospitals couldn't accommodate them.

6 www.drspock.com, Retrieved 8/14/09.

7 Ibid. 8/14/09.

8 Ibid. 8/14/09.

9 This concept represented here: Croker, Richard. *Boomer Century*. Springboard Press, New York. 2007.

10 Ibid. 2007.

Schools couldn't accommodate them. Everywhere they've been throughout their lives, they've been a crowd. They had to stand out. Their need for distinction may also be linked to growing up during Sputnik,[11] when schools were admonished to boost math and science curricula to 'keep up with the Russians.'"

Whether they were protesting the Vietnam War, questioning the relevance of sexual and social mores, or launching the next great idea, the Boomer generation has never been afraid to challenge the status quo. Many experts—and Boomers themselves—trace these attitudes to childhood.

Boomers' confident, individualistic attitude has found its way into every aspect of their lives, and the workplace is no exception. Let's start with Boomer women, the face of just one of the women's movements in U.S. history. In 1950, when the youngest Boomers were still babies, the highest participation rate among all age groups was 43.9 for women aged 16 to 24.[12] During the 1970s and 1980s, women began joining the workforce at a greater clip, pushing the rate to nearly 60 percent by 1991.[13] But more women in the workforce were just part of the story. The 1970s and 1980s were also periods of occupational desegregation, with more women moving into male-dominated occupations. Many factors contributed to this trend, including the women's movement, laws prohibiting sex discrimination, education gains, the steady increase in women's labor force participation, and reductions in gender stereotyping in education and employment, BLS economist Barbara H. Wootton wrote in 1997.[14] As time went on, women began to rise through the ranks in the workplace. In 1995, women accounted for 43 percent of managerial jobs, up from 22 percent in 1975.[15] In 2008, women accounted for 37.4 percent of these jobs.[16]

Boomer Characteristics

While more women in the workforce have been a huge part of the Boomer experience, when you talk to Boomers about their careers, one theme always seems to rise to the top: work ethic. Generally speaking, men and women, in characteristic Boomer style, can all think of a job or a situation where their work ethic has contributed to the success of the company.

---

11 Launched by the Soviet Union in 1957, Sputnik was the first earth-orbiting artificial satellite. The Soviet Union's launch of Sputnik inspired educational leaders to revamp science and math curriculum in schools.

12 Fullerton, Howard N Jr. *"Labor Force Participation: 75 years of change, 1950-98 and 1998-2025." Monthly Labor Review.* December, 1999. pp. 3-12.

13 "Women at Work: A Visual Essay." Bureau of Labor Statistics, *Monthly Labor Review.* October, 2003. pp 46-50.

14 Wootton, Barbara H. "Gender differences in occupational employment." Bureau of Labor Statistics, *Monthly Labor Review.* April, 1997. pp. 15-24.

15 Ibid. pp. 15-24.

16 U.S. Bureau of Labor Statistics, Household Data Annual Averages, 2008.

Other generations agree.

"Younger workers tend to want to do their work and leave to attend to their personal lives," said Janet Michael, a human resources director. "We don't see the same desire that older generations have to go above and beyond."

Michael, who handles personnel issues for an insurance company, said many of the top sales people at their 70-year-old company are accustomed to socializing at golf tournaments and meeting with clients after hours, if needed.

"That's how the older generation built this business," Michael said. "That's what clients are used to, and that's what they expect."

Boomers are also known for their high levels of knowledge and skill they have amassed after several decades in the workforce.

In 2005, Towers Perrin prepared a report for AARP that made a business case for workers over age 50.[17] Researchers interviewed 10 major U.S. employers for this report and found that "without exception," employers said that the experience, maturity, and positive attitudes of their 50+ workers provided enormous value to their businesses.[18]

"They know more than they can tell," said Debby Mc Nichols, who wrote her dissertation on transferring Boomer knowledge to Gen X in the aerospace industry.[19] "They really can't *tell* younger generations what they know. They have to *show* them."

Some experts say the economy has given businesses a reprieve—another chance to capture Boomer knowledge before they leave the workforce.

The recession of 2007 has provided a wake-up call for Boomers with a "live for today" mindset, said Matt Thornhill, co-author of *Boomer Consumer*. They've realized that overall, they have a poor track record of saving for retirement, and while they're optimistic by nature, they may not be able to retire in the timeframe they may have planned. And whatever savings they once had are worth 30 percent less after the economic collapse, he added.

"The plan for many is to put off retirement," Thornhill said. "They'll be staying in their jobs for some time longer."

---

17 AARP (Report prepared by Towers Perrin) "The Business Case for Workers Age 50+: Planning for Tomorrow's Talent Needs in Today's Competitive Environment." 2005. Executive summary.

18 Ibid. p. 13.

19 McNichols, Debby. Tacit Knowledge: An Examination of Intergenerational Knowledge Transfer within an Aerospace Community. 2008. University of Phoenix.

Can Older People Be Creative?

David Galenson, a University of Chicago economist, has been answering this provocative—and perhaps controversial—question for nearly a decade. The author of *Old Masters & Young Geniuses: The Two Lifecycles of Artistic Creativity* (2006), Galenson has become known for delving into what he calls "a damaging, ancient concept that creativity is the province of the young." There is an assumption and bias, built over hundreds of years, that young people are creative and older people are wise and therefore not creative, he said. Galenson disagrees, and has a long list of artists and others from Rembrandt to director Robert Altman whom he suggests completed their best work late in life.

Galenson's findings show there are two types of creativity: conceptual and experimental. Conceptual innovators often enjoy a flash of genius—their work is based on ideas and sudden breakthroughs, which often come at a young age. On the other hand, experimental innovators often start with a vague concept and develop their contribution over time.

Galenson's research, while focused on the arts, answers the question about age and creativity. Can older people—specifically, older workers—be creative? His findings show the answer to be a convincing "yes."

Boomer Cross-Generational Dynamics

The Boomer generation spans 18 years, which makes for some interesting differences within the group itself.[20] Some say the giant group is really two generations in one—the "leading-edge" Boomers born in 1946 and the "trailing-edge" Boomers born in 1964.

The oldest Boomers, now in their late 50s and early 60s, have received most of the attention from the media and books about the generation, according to a 2009 MetLife Mature Market Institute study on the differences between the two groups. The oldest Boomers tended to live in a traditional household with stay-at-home-moms and grew up during economic times that fed the growth of suburbs and consumer demand, the study found. By the time this group graduated from high school, "they found themselves at the forefront of a decade of social unrest as well as social progress." Now, they face a new stage of their lives that includes retirement and thinking about how to pay for it.

---

20 MetLife Mature Market Institute. Boomer Bookends: Insights into the Oldest and Youngest Boomers. February, 2009.

The youngest Boomers, now in their mid-40s, are in a completely different stage of their lives. They are in their peak earning years and may have young children at home. Their experience growing up was very different from the oldest Boomers. "Instead of living in families where their mothers stayed at home to raise the family, they were more likely to be latch-key children," the study found. "Women were entering the workforce in growing numbers, and the divorce rate was increasing." The economy wasn't as strong for the youngest Boomers, so they were less likely to see the world as a place brimming with opportunity. This group looks into the future and knows it will need to take more responsibility for its financial future.

While the majority of the oldest Boomers embrace the Boomer label, the youngest Boomers do not want to be known as Baby Boomers. In fact, about one-third prefer to be known as Generation X, the study found.

There are a great number of differences between the oldest and youngest Boomers, said James of Boston College. She illustrated the point by reminding us that the last three U.S. presidents, Bill Clinton, George W. Bush, and Barack Obama, were all Boomers.

All this analysis of generational differences has started to wear on some observers.

"Well, frankly, I'm a bit tired of the whole thing," management psychologist Betty Doo wrote in a 2009 blog entry[21] about all the generation talk in books and the media. "I'm tired because these discussions are based upon such gross generalizations, and they do not seem to move us any closer toward a shared understanding."

Others share Doo's annoyance with the recent barrage of generational research, studies, and conjecture, which she said are frequently simplistic and overstate the importance of generational differences. However, some leaders and managers find research about the generations helpful, even insightful.

While it's important to consider the individual, people are shaped by the era in which they grew up, and that influences how they work. An era's prevalent events, products, and attitudes become part of their lives, whether they participated or not. While we acknowledge that there are differences within and between generations, generalizations about groups help to highlight trends.[22] Table 2.2 presents some differing societal viewpoints among the generations.

---

21 Betty Doo's blog is titled The Resilient Leader.
22 Oblinger and Oblinger. Educating the Net Generation. 2005. p. 2.9.

Table 2.2   Societal Viewpoints: Differences Among the Generations
(Based on NASA Knowledge Management presentation dated December 16, 2008)

Era	Viewpoints
1930-50	Focus on society Friendships are forged through adversity.
1960-70	Focus on community Friendships are forged through identifications with a cause.
1980-90	Focus on the individual Friendships are forged through individual goal accomplishment.
2000s	Focus on common interests Friendships are created or thrive in a virtual environment.

When generational research is industry-specific, the findings may even help managers craft a knowledge transfer plan that really works.

Take McNichols' research on Boomer knowledge transfer to Gen X in the aerospace industry. McNichols chose to focus on Gen X because they are the next recipients of knowledge in the aerospace industry; Gen Y is still too young, she said. During her research, McNichols found that Boomers in aerospace said they wanted to share what they knew, but they didn't like Gen X's attitude.

"They admitted they had egos," McNichols said. "But they also said the younger generation was arrogant in their approach to asking for knowledge."

McNichols' Boomer subjects wanted more of a "you have so much to offer, and I am ready to learn" approach, McNichols said. Instead, they found Gen X wanted to approach Boomers in a less adoring manner. In fact, some Gen Xers felt Boomers owed it to them to provide the knowledge they needed to advance in their careers, McNichols' research found. Industry-specific research such as McNichols' can help steer companies that may be aware of hostility in their workforce but not know where it's coming from.

Experts have also noted major differences in the way generations like to come together to make decisions. Boomers tend to want to be seen as valuable, and they like to work in teams, Thornhill said. They want to have a role, and in team meetings, they often have higher status.

"Boomers want to huddle up and talk," Thornhill said.

Gen X on the other hand "wants to get stuff done and go have a life," while Gen Y sides more with Boomers in this respect, Thornhill said, because they want opportunities to contribute and participate during these early days of their careers.

How Boomers Learn Best

Ask Boomers to describe a typical school day growing up, and they will likely recall a very structured environment where memorization was king. For some, the structure worked well. For others, it was dull as dirt.

As a child, you could take comfort in the overall routine, said Deborah Osgood, a Boomer and owner of the Knowledge Institute, a New Hampshire firm that specializes in entrepreneurial education, development, and marketing communications. However, there was little real-world application of what students learned. Students studied math, science, and history from text books, and there were few in-class experiments or exercises to give context to the lessons.

"It was my job to understand what was expected of me, to deliver it in order to get the 'A,' and that's what I did," Osgood recalled. "There was very little opportunity to think outside the box, and a lot of reinforcement that doing so would result in provoking the wrong attention."

Today, some Boomers still prefer highly structured learning environments, experts say. Here are some other approaches to consider when working with Boomer learners:

- Lectures can work well when introducing new topics and ideas.

- Hands-on learning with expert feedback provides context and helps with specific skills development.

- Demonstrations by experts give learners the visual guidance they need before they try the task themselves.

Michael Frost, who recalled his school days as structured, orderly, and not overly complicated, said as he grew older, the idea of a teacher at the head of the classroom controlling the group didn't work for him anymore. As a trainer in law enforcement, he found that he was arriving to classrooms where some students had 30 years' experience and some had 30 days' experience. Instead of standing at the front of the room as the only expert, he began to facilitate conversations between the students, each of whom had varying degrees of knowledge. This approach gets everyone in the room, regardless of age, learning from someone else, and not just the teacher.

"I empower everybody," Frost said. "I want everybody to be engaged and involved."

Mature Workers Make a Difference

Before we move on to Generations X and Y, let's look at the parents of the Boomers. Born before 1945, Mature workers made up four percent of the workforce[23] and often worked on a part-time basis.[24] Experts acknowledge Matures' contribution to the workplace, but Boomers often grab center stage because the cohort is such a huge part of the workforce. Still, as longtime contributors, Matures may be asked to play a role in knowledge transfer efforts at their organizations. This will be especially true in organizations they have founded or in businesses they have run for decades. A greater understanding of their unique experiences can help managers looking for ways to bridge the gap between older and younger workers.

Generational observers have bestowed more names on this cohort than any other: they are known as Matures, The Greatest Generation, Traditionalists, Silents, and Veterans. Generally speaking, people from this generation stand for traditional values—patriotism, loyalty, and respect for authority. They are known for having an upbeat, positive attitude in the workplace, a strong work ethic, and good customer service skills.

This generation's trials made them who they are; many endured a tremendous amount of hardship early in their lives. Many tell stories of families struggling in poverty through the Great Depression, while others talk about fighting abroad during World War II and returning home to a country that was far from stable. This is a generation that has seen its share of pain. Generally speaking, they are willing to make sacrifices if it helps to get the job done.

Small and Mighty: Generation X

While Generation X is a smaller group than Boomers and Millennials, they have had a sizeable impact on the way organizations run today. For example, we've all heard of "work-life balance," the corporate buzz word most people don't bother to define anymore; everyone knows it means you can have a job and a life, too. Maybe you say no to overtime when it doesn't fit your schedule, or you work from home if your child is sick with the flu. You have control of your work life and your home life, and ideally, that leads to work-life balance.

23 U.S. Bureau of Labor Statistics, Table 16, Employed persons by detailed industry, sex and age, Annual Average. 2008.
24 National Institute on Aging. Growing Older in America: The Health and Retirement Study. 2007.

If you like your work-life balance, just turn to the nearest Gen Xer and say thanks. Born between 1965 and 1979 and 51 million members strong, this group initially puzzled managers when it arrived with this new idea that their life outside of work deserved consideration and respect.

Dr. Breda Bova, professor of education at the University of New Mexico, remembers the call she received in 2000 from a company asking if she had any experience with Generation X.

This new group of workers was driving managers crazy, Bova recalled. Managers couldn't understand how this new generation viewed work and careers. And managers had no experience with the concept of work-life balance, which Gen X introduced to the workplace, Bova said. Generation X had a work life, a home life, and recreation, and they immediately drew the line in the workplace. Many had been latchkey kids and had fended for themselves while both parents worked. Many simply were not willing to live by the same rules and rejected the idea of raising their children the same way.

"The Baby Boomer generation missed a lot of their kids' firsts because that's just how things were," Bova said. "Generation X wasn't willing to work this way. They owned their careers and their lives, and this gave way to a free agent approach. A lot of managers had a hard time dealing with that."

Organizations realized they were going to lose a lot of highly qualified people if they didn't incorporate more flexibility into the workplace, Bova said. The result is life as many of us know it today, with more companies encouraging work-life balance and introducing perks that include working virtually when possible, or necessary.

Companies Encourage Employees to Get a Life

From commuter benefits to health fairs, more organizations are offering work-life balance perks. This certainly wasn't always the case—just ask a Mature or a Boomer to recall their first jobs. You can be sure work-life balance didn't come up a lot. But today, there are all kinds of ways to enjoy your life while you're at work. For SAS, a Cary, North Carolina-based business analytics and software services company, employees who experience work-life balance are more engaged, innovative, and productive. With this ideal in mind, SAS has built an organization that focuses on accommodating employees at its sprawling Cary campus and across the globe in fun, unique, and practical ways.

Jennifer Mann, vice president of human resources said SAS, founded in 1976 by Jim Goodnight, has offered benefits such as day care and recreation facilities since its earliest days. What started as a one-person nanny service for a few children on the Cary campus has evolved into two onsite day care facilities, one for infants and one for pre-school children. There is also a summer camp for school-age kids. Likewise, the workout room stocked with weights and a treadmill is now a full-service recreation facility that includes an aquatics center, gymnasium, pool tables, and basketball courts.

Employees can also take advantage of the on-campus Healthcare Center and hair salon and receive manicures, pedicures, even massage therapy.

Other organizations also make employee health and wellness a high priority. AAA Northern California, an insurance and membership company based in Walnut Creek, California, offers cash incentives to employees to complete online health risk assessments and also holds prize drawings for employees who participate in a "10K-a-Day" walking program. Some locations offer health and wellness fairs, biometric screenings, exercise classes, and, to help keep personal finances in check, a year-long series of financial fitness classes.

At Austin, Texas-based Whole Foods Market, employees can take personal leave for up to 30 days or sabbatical leave for extended periods of time, depending on their length of service. Many stores also showcase the artistic talent of their team members, allowing them to perform at store events or display their art work. Each of the company's 12 regional offices chooses its own additional benefits, which could include bringing your dog to work, gym membership discounts, and telecommuting.

Whole Foods even has a name for their work-life balance initiative: *Supporting Team Member Excellence and Happiness.* Employees vote every three years on the benefits they receive, ensuring company offerings remain relevant to the group.

Generation X Characteristics

Generation X can't take all the credit for companies' move to create a more remote workforce, but they certainly played a role in this change over time.

"Some changes had to do with the whole notion of work," Bova said. "After all, how can you be working if someone can't actually see you working? Generation X had a much higher level of comfort with technology, which made working virtually possible."

Gen X also turned the concept of loyalty on its head. Many had seen their parents laid off during the economic downturn in the late 1970s and early 1980s. They emerged from this experience with a different view of what work and career should be. Before Gen X, other generations looked at loyalty as "seat time," or how long people stayed at a job, Bova said. Generation X, on the other hand, tends to be loyal to people who motivate them and projects that excite them, not necessarily to companies.

Experts say the recession that began in 2007, when many Gen Xers were in their late 30s and early 40s, caused an attitude adjustment.

Generation X has been loyal to its career and its resume, jumping from job to job in a quest for all the right experiences, Thornhill said. In the past, every job was a stepping stone to the next job. But now, Generation X is settling down.

"Along comes the recession and the opportunity to move on isn't there any-more," Thornhill said. "They're saying, 'I have to put up with it. I need to work my way up here. I have to put my kids through college.' The recession is going to make them a more stable workforce."

High unemployment caused by the recession means there may not be a better job out there. Gen Xers are hunkering down, Thornhill said, and staying in their jobs so they can furnish their homes, educate their children, invest in their retirement, and take vacations with their spouses.

For many Gen Xers, the independent, free agent spirit remains, and security at work is still considered an illusion—a feeling that maps to their interest in lifelong learning. In a 1999 study, Bova and Dr. Michael Kroth, reported that Generation X, the so-called "business casual" generation, placed a very high value on companies that supported continuous learning on the job.[25] They also stressed the importance of continuous individual learning and personal development. The more they know, the more marketable they are, which makes it easier to find interesting work should the need arise.

Gen X Cross-Generational Dynamics
Communication is the primary cross-generational issue in the workplace—for everyone, not just Gen X.

"It all comes down to how the generations like to communicate, and how they want others to communicate with them," Bova said. "People in the two more junior generations (Gen X and Y) expect communication to be fast. They'll say something like, 'get back to me soon.' Boomers might say, 'well, define *soon*.'"

---

25 Bova, B and Kroth, M. "Closing the Gap: The Mentoring of Generation X." *Journal of Adult Education* Vol XXVII No. 1, Summer, 1999. pp. 7-17.

Generational observers often lump Gen X and Gen Y together, mainly because their life and work experiences were shaped by the Internet and Internet-enabled tools, said Pat Galagan, executive editor with the American Society for Training and Development. Boomers are in their own category because their early work experiences were not shaped as much by technology.

Gen X and Gen Y grew up playing video games and watching shows such as "Sesame Street" that couched lessons as games with humor, Galagan said. They have grown up with the expectation that learning should be fun. And thanks to their interest in Web 2.0 technologies, they tend to be more collaborative than previous generations, especially as it relates to learning and work.

So, how does a love for social media tools play out in the workplace? Say a Gen Xer has a question about some factor of their job. They may forgo sending an email, opting instead to send a text message. The defining characteristic of this generation and Gen Y is *speed*.

"By texting a question to someone in their company and receiving an immediate response, they're doing more than creating a 'just-in-time' learning environment," Galagan said. "They are learning from a community, which is very different from the classroom model where an instructor opens your head and fills it with information. These learners take the initiative. They do everything in the moment. They don't wait until it's time to go to class. They get the answers they need, and they apply the information and move on."

Indeed, Gen Xers are a task-driven bunch, content to work independently, Thornhill said.

"Gen X just wants to be left alone to get the job done," he said. "And, they are much more likely to want to mentor each other than to seek out Matures or Boomers."

How They Learn Best

Bova and Kroth in 2001 joined forces to study the ways Generation X prefers to learn in the workplace.[26] Using a five-point Likert scale (1 = strongly disagree to 5 = strongly agree), they found:

■ Gen Xers prefer action learning above all, rating it at 4.8. They like to learn by doing and find real solutions to real problems.

■ The group rated incidental learning, or learning that is unintentional and spontaneous, at 3.9.

---

26 Bova, B and Kroth, M. "Workplace Learning and Generation X." Journal of Workplace Learning. Bradford: 2001. Vol. 13, Issue 2. pp. 57-65.

■ Gen X's least favorite learning method was traditional, classroom-based learning. Rated at 2.1, the study served as a reminder to companies that Gen X prefers self-directed learning, a departure from generations before them.

The best way to transfer deep knowledge to Generation X may be through mentoring, Bova said. On the other hand, transferring lower-level, procedural knowledge requires a completely different tack.

"You have to be incredibly explicit when transferring lower-level knowledge," Bova said. "Generation X and Millennials grew up having tons of options. So, if you have a procedure with A, B, and C, people might think they could do A and C and skip step B. You need to be very, very specific with younger generations."

Bova suggests giving instructions and imagining all the exceptions that could exist. Expect younger generations to ask for exceptions. This is what they have done since they were children, and it is very much a part of their experience.

Pushing the Envelope: Generation Y

The newest entrants to the workforce, this generation was the first to use "text" as a verb. Also known as "Millennials" and "Echo Boomers," Generation Y represents what the Bureau of Labor Statistics reports call the "baby-boom echo,"[27] a modest increase in births from the late 1970s through the early 1990s.

There has been some debate about the period of time Generation Y (and Generation X) represents. Some writers and generational experts say Gen Yers were born between 1977 and 1994, while others say between 1980 and 1995 or 1999. Another camp leaves the dates open and says Gen Y is anyone born after 1980. Some experts have said that this generation is larger than the Boomer generation, although there is still a great deal of ambiguity around the time periods it encompasses. Debating this generational time period may seem like we're over thinking the issue, but when counting heads, a few years either way can make a difference.

To make matters even more confusing, the U.S. Census Bureau does not classify people as Generation Y, Generation X, or Matures, so it's impossible to simply pull up a Census table online and search on these groups by name. The only group the bureau classifies by years of birth in some of its data is the Boomer generation. Go figure.

---

27 Toossi, Mitra. "Labor Force Projections to 2016: More workers in their golden years." Bureau of Labor Statistics, *Monthly Labor Review*. November, 2007. p. 33-51.

Gen Y has caused a stir, no matter how you look at them. This is the largest generation since the Boomers, with nearly 62 million members, if you use dates ranging from 1980 to 1995. Using these dates and statistics, there are nearly 22 percent more Gen Yers than there are Gen Xers. Still, the Boomer generation—in regards to sheer numbers—remains unmatched, possibly because it's the only generation with clearly defined time periods.

Gen Y Characteristics

In training circles, members of Generation Y are often called "digital natives." They have grown up during the Information Age, in a world where technology (and technological aptitude) is a way of life. This generation uses high technology for everything from taking a picture to connecting with friends to researching facts and figures and finding their favorite songs. In many ways, their Boomer and Generation X parents have promoted their use of technology and their constant contact with the outside world.

From laptops to cell phones, Gen Y has never known a world without gadgets that connect them to others. Pew Internet & American Life Project studies[28] have shown that 58 percent of people living in married-with-children households own two or more desktop or laptop computers, and 63 percent of those households link to a home network. Both spouses use the Internet in 76 percent of these households, as do 84 percent of their children aged 7 to 17. And 89 percent of married-with-children households own multiple cell phones; 47 percent own three or more mobile devices.

All this technology may have helped fuel what are known as "helicopter parents," moms and dads who hover over their Gen Y children's lives. While this parenting style is not new, there is little doubt that society's acceptance of technology and connecting intensified this phenomenon in Generation Y.

Without a doubt, the advent of new technologies and the speed of technological change have shaped this group's experience and have made them who they are, said Dr. Jan Ferri-Reed, president of KEYGroup®, a Pittsburgh, Pennsylvania-based consulting firm, who co-authored *Keeping the Millennials* with company founder Dr. Joanne G. Sujansky.

Millennials are used to getting the information they need, when they need it, and their comfort and confidence with technology and the Internet mean they move on if they don't find what they're looking for quickly.

---

28 Pew Internet & American Life Project, Summary of Findings. October, 2008.

High-speed technology has also contributed to Gen Y's dislike of the word "wait." Some call it *ambition*. Others call it *impatience*. No matter how you look at it, Gen Y's energetic, multitasking nature plays a role in the workplace.

Millennials have also had greater exposure to the media than previous generations. Easy access to media and information has helped them form their preferences and opinions about the world around them, and the workplace is no exception.

Millennials like working for companies that have a strong mission and focus—they are used to interacting in a global environment, according to Ferri-Reed. Diversity is not usually a concept that they need to learn to embrace—it's what they expect to encounter in school and at work. As for social consciousness, Millennials expect leaders who espouse a social awareness and support for worthwhile causes to demonstrate those values on a daily basis. For example, they expect to see evidence of "recycle, reduce, reuse" if an organization is environmentally conscious.

Gen Y Cross-Generational Dynamics

Human resources managers and experts often cite Gen Y's need for more regular—some say constant—feedback and communication as a source of conflict in the workplace.

"On the flip side, everyone wants feedback," Ferri-Reed said, speaking for other generations in the workplace. "Maybe Millennials are just asking for it more often."

While they are on the opposite end of the age spectrum, Boomers may be the perfect companion to Gen Y in the workplace. Here's why: "Boomers at this stage of their careers are either running the company or realizing they are never going to run the company," said Thornhill. "Either way, they still want to contribute, but many are feeling a little unappreciated. The culture is about bringing up the next hot shot and finding the next leader, so Boomers who have reached their pinnacle may not feel there is anywhere to go."

Gen Yers who grew up with highly involved, hovering parents appreciate having mature direction in the workplace and often want feedback on everything they're doing, Thornhill said. This creates a cross-generational dynamic that gives Boomers the opportunity to mentor a younger employee, and it provides Gen Y with the guidance they want in the workplace. Everybody wins.

Other cross-generational dynamics exist—some are not as easy to overcome as others. Gen Y also tends to want juicier job assignments early in their career, said Ferri-Reed, an urge that may draw resentment from Boomer and

Gen X workers who had to wait for more challenging roles. Even in the area of promotion, generational attitudes differ. For Boomers, it's about paying your dues; for Gen X, it's about showing you are competent, Thornhill said.

Gen Y's confidence with technology feeds their desire to take on new tasks in the workplace. "Millennials ask, 'Why can't I leverage technological tools at work to get ahead?'" Ferri-Reed said. "It's very hard for them to watch other people who are archaic in their use of technology."

The same people who comment on Gen Y's impatience also tend to label them as overly casual (some say warm and friendly) in the workplace, especially around superiors or customers who may expect a more formal approach. Gen Y also catches heat from co-workers who don't appreciate Gen Y's assumption that text messaging is an appropriate means of communication for every occasion.

"We have a Gen X manager who asks that workers call in if they are going to be out sick," Michael said. "Gen Y employees will instead send a text message, because that's the way they're most comfortable communicating. The Gen X manager said, 'I don't check my text messages much during the work day. That's why I want a phone call.' There's a difference in the way the two groups communicate, no doubt about it."

But how different is Generation Y, really? Every generation has its youthful, impetuous phase, and every generation has its fascination with the newest toys and technologies. How are their preoccupations with hand-held gadgets different from Boomers' passion for television in the early 1950s and Gen Xers' love of Atari and *Space Invaders* in the 1980s? And how is their casual manner so different from Gen X's attitude during their early days in the workplace?

While there are some similarities between Gen Y and other generations, Ferri-Reed said trends and experiences make this group unique.

"For one thing, they are often perceived more negatively than positively," she said. "Then there is the media hype and exposure about who they are and that sometimes leads to resentment among other generations who ask, 'Hey, why are they getting all the attention?'"

Media outlets ranging from *Ladies Home Journal* to *Training and Development* magazine have weighed in on the business world's effort to understand Gen Y. In some articles, it's easy to see how Gen Y is a group that business leaders are still getting to know.

There's no denying that Gen Y's lifelong access to quickly changing technologies also makes them unique and valuable assets in the workplace, Ferri-Reed said.

Millennials are highly educated and accustomed to competing to get what they want, she said. Their strengths in technology and their rich educational background do more than just make them a unique group—they also influence what they want and need in the workplace, and how other groups perceive them, she said.

How They Learn Best

Gen Y wants to learn by doing. Don't count on this group to read an instruction manual cover-to-cover when they're learning a new task. They simply do not operate this way. Thornhill reminds us that Gen Y grew up playing video games, and they're accustomed to starting tasks spontaneously with little or no instruction.

"With video games, you just put it in and start," Thornhill said. "That's how they come to the workforce, too, with a trial-and-error learning style. They want to learn by doing."

Here are some Gen Y learning preferences to consider:

- Trainers passing on procedural or explicit knowledge to Gen Y may find they lack patience for a "must-do-it-this-way" approach to learning.

  "It really varies per individual," Ferri-Reed said. "For example, you may want to use a mix of traditional methods, such as job aids, but also be available to offer face-to-face coaching as needed."

- Transferring deep knowledge may also require a blended approach. Ferri-Reed suggests a combination of traditional as well as current learning theory.

- This generation wants practical information when they need it, according to Ferri-Reed. Traditional methods to transfer deep, intuitive knowledge could be mentoring and on-the-job training, which offers an approach that maps to their preference for feedback and communication.

- Gen Y also benefits from job shadowing to learn the ins and outs of a business or department, Ferri-Reed said. Self-study, including e-learning or videos, also works well.

"This group is used to doing research on their own," she said. "Think about using training that's on demand and easily accessible to them when they need it, as opposed to posting a notice saying, 'We're holding training from 9 to 4 on Tuesday.'"

Some HR managers have also observed that Gen Y has little interest in Boomers' storytelling communication style. "Just get to the point," they seem to want to say. "I don't have time for a story."

Denise Lee, an adjunct professor at Johns Hopkins University, disagrees with the view that Gen Y doesn't learn through stories. A consultant and educator who uses narrative practice for knowledge transfer in the federal, academic, and private sectors, Lee said people think and process knowledge and even dream in the form of stories. Cognitively speaking, every experience, relationship, and object is stored in the mind as a story.

There's no getting around it—people find great value in stories, she said. For instance, each year, the President of the United States gives the State of the Union address. When it's over, it's the story of the war hero or the single mother or the elderly marathon runner that we remember.

Lee's advice is to use narrative at every opportunity but without necessarily using the label of storytelling. This distracts from the purpose—sharing knowledge—and may cause the listener to lose interest. Just tell the story, blending it into your work, and integrating it into your conversation.

Whatever approach managers take, they must remember that many different technologies and media compete for Gen Y's attention at any given time.

"They have learned to process a lot more information simultaneously than we did or had to growing up as Boomers," said Deborah Osgood. "This means that to maintain their interest in the classroom or in the workplace, learning must be dynamic and multifaceted if it's going to hold their interest."

What Do All Three Generations Have in Common?

While we certainly have our differences, Boomers, Gen X, and Gen Y have more in common than they may realize.

"We are all trying to do something positive," McNichols said. "We all want to make a contribution at work."

Leaders play a role in noting the differences *and* similarities between groups; the ability to assess these is the first step toward successful knowledge transfer.

"While we have societal norms that fluctuate, each generation has a necessary distribution of personality styles. This will include those who are more outgoing (gregarious and extroverted) in their behavior and those who are more introverted (quieter and less aggressive) personality types," said Sharon Birkman-Fink[29] of Birkman International.

---

29 This concept represented here: Sharon Birkman-Fink, "Manage Multigenerational Communication." *Training.* July/August, 2009. p. 17.

man-Fink is no stranger to personality types. During the late 1940s, her father, Dr. Roger Birkman, designed a psychological instrument for pilot selection for the U.S. Air Force. Ultimately, he developed this instrument into The Birkman Method®, an assessment tool that businesses and other organizations use to measure people's social expectations, self-concepts, interests, and stress behaviors. The goal of this tool is to facilitate team building, executive coaching, leadership development, career management, and interpersonal conflict resolution by measuring what people really need to be productive on the job.

From its 298 simple questions answered online, The Birkman Method looks at an individual from five different perspectives.

- **Interests:** What activities does an individual enjoy? Individuals who perform jobs that align with their interests are much healthier and happier.

- **Usual Behavior**: How does the individual see himself or herself? What are their effective, everyday social behaviors that others can see?

- **Underlying Motivational Needs**: An individual can be sociable and friendly, but that doesn't tell you how much alone time the person needs to recharge after a challenging day or hours of intense social interaction. Some will need a little; others need a lot. "It's kind of like watering your plants," Birkman-Fink said. "You have to know how much is appropriate to keep it healthy."

- **Stress Behaviors**: When an individual's needs go consistently unmet, they will go into stress, Birkman Fink said. Employers who assess these needs in their employees can help ensure that the individual's personalities and behavioral needs align better with their jobs.

- **Organizational Focus**: This is a composite score of all the responses and can tell an employer how and where an individual will contribute to the organization in the strongest way.

Birkman-Fink says that while our social intelligence is still actively developing throughout the teen years, and this continues throughout adulthood, our dominant areas of interests appear to be in place by the time we reach seventh or eighth grade. Birkman International is conducting further research on this topic. Meanwhile, for six decades, Birkman has continued to provide data on essential personality needs. These have not really changed dramatically.

"In terms of people's temperament, core needs, and interests, we have seen relatively little change over the years," Birkman-Fink said. "Sure, we've seen stylistic differences along with shifting social mores and, of course, vast changes in the way we use technology. To stay current, we re-norm[30] from time to time, but when the last re-norming was completed in 2000, while there were some minor fluctuations, there were no significant personality changes in the general population."

Jackie James and Kathy Lynch of the Sloan Center on Aging & Work at Boston College say there are many differences within generations and similarities across generations. Their Age & Generations Study suggests that everyone, regardless of their generation, is looking for meaningful work, fair compensation, and good benefits. And Matures, Boomers, Gen X, and Gen Y all want job security, flexibility, and some autonomy on the job, Lynch said.

In fact, James and Lynch say their ongoing research shows that generational differences are overblown.

In the text of a 2008 report, the Center for Aging & Work pointed out the fact that for much of the 20th century, people used age as an indicator of the "seasons of our lives," in part because it seemed our lives unfolded in a way that corresponded with age. Since then, major changes have made chronological age an unreliable indicator of a person's work and life experiences. Those changes include life course events and variations in the timing of transitions such as education completion, career entry and exit, marriage, divorce, and retirement.

"There is so much to a person beside what generation they were born into," James said. "You have family history, education, race, gender, and where people are in their lives."

James uses her experience as an example. A Boomer, James was earning her PhD during the mid-1980s, when the technology revolution was already underway.

"I had to learn how to use technology to do my dissertation, so I was shaped by the technology revolution the way a Generation Xer might have been. I'm a Boomer, but I don't feel I'm at the end of my career. I still feel I am in mid-career."

How Can Understanding Generational Differences Help Knowledge Transfer?

Understanding generational differences is an important step to breaking down barriers that hinder knowledge transfer. For example, years ago, seeing the differences between Boomers, Gen X, and Millennials in his department, Michael Frost initiated intergenerational courses to get everyone on the same page.

---

30 Re-norming is the practice of updating the stratified normative sample that is representative of the population to which examinees are compared.

He started by bringing together Boomers and Gen X and asking the group to rattle off all the negative labels they used to describe Millennials. Overvalued, pompous, self-serving, entitled…the negatives were flying. Then Frost asked them to characterize what they had experienced from the generations before them. Once the group had expressed all their less-than-positive feelings about the younger and older generations, Frost asked them to come up with some positive contributions that Millennials make to law enforcement and discuss what the generations have in common. Before long, Boomers and Gen Xers were talking about Millennials' general optimism, their confidence with technology, and the opportunities to develop mentoring and reverse mentoring relationships.

Then he conducted a similar course with Millennials. His goal? To demystify the generations and increase understanding to facilitate effective knowledge transfer.

"There has to be a mutual language of understanding," Frost said. "I will not accept knowledge from you if you are not educating me in the language I understand. If you don't connect with me, I am not going to be paying attention. Your effort will be an exercise in futility."

Remember the Recipient

Considering the needs of the recipient of knowledge is at the heart of Frost's lesson. Historically, the source of knowledge is the focus of knowledge transfer efforts. After all, senior and experienced workers have the knowledge, so they are often viewed as a more significant part of the equation. However, research shows that knowledge transfer efforts must also focus on the receiver if they are to succeed.[31] In a workplace where several generations converge, understanding generational differences and learning styles is a vital piece of any successful knowledge transfer work.

"If you don't understand different learning styles and take into account the needs of the receiver, you won't be able to facilitate knowledge transfer to the extent that it will provide value to your business," said Diane Piktialis, Research Working Group and program leader at The Conference Board.

In its report titled "Bridging the Gaps," The Conference Board recommends that organizations involve younger employees in discussions about how they want to receive knowledge. Boomers and Matures often include history and context as they share knowledge to give "the big picture"; but younger

---

31 This is one of the major findings of The Conference Board's research presented in "Bridging the Gaps: How to Transfer Knowledge in Today's Multigenerational Workplace." 2008. pp. 9-11.

employees tend to seek what they need, when they need it. While this attitude may puzzle some older workers, research shows that younger workers respond more favorably to knowledge that is packaged with their needs in mind.

Piktialis recalled one Boomer manager who was the keeper of the company's knowledge database and confident that knowledge management in his firm was cutting edge. During a discussion about younger employees' preferences, a young woman in her twenties described Second Life, an online virtual world. Her generation used Second Life to meet, chat, share information, and so much more. She told the group, including the manager, that this, and not a static database, was the technology her generation used. Learning more about this and other social networking sites would help him get her generation's attention in the future, the young woman told the manager.

It's also important to remember that knowledge transfer is one step in the learning process—it is not the end goal. After all, knowledge transfer efforts are only successful if the recipient applies the knowledge that has been shared, Piktialis said. This is why paying attention to the recipient's learning style can mean the difference between a person capturing and applying knowledge and tuning out.

Remember, it's easy for conversations about the generations to spiral into stereotype and myth. To avoid this trap, focus on the generations' different learning styles and what's important to the workplace, Piktialis said. When you talk about the generations in this context, you can provide a foundation for respect and trust, which is one of the first steps to successful knowledge transfer.

3

Knowledge in the Workplace

When you think about your company and the factors that contribute to its success, the first things that likely come to mind are the people and what they know, i.e., their knowledge. From the factory floor to the supervisory desk to management "upstairs," it is what each employee knows about his or her job or role in the business that creates continuity in a company's operations.

The challenge for managers is that most workers don't think much about what they know. They arrive at work each day and barely give a thought to how they use their knowledge to complete various tasks. And workers may not realize how valuable their knowledge is to their co-workers and to the organization as a whole. If asked to share what they know with another, less experienced worker, they may not know where to start. This is why managers need a plan when it's time to capture and transfer Boomer knowledge. But first, they need a basic understanding of what knowledge is and how it differs from data and information.

To illustrate why it's important to distinguish[1] these concepts from one another, imagine for a moment you are shopping for a new pet. As you walk down the aisles of the pet store deciding what to buy, consider how you would care for a goldfish, a snake, and a kitten. If you buy a goldfish, you'll

---

1 In their article, "The Eleven Deadliest Sins of Knowledge Management" (*California Management Review*, Vol. 40, No. 3. Spring, 1998. pp. 265-276), Liam Fahey and Laurence Prusak discuss the importance of making distinctions among data, information, and knowledge. Prusak and Thomas H. Davenport also discussed this concept in their book *Working Knowledge: How Organizations Manage What They Know*. Harvard Business School Press. 1998, 2000.

need water, fish food, and a new bowl. If you buy a snake, you'll need a container with enough room for the snake to slither around and a heating unit to keep it warm. If you buy a kitten, you'll need space for it to roam, and you can expect it to hide under the bed from time to time. Each animal requires a specific kind of care, and you won't be able to properly care for it until you understand what it needs.

Likewise, in the workplace, you need to know what you are working with: data, information, or knowledge, so you can effectively capture it, transfer it, and maintain it. If you don't understand what you're working with, you'll attempt to treat these concepts as interchangeable when they really aren't. This is the equivalent of putting the kitten in the fish bowl and leaving the snake to slither around the house and hide under the bed.

With the understanding that data, information, and knowledge differ, let's define them. By defining these terms, you'll gain a better understanding of what you're working with, and you'll make better, more effective decisions when it's time to transfer knowledge to the next generation.

Data—Diamonds in the Rough

Data is the backbone of every organization. It is how we know how many people we employ, how much we pay them, how much our customers pay us, and how much we earn each quarter. But data by itself has no meaning or context, so sharing it with others is not really a great challenge—simply print out a spreadsheet and hand it off. Knowledge on the other hand, is not as easy to transfer, as you'll learn later in this chapter.

Consider Judith, a fictional human resources manager we conceived to help us illustrate our terms. Judith knows her company could experience a wave of retirements, so she has collected data on the number of employees in each job and function, how long each has been on the job, the age of each employee, and who is eligible to retire.

Judith's data-filled spreadsheet is a numeric snapshot of the company's workforce, but it has its limitations. The data is flat, which means that it doesn't provide information about how retirements could affect the company, the relationships among affected jobs and roles, or the attitudes or intentions of employees. As is the case with most data, there's no context to Judith's spreadsheet. However, the numbers are the essential pieces that, when collected and analyzed, become the basis for creating information.[2]

---

2 Davenport, Thomas and Prusak, Laurence. *Working Knowledge: How Organizations Manage What They Know.* Harvard Business School Press. 1998, 2000.

Information—Give Data Some Shape

Information based on data gets you closer to making decisions. Let's go back to Judith, the HR manager. She takes her data on the company's workforce and interprets what the numbers mean. For example, three of her 10 salespeople have been with the company for more than 10 years and are eligible to retire. Four of the 10 salespeople are relatively new to the company and show some promise for bringing in new accounts and raising the company's revenue. According to her data, the three salespeople nearing retirement are vital to company operations, and they nurture a handful of the company's longtime clients. Looking over the data and client surveys that praise the company's experienced salespeople, Judith knows the company could lose these clients if key staff people retire.

Judith prepares a presentation for company executives to make a case for a knowledge capture and transfer initiative at her company. Using her data, she creates a narrative to accompany a slide presentation. The slides present the data; Judith's narrative gives meaning to the data by illustrating how the three mature salespeople influence the company's future. When she has finished discussing their sales and clients and their role in the company, she introduces HR's idea to create a mentoring program that pairs these experienced salespeople with newer workers.

Judith has given her data shape; she has used it to tell a story and propose a solution. If she had simply emailed executives her data with "Please Advise" in the subject line, she would have done little to influence the situation. By using her data to create a presentation and narrative, she infuses the data with meaning and influences her audience to make a decision based on information, not data.

Pamela Walshe, vice president of user research for Wells Fargo Bank, gave an example of how data without information and information without knowledge could wreak havoc on an entire industry. During a 2009 conference, Walshe witnessed a panel discussion where the moderator asked panelists to discuss the challenges the marketing research industry faced.

"The panelists were people who were very accustomed to interpreting survey data," Walshe said. "They were big consumers of data that showed X percentage of consumers think this or that. So it was very telling when the panelists responded that the challenge the industry faced was too much information and not enough knowledge."

In other words, they had the facts, but knowing how to apply them required a completely different set of skills and experience.

"Data and information are only valid if you can use it all to effect change," she said.

Knowledge—Transforming Data and Information

Looking back on our work and personal lives, we can trace how we have come to know some of the things we do. We develop knowledge in many ways: education, hands-on experience, and our relationships with others all contribute to what we know. We build knowledge over time, using data and information as building blocks.[3] These three elements are parts of a whole.

Having knowledge about a topic allows you to give context to data and information, to bring it to life for yourself and others. Let's go back to Judith. Her work is done, right? Probably not. Once she completes her presentation, management executives will likely come back with questions about the company's workforce, employee attitudes, and statistics on successful knowledge capture and transfer initiatives. Judith's ability to sell her solution to executives will depend on a well-rounded discussion of the situation her company faces. Essentially, her *knowledge* of the industry, her company, and capture-and-transfer efforts will carry her through her presentation and subsequent conversations with executives.

Each of us has unique experiences that contribute to what we know about ourselves, our jobs, and other people. We rely on this knowledge to get us through life, but we barely think about how much it means to whom we are. That's why defining what knowledge we possess and how it can benefit others can be incredibly difficult. Why? Because we don't always know what we know.

For example, think about a great cook you know. When you ask her how she makes her signature dishes, she probably responds with an answer that translates to "I just use a little of this and that." When she makes the dish, you can be sure she doesn't level the flour and measure the sugar. That's why when you ask her for the recipe, she has to sit down and really think about all the ingredients that go into the bowl. Creating her signature dish has become automatic. She has such deep knowledge of how everything (data and information) works together that it's difficult to explain on a recipe card. She almost has to *show* you how she makes the dish. By doing this, she shares—or transfers—her knowledge to you.

Let's take this example a step further. Because this great cook makes a dish you love, does that mean you want her to share every dish she knows? Probably not. Perhaps you don't want to learn how to make the high-fat, buttery dishes, or the ones that contain brussels sprouts. Now you begin to analyze what she knows and zero in on what you need her to share with you to improve your cooking practice. Analysis is an important part of knowledge transfer, and we'll cover it in detail in Chapter 5, "Boarding the Knowledge Train."

---

3 This concept represented here: Davenport, Thomas and Prusak, Laurence. *Working Knowledge: How Organizations Manage What They Know*. Harvard Business School Press. 1998, 2000.

Different Tasks Require Different Knowledge

A longtime assembler at an aerospace company was working on a development project that required multiple pieces to create a single unit. The assembler had no trouble with the units, and easily completed numerous batches for the company's engineers to continue their testing.

The assembler later went on extended leave while the development project was still in progress. Another assembler stepped in, but she could not match the first assembler's skill at putting the pieces of the unit together. Nothing seemed to fit when the fill-in assembler performed the work. How had the first assembler completed the units so successfully?

Company tests later found failures in some of the units. More careful examination revealed that other assemblers, not the first assembler, created the failing units. The company implemented a process improvement project and began searching for answers. Eventually, the company discovered that the first assembler used a toothpick when putting her units together. When the pieces gave her trouble, she wielded her handy toothpick and gently finessed everything into place.

Pamela Holloway, knowledge and management consultant and owner of AboutPeople, defined the assembler's knack for assembling units as procedural knowledge, but she didn't stop there. Knowledge has many layers, and revealing the types of knowledge people use in the workplace is like peeling an onion, she said.

While the assembler followed a step-by-step procedural process to put the units together, her use of the toothpick as a tool added an important nuance or overlay. It's the kind of critical knowledge that so easily gets overlooked.

While Holloway's multidimensional approach to analyzing knowledge may seem like splitting hairs to some, understanding the kinds of knowledge that exist in the workplace is critical to successful knowledge capture and transfer. In other words, if you know what kind of knowledge that your employees possess, you will have a better idea of how to draw it out and make it accessible to the next generation of workers.

For now, let's look more deeply at the kinds of knowledge that exist in the workplace.

Explicit Knowledge—It's on the Shelf

Knowledge is generally classified as either explicit or tacit.[4] Explicit knowledge is knowledge that has been articulated and documented, while tacit knowledge is knowledge that cannot be articulated. Some knowledge experts even characterize tacit knowledge as knowledge that people don't even realize they have, that is, "They don't know what they know." There have been plenty of arguments around the ability to articulate and transfer tacit knowledge—more on that in this chapter.

Knowledge experts Dorothy Leonard and Sylvia Sensiper described knowledge as existing on a spectrum; at one end, knowledge is almost completely tacit, or semiconscious and unconscious.[5] At the other end, it is almost completely explicit, or captured and accessible. Most knowledge, they say, exists somewhere in the middle. Figure 3.1 illustrates this concept.

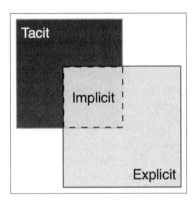

Figure 3.1   *Tacit and explicit knowledge are at opposite ends of the spectrum. Implicit knowledge exists somewhere in the middle.* Source: Larry Todd Wilson

Some examples of explicit knowledge are:

- Documented processes
- Presentation slides
- Manuals
- Flow charts
- Videos

---

4 DeLong, David. *Lost Knowledge: Confronting the Threat of an Aging Workforce*, Oxford University Press. 2004. p. 83.

5 Leonard, Dorothy and Sensiper, Sylvia. "The Role of Tacit Knowledge in Group Innovation." *California Management Review*, Vol. 40. No. 3. Spring, 1998. p. 113.

Explicit knowledge can be easily transferred from person to person[6] —think of the emails that contain a series of slides with case studies about your clients. These slides contain your team's explicit knowledge.

Some companies regularly update their documented explicit knowledge and even tie performance reviews to keeping documents current. On the other hand, tacit knowledge is not as easy to put your finger on. Explicit knowledge is objective and rational, while tacit knowledge is subjective and experiential.[7]

Implicit Knowledge—It's Still in Your Head

Implicit knowledge is knowledge that an individual has the ability to articulate but hasn't yet done. In some organizations, implicit knowledge is a source of frustration to others because the "knower" is aware that he possesses knowledge that others could benefit from. Often, he simply can't find the time to sit down and articulate what's in his head.

Some examples of implicit knowledge are:

■ An executive has a list of preferred contact names and numbers that she never documents or shares with her team.

■ A longtime worker who has used the company's computer system since the earliest days of the business has in-depth knowledge of the system that he has never documented.

■ A longtime worker knows where specific documents exist on the server, and only shows co-workers where they exist when asked.

Figure 3.2 provides an easy way to answer the question if knowledge is explicit, implicit, or tacit.

Indeed, the goal in many organizations is to make *implicit* knowledge *explicit* so that it can be accessed, leveraged, and adapted by all. This is no small feat. Eliciting implicit knowledge requires time, preparation, and targeted questioning to draw out what an individual knows. Essentially, when you bring people together, you set the stage for transferring implicit knowledge. Some effective methods for transferring this kind of knowledge include mentoring, participating in communities of practice and social networks, and facilitating After Action Reviews. The use of stories in the workplace can also give longtime workers a way to communicate their knowledge and give context to data that isn't very interesting on its own. We cover each of these methods in Chapter 6, "Knowledge Retention by Design."

---

6 This concept represented here: Davenport, Thomas and Prusak, Laurence. *Working Knowledge: How Organizations Manage What They Know*. Harvard Business School Press. 1998, 2000.

7 Ibid. 1998, 2000.

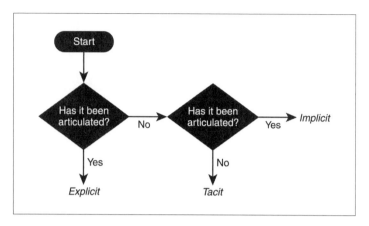

Figure 3.2 *Follow the arrows and answer the questions to understand what kind of knowledge you are working with.* Source: The Knowledge in Knowledge Management, 2003 by Fred Nickols, http://home.att.net/~OPSINC/knowledge_in_KM.pdf

Tacit Knowledge—Too Deep to Articulate?

Michael Polanyi summed up the essence of tacit knowledge when he suggested that "We can know more than we can tell."[8] For example, we can recognize a person's face and could recognize that face among a million other faces. "Yet we usually cannot tell how we recognize a face we know," he wrote. Some knowledge simply cannot be put into words. That's tacit knowledge.

But is the theory that tacit knowledge can't be articulated really that cut and dried? Are there ways to elicit tacit knowledge and make it explicit, or at the very least share it with another person? Ask these questions in a room full of knowledge experts, and you are guaranteed to have a lively and long conversation.

There are no right answers, but there are many theories, ideas, and methods for revealing a person's tacit knowledge to others.

For Pamela Holloway, it's all about asking the right questions and looking for the not-so-obvious influences. Years ago, Holloway worked with a chemist who was especially adept at coming up with new and highly marketable chemical compounds. The company he worked for wanted to know why he was so much better than his peers who had similar credentials and experiences. They wanted to know how he did it.

---

8 Polanyi, Michael. *The Tacit Dimension*. Doubleday & Company, Inc., Garden City, New York. 1966.

Holloway spent hours asking questions to get at the chemist's tacit knowledge. She started by asking "day-in-the-life" questions that zeroed in on his typical day. These questions proved too topical, and didn't reveal his thought processes or mental models.[9] In fact, the chemist's tacit knowledge around his skills was so deep, he really couldn't say how he came up with new ideas, Holloway said.

In an effort to determine influences and triggers, Holloway asked about hobbies and the types of things the chemist did outside the realm of chemistry. One of the things she discovered was that he liked electronics and often read electronics magazines. Holloway followed the thread.

Does reading about electronics or tinkering in your workshop help you in the lab? Holloway asked. Are there any similarities between electronics and chemistry?

He replied, "That's interesting. I never really thought about it, but they are similar. And in fact, I get some of my best ideas after studying electronics designs."

Bingo.

"Until our conversation, it probably had not occurred to him (at least not consciously) that reading electronics magazines helped him come up with new ideas for chemical compounds," Holloway said. "Most of this process was at a subconscious level. This doesn't mean that we'd instruct everyone who wanted to be a chemical inventor to read electronics magazines, but we might suggest they look outside their domain to expand their perspective."

Some other examples of tacit knowledge include:

■ The innate way individuals speak and use grammar rules in their native language. They are unable to explain some rules because they acquired them naturally during childhood, rather than through explicit instruction.

■ Driving a car, for example, knowing how far to turn the wheel when going around a corner.

■ Penning your signature.

---

9 A mental model is an internal representation of an external reality. According to Larry Todd Wilson, the term "mental model" has been used in many contexts and for many purposes. Psychologist and philosopher K.J.W. Craik made some of the earliest mentions of this concept in the 1940s.

The Debate over Tacit Knowledge

Some managers and executives don't use Polanyi's definition of tacit knowledge and opt for a less literal explanation. In fact, it's not uncommon for knowledge workers to argue over just how deep and unreachable tacit knowledge is.

Mary Newell, manager of leadership training at Pratt & Whitney Rocketdyne, talks about tacit knowledge as deep knowledge on any given topic. Sharing this knowledge is critical, and the company has found great success using organized mentoring circles as a way to draw knowledge out of individuals.

During the late 1990s, the organization's Program Management Council was looking for a way for top program managers to spend more time mentoring and sharing tacit knowledge, but there just weren't enough hours in the day. So the Learning and Development team created the mentor circle process, which allowed very experienced leaders to share knowledge with less experienced program managers and leads.

In 2001, the Program Management Council sponsored the first Rocketdyne[10] mentor circle, a formal group of about 12 people who met once a month for about 14 months. The company created the first mentor circle for program managers, creating a forum for people to share tacit knowledge about programs they had worked on and people they had worked with.

After the first circle, participants and the circle leader (a key program manager) noted that the same areas of concern were appearing in each of the organization's programs. Participants passed this information to the Program Management Council, which, in turn, noted that program managers were repeating some of the same mistakes their predecessors had made.

The mentor circles helped remedy this. During the circles, program managers talked about their personal choices and other factors that led them to make mistakes in the first place. Participants shared the how and why with their program peers, which kept critical knowledge moving throughout the group.

Today, Pratt & Whitney Rocketdyne has expanded the program to include mentor circles for women in leadership, chief engineers, and product development. While the program has evolved, the goal of transferring deep, tacit knowledge remains the same, Newell said.

"What is discussed in the room stays in the room," Newell said of the mentor circles. "It's not a presentation event. There are no video cameras or notes. The conversations in there are tacit—they are the personal point of view of someone who has managed a difficult project."

---

10 Pratt & Whitney Rocketdyne had not yet merged with Pratt & Whitney in 2001.

Transferring Tacit Knowledge: Face-to-Face Is Best

During her research into knowledge transfer between Boomers and Gen X in the aerospace industry, Debby McNichols learned that younger workers wanted to tap into tacit knowledge on their own terms.

"Gen X says 'we want to be sitting right next to Boomers when we receive tacit knowledge,'" McNichols said. "It really surprised me because Generation X is so tech-savvy. But they responded that they prefer to receive tacit knowledge when they are in close proximity. If it's any other way, they say they won't hear important conversations when they're happening, and they'll end up receiving second-hand information."

Aerospace Gen Xer's desire to receive tacit knowledge directly speaks to a long-held belief that this is the best way to go. In *Working Knowledge: How Organizations Manage What They Know*, Davenport and Prusak said that the best way to transfer knowledge in an organization is to hire bright people and let them talk to each other. Nearly 10 years after the book was published, Prusak still says that the best way to transfer knowledge is by working with another person, one-on-one. "I believe it even more now than I did then," Prusak said. "If you want someone to know what you know, you have to be with them. They have to see what you do—you can't tell them what you know."

In 1998, Dan Holtshouse noted that some scholars and business leaders thought that sharing tacit knowledge required an interactive, face-to-face work environment.[11] Holtshouse, who was director of corporate strategy at Xerox at that time, agreed but pointed out that corporate cost-cutting had led to a decrease in permanent office spaces for some. This resulted in more mobile workers, a phenomenon that disrupted social connections in the workplace and made sharing tacit knowledge more difficult. Holtshouse still believes that face-to-face interaction is the best way to share the very deepest tacit knowledge. However, some of this knowledge can be drawn out by asking the right questions—in other words, the recipient may not necessarily need to be in the same room. Knower and receiver may even communicate online, via social networking sites and chat rooms, he said. Prerequisites for drawing out this kind of knowledge are trust and reciprocity, both of which can be developed online if a face-to-face environment is not available. Asking the right questions to allow tacit knowledge to surface in a virtual environment is key, Holtshouse said, but not an easy task as the receiver does not have visual prompts as they would with face-to-face interaction.

11 Holtshouse, Dan. "Knowledge Research Issues." *California Management Review*. Vol. 40, No. 3. Spring, 1998. pp. 277-280.

Ask the Right Questions in a Virtual Environment

For Dan Holtshouse, communicating virtually takes more concentration and work than face-to-face interaction does. To help you ask the right questions to "surface tacit knowledge," create a mind map (see Figure 3.3) with questions before the virtual meeting. As the discussion progresses, add new material to the map as it comes up. This exercise will help draw new questions at the boundaries of different elements on the map. Listen intently to the subject matter expert's vocal inflections and choice of words. Picking up these elements in the conversation will give you clues as to what you would have picked up in a face-to-face conversation.

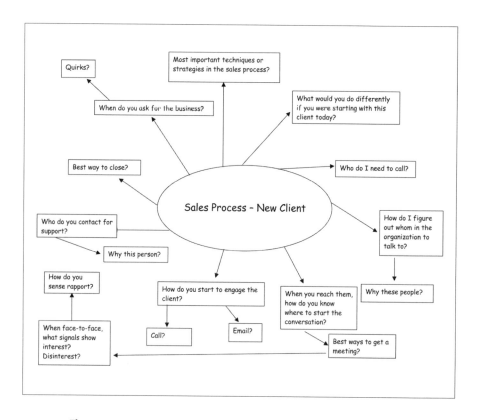

Figure 3.3   *This mind map of the sales process illustrates the various directions conversations can take. Creating a mind map is a good way to prepare when you want to draw out deep knowledge.*

Three Questions for Successful Knowledge Transfer

Explicit Knowledge: What is typically written down and can be effectively communicated?

Support information about a topic or a domain

Guidance about what to do to accomplish a task

Implicit Knowledge: With the right facilitation or technologies, what is possible for a knowledgeable person to express?

Guidance about how to accomplish a task

Information about when to or why to act or decide

Information about how to relate to others

The big picture of how it all fits together

Tacit Knowledge: What can never be verbalized?

When observing a knowledgeable person's results, we may infer that his or her experience originates from knowledge that cannot be written or spoken.

Source: Larry Todd Wilson, Knowledge Harvesting, Inc.

Other Types of Knowledge

As we have discussed, most knowledge falls somewhere between explicit and tacit. Here are some additional types of knowledge that exist in the workplace.

Declarative and Procedural Knowledge

Declarative knowledge is a close cousin of explicit knowledge. It is knowledge that a knower can communicate. Declarative knowledge is often associated with rote memory, said Dr. Renay Scott, Dean of Arts and Sciences at Owens Community College in Toledo, Ohio, and a former instructor of education at Central Michigan University.

Declarative knowledge is the foundation for procedural knowledge. For example, at Owens, critical thinking is one of five learning outcomes to complete general education requirements. Administrators regularly assess students' critical thinking abilities to ensure that the college is providing optimal learning opportunities and instruction. Dr. Scott's staff has two assessment choices: They can use a standardized test, known as the Collegiate Assessment of Academic Profile, or they can create their own test in-house to give to their students.

Dr. Scott's staff needs declarative knowledge before they can exercise procedural knowledge in selecting the strongest tool for assessing students' abilities. They need to know about validity and reliability, whether the test is norm-referenced or criterion-referenced,[12] and the differences among mean, median, and mode. Knowing these facts and committing them to rote memory are examples of declarative knowledge. Once the staff has this declarative foundation, they can leverage their procedural knowledge and select the best assessment tool to measure students' abilities.

If the staff does not have a declarative foundation, their procedure for choosing an assessment tool will be flawed because they won't have a basis for analysis, Dr. Scott said.

"We all come to any procedure with prior experience, most of which is declarative in nature," Dr. Scott said. "But then we need more declarative knowledge to engage more in the procedure."

For example, if her staff decides to forgo the standardized test and create a test in-house, they will refer to their declarative knowledge for steps to create the test. They would then use procedural knowledge to create the test.

To successfully use the in-house test to assess critical thinking, the faculty would need to write effective, multiple choice questions that:

- Align with the learning outcomes being assessed.

- Adhere to principles when creating a tool to measure students' knowledge.

Multiple choice questions need to include sufficient information and cues that prompt the respondent to review the multiple options included as part of the question. The options should be reasonable enough that any of them could be the answer to the question. These procedures, when followed, lead to valid and reliable tests that help educators determine a program's efficiency by assessing students' level of knowledge, Dr. Scott said.

---

12 Norm-referenced—Assessment process used to make comparisons across large numbers of students. Criterion-referenced—Method for assessing what concepts and skills students have learned from a segment of instruction.

Political Knowledge

Pamela Walshe suggests that political knowledge in the workplace is also vital, especially in large organizations. For example, a manager may hand new hires an organization, or "org" chart, on their first day and claim to bring them up to speed on who's who in the company. But an org chart only provides part of the story.

Highly influential people within the organization may exist at a lower level on an org chart, so their positions may be misleading in terms of what kinds of power they may actually wield, Walshe said. Political knowledge is tacit and sensitive. It's the kind of knowledge that people share in off-the-cuff conversations around the water cooler when they talk about people and projects.

"A more seasoned person may give a new hire insight into how other people work," Walshe said. "They may say, 'This is the person who can really make things happen.' Political knowledge is nothing you'd ever put on paper."

Cultural Knowledge

Cultural knowledge refers to the way you navigate organizations *and* interact with others in the workplace. In both examples, if you don't have knowledge of how a culture works, you risk falling outside the circle of trust.

Arti Kirch, a project and program manager who has worked on staff and as a consultant for some of the country's largest financial institutions, has first-hand knowledge of the importance of cultural knowledge. For example, the staff at one brokerage firm she worked with did not want to hold meetings. Ever. When an issue needed to be resolved, stakeholders simply communicated via email, avoiding meetings whenever possible.

Her next employer worked in a completely opposite way, and regularly called meetings for even trivial issues, she said. At first, Kirch resisted going to meetings. Soon, she realized decisions were being made without her. She also learned that people were working during the meetings, and were resolving issues together instead of on their own in small groups.

"If I had ignored this, or stayed tone deaf to it, I wouldn't have gone anywhere," Kirch said. "In a corporate setting, if you don't do it their way, you aren't going to be on the knowledge train. People would have assumed I was either unreachable or not part of the need-to-know group. In other words, in this organization, you need to show up to find out."

In the health-care industry, cultural knowledge goes beyond being aware of organizational culture, said Amy Wilson-Stronks, project director for Health Disparities with the Joint Commission. It also means health-care workers are sensitive to cultural differences among individuals in the workplace *and* among their patients. Today, hospitals experience shifting patient demographics and a growing number of languages and dialects, realities that require increased cultural awareness, sensitivity, and knowledge.[13]

In healthcare and other industries, practitioners use the term "cultural competence" to describe practices and policies aimed at increasing understanding. Sensitivity about sexual orientation is also a component of being culturally competent.[14]

One of the ways the healthcare industry has tried to address and accomplish cultural competence is by hiring a diverse workforce, Wilson-Stronks said. That often means bringing together individuals from different cultures that may not have familiarity with one another.

Sometimes, workforce shortages require hospitals to hire a diverse workforce. For example, the nursing shortage has led to efforts to recruit nurses from other countries. In some instances, hospitals target their efforts. That is, if they have a large Spanish-speaking population, they may try to recruit nurses from Mexico or other Spanish-speaking countries, she said.

In these situations, Boomers may be sharing knowledge with individuals who are from different generations *and* from different countries, she said. In these cases, Boomers may face a cultural double-whammy.

Wilson-Stronks reminds those who fear making a cultural faux pas that the "competence" in cultural competency is misleading.

"Cultures will always change and evolve, and while we may be different on the basis of national origin, we also live by different sets of norms based on religion and differing values," Wilson-Stronks said. "As we become more diverse and more integrated, the evolution of different cultures will perhaps be more rapid. Basically, a person achieves cultural competence by recognizing they are never going to achieve it."

Knowledge Within Your Organization

As you can see, all knowledge is not created equal. Understanding what kind of knowledge exists in an organization is a critical part of any knowledge initiative.

Organizations that have a clear understanding of the types of knowledge they want to transfer will be more successful when it's time to elicit knowledge from

---

13 This concept represented here: Gotsill, Gina. "Cultural Consideration." *The Hospitalist.* December, 2008. pp. 33-35.
14 Ibid. p.34.

subject matter experts and package it for their target audience, said Larry Todd Wilson, of Knowledge Harvesting, Inc. Considering the learners' needs while also understanding the knowledge you want to transfer is also critical.

Some companies use various analysis methods to gain a better understanding of their audience and the knowledge they have—or don't have. We will cover methods for analyzing the workforce in Chapter 5. Taking time to look at the knowledge that exists in the workforce before launching a knowledge initiative helps ensure that their efforts will be successful and well received. It also gives managers the data and information they need to tie the program to organizational goals.

Hospital's Nurse Mentoring Program Helps Transfer Skills

Here's an example of an organization that designed a long-term knowledge program in line with its short- and long-term goals and strategies. In 2003, Scripps Health, a five-campus healthcare system in San Diego, California, noticed some difficult industry trends and decided to do something about them. Like other healthcare organizations, Scripps Health faced losing experienced members of its workforce as the Boomers neared retirement. Thirty-four percent of the Scripps Health population was 50 or older and about 27 percent of the system's workforce had been with the organization for more than 10 years. About 10 percent of the workforce had been with Scripps for more than 20 years.

Hospital administrators and executives also saw knowledge gaps among new nurses fresh out of college, as well as high turnover rates.

Another sign of the times was the changing role of the charge nurse. Traditionally, charge nurses served as mentors to new nurses, but fewer resources left less time for coaching. Charge nurses had become the equivalent of traffic cops, moving patients in and out of the unit. New nurses, though highly trained and proficient, didn't have access to much-needed mentors to provide support through their first challenging years.

Knowledge and expertise are the foundations of care at Scripps Health, said Vic Buzachero, Corporate Senior Vice President of Human Resources. Providing support for new nurses was also a high ideal and a strategic objective to reduce turnover and improve care. In response to industry trends, and with an eye on their organizational objectives, Scripps Health administrators and executives launched a formalized nurse-mentoring program in 2004. The health system started with a pilot at their La Jolla campus, one of the main trauma centers in San Diego County.

One of the first steps in creating the program was identifying the nurse mentor role. What kind of person would make an ideal nurse mentor? And what kind of knowledge should nurse mentors possess? Hospital leaders looked for clinical experts who could assist a new nurse with care plans and patient and family relations, in addition to collaborating with physicians and interdisciplinary teams.

Scripps Health wanted new nurses to be drawn to their nurse mentors, Buzachero said.

"We were hoping to transfer their skills to everyone else and multiply their ability so it wouldn't be lost," Buzachero said.

By November 2004, Scripps Health had implemented its nurse-mentoring program in all five of its hospitals. System leaders credited the nurse-mentoring program with the decrease in new nurse turnover rates, which dipped from 20.3 percent in 2005 to 12.1 percent in 2008.

Where Does Knowledge Management Fit?

Look around your workplace, and you will see that knowledge in all its forms exists in every office, area, and department. Knowledge, as Davenport and Prusak wrote, makes organizations go.[15] Knowledge is not new to the workplace, and neither is the concept that experienced workers will share their knowledge with the next generation. However, the concept of knowledge as a corporate and competitive asset that must be managed is new.[16]

Enter the term *knowledge management*, or KM, the discipline that encompasses knowledge capture, transfer, and retention.

Looking Back, Looking Forward

More than a decade ago, knowledge management (KM) was a burgeoning field, and there was a tremendous amount of excitement around new technologies that could help companies capture, access, and share the knowledge in people's heads.

---

15 Davenport, Thomas and Prusak, Laurence. *Working Knowledge: How Organizations Manage What They Know.* Harvard Business School Press. 1998, 2000.

16 Ibid. 1998, 2000.

Experts Trace Knowledge Management Roots to Drucker

Peter Drucker, one of the most influential writers and thought leaders on modern management in the 20th century, also wrote about knowledge and its new-found place in American business as the country shifted from being industrial-based to knowledge-based, especially in the latter half of the century. Drucker joined others in observing that American business was moving to a foundation built on information rather than manual labor—"Work that is based on the mind rather than the hand."

By 1964, Drucker was making distinctions between manual work—the engine of American business for the previous 100 years—and knowledge work, where the worker processed information and configured creative and spontaneous responses to situations. The thought processes behind knowledge work were a departure from standard procedures characteristic of manual work.

Drucker returned to knowledge themes throughout the 1970s and 1980s, and even late in his career in the 1990s. He died in 2005. His observations on the role of knowledge in organizations have endured; even today, experts trace knowledge management's roots to Drucker's research and writings.

"The most valuable assets of a 20th-century company were its production equipment," Drucker wrote in *Management Challenges for the 21st Century* (1999). "The most valuable asset of a 21st-century institution, whether business or nonbusiness, will be its knowledge workers and their productivity."

In a 2001 white paper,[17] A. Andrew Anderson, formerly a consultant with Robbins-Gioia, wrote about three business factors that drove the need to improve knowledge management processes and create a knowledge management infrastructure. They were:

- Capture the knowledge of the Boomer generation and "harness it for workers with less knowledge."
- Offer better and more efficient services to customers, which would provide a more cost-effective way of doing business.
- Improve organizations' "ability to thrive in a constantly changing environment through the efficient use of knowledge."[18]

17 A. Andrew Anderson. Building a Knowledge Culture. Robbins-Gioia LLC. 2001.

18 This concept represented in an executive overview of the "Knowledge Management, Response Ability and the Agile Enterprise," excerpts from the paper published in *Journal of Knowledge Management*. March, 1999.

Anderson noted that organizations were approaching knowledge management (and these three drivers) through two different initiatives. First, there were knowledge management initiatives to capture tacit knowledge. Then there were initiatives to build a knowledge management infrastructure within the organization.

Throughout the 1990s and into the 2000s, companies bought high-tech tools to launch knowledge management initiatives, hired Chief Knowledge Officers (CKOs), and set about to create a "knowledge culture" that would covet institutional knowledge. Some companies succeeded during this first phase. Others failed.

Today, business leaders' hindsight illuminates what went wrong with KM in the 1990s. Initially, KM was treated as a technical issue, and companies made large investments in technologies that gave them the capability to sort, store, and distribute corporate knowledge. *Repository* became the new buzzword, and everywhere companies were trying to stuff data, information, and knowledge into portals and databases for easy retrieval.

This was the first phase of KM, said Neil Olonoff, a 25-year knowledge management practitioner and consultant for the federal government. The second phase was more about sharing knowledge and less about collecting and storing. Now, KM is moving into a phase that focuses on leveraging social networks and the collective energy of the organization, Olonoff said.

It's plausible that some of KM's early failures were caused by the discipline's identity crisis.

"Knowledge management is a new discipline, which at its inception, had no literature or foundational basis," said Olonoff. "It's a discipline that didn't know if it was IT, organizational development, sociology… certainly it has roots in all those fields. We're still trying to figure out if it's one discipline or if it will have multiple paradigms."

He added: "It can be too much for outsiders to get KM and accept it. KM practitioners themselves are still learning."

Experts and students of KM say the discipline's initial high-tech approach brought many companies right back where they started. Sure, they had archived documents, data, information, and knowledge in their repositories, but after a short time, it became stale, static, said Walshe. Essentially, companies had implemented systems and new technology, but they still had the same problems, observes Jody Holtzman, senior vice president of research and strategic analysis at the AARP.

Serendipitous Knowledge Transfer

Sometimes, knowledge management and knowledge transfer happen serendipitously. Here's an example: Based in Southlake, Texas, Sabre Holdings supports a range of customers including travel agents and corporations through its companies, Travelocity, Sabre Travel Network, and Sabre Airline Solutions. Sabre Holdings, known as *Sabre*, employs about 9,000 people ranging from Matures to Gen Y in 59 countries.

Because of global presence and workforce, Sabre had a broad telecommunications policy that allowed a large number of employees to work remotely, said Erik Johnson, general manager of cubeless, a product developed by Sabre Travel Studios. After a while, Sabre's corporate communications staff began to hear requests from employees for opportunities to get better acquainted with their co-workers around the globe. With some workers in the United States, others in Europe, Australia, and other parts of the world, it was impossible for employees to feel connected.

To meet the needs of its global workforce, Sabre implemented its own social network to promote communication and collaboration among its employees. The result was SabreTown, a social networking platform built on top of the company's content management system that uses some of the same concepts as LinkedIn and Facebook. Seventy percent of Sabre's employees use the system at least once a month, Johnson said.

Since its launch in 2007, SabreTown has given employees a place to collaborate and share information and knowledge. It all starts with the employees' profile, which goes way beyond name, title, and contact information. Profiles include questions about places you've traveled, schools you've attended, "corporate gigs and contacts," and "skills, expertise or things you rule in." The profile also asks about sports and music interests and favorite lunch spots and watering holes.

When employees have a question, they enter it into SabreTown's question-and-answer function. For example, employees can ask how to complete a process, how to handle a unique situation, or where to look for data. Using an inference or relevance engine, SabreTown sends the question to 20 employees, based on their profiles. Most questions are answered within an hour and each question receives an average of nine responses.[19] Answers to questions are then stored within the network.

---

19 Prescient Digital Media case study on Sabre Town. http://www.prescientdigital.com/articles/intranet-articles/employee-social-networking-case-study/ Retrieved 9/29/09.

"There is a lot of experience out there," Johnson said of the Sabre community. "There are people who have worked for Sabre for many years. Younger employees can ask questions and have access to employees who have been here for awhile and have a wealth of expertise to share."

So what's the difference between SabreTown and a knowledge base?

"The difference is in its connectivity," Johnson said. "Knowledge bases don't have profiles, the blogging component, or the group component. SabreTown has more of a community feel than a system feel. When we designed it, we talked about it in terms of adoption, not deployment. We don't look at it as a technology solution; it's a people solution. SabreTown is not a database of information. Its value comes from the ease in which it connects individuals."

"Companies got burned in the 1990s," Holtzman said. "Today there's the reality that companies have limited resources and limited time. I think today one of the keys to KM is not formal systems, but informal networks."

Global technology trends may be proving him right. In 2009, Prescient Digital Media, a technology-consulting group, surveyed 561 organizations on their use of Intranet 2.0 and social media networks. Organizations from around the world responded to the survey, and their participation was broken down this way:

36% were from the United States

24% from Europe

11% from Canada

11% from Australia and New Zealand

10% from the United Kingdom

8% from Asia, Africa, South and Central America

The number of employees with access to the company Intranet varied:

61% of the organizations had more than 1,000 employees

32% had 6,000 or more employees

39% had less than 1,000 employees

Of the companies Prescient surveyed, 71 percent said they used Intranet 2.0 tools for knowledge management, but 77 percent said they used these tools for employee collaboration.

The key to informal networks within an organization is that they don't remain virtual, said Holtzman. As colleagues meet online, they become a resource for each other off line as well, which contributes to breaking down silos across the organization. And, the fact that this activity is self-motivated means that the new relationships will be stronger than formal, structural mechanisms the executive suite imposes.

"There Has to Be a Need"

In 2005, a group of Northern California oil refineries, steel processors, chemical manufacturers, power production and distribution companies, and water and waste treatment plants came together to discuss the industry's troubling workforce trends. Each company realized that 20 to 50 percent of their production workers would be eligible for retirement within the next five years. Together, over 100 new employees would need to be hired and trained every year to replace workers who would elect to retire.

The companies had to do something. In 2006, the manufacturing industry in two San Francisco Bay Area counties employed 100,000 workers. Projections showed that by 2012 it would employ 102,000 workers.

Company leaders created an industry partnership and approached Los Medanos College, a community college in Pittsburg, California, with an idea. Rather than creating training courses at each company, the partners proposed a community college program, a move that would save money, create a standardized curriculum, and ensure a steady stream of well-trained workers to replace retirees. And, as a program designed by industry for industry, the program would serve as a way to transfer knowledge from more experienced workers to new hires.

"Plants are becoming more reliable," said David Kail, PTEC director and instructor, who spent 30 years as a chemical engineer working in manufacturing before joining the team to design the new program. "If you have 30 years' experience at a plant, you've seen things that a new operator won't see in their lifetime. All instructors in this program are from industry. We want the stories because while plants are more reliable now, there is always a chance problems could occur. We want students to be able to respond to those problems. This is why sharing is a huge part of what we do here."

Excited about the prospect of creating good-paying jobs for its residents, the county's workforce development board and municipal groups joined the partners' effort to create the Process Technology Program (PTEC) at Los Medanos College (see Figure 3.4). A Department of Labor grant provided funding, and in December 2006, the PTEC program graduated its first class of 19 graduates.

Of course, this is an abbreviated version of the work that went into creating the PTEC program. But it illustrates the way organizations can come together to find solutions to Boomers leaving the workforce—and filling the inevitable knowledge gaps.

"There has to be a need," Kail said. "And industry has to be willing to invest in filling the need."

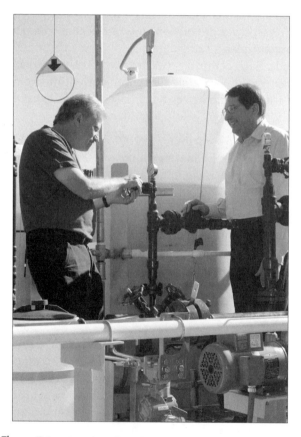

Figure 3.4 *David Kail (right), director and instructor of the PTEC program at Los Medanos College in Pittsburg, California, works with a student at the college's outdoor, hands-on project lab.*

Barriers to Knowledge Transfer...and Solutions

Many organizations are concerned about transferring knowledge from older to younger workers, but few are doing anything about it.[20]

"We know that companies take knowledge transfer seriously because our research shows that companies have identified it as a critical issue," said Diane Piktialis, Research Working Group and program leader at The Conference Board. "They're not doing much about it because they don't know what to do about it. They don't know where to start."

Prusak agrees with the idea that organizations may not know how to get started with knowledge transfer efforts. There are a few reasons for this. First, most people don't really understand what knowledge is, and often confuse knowledge transfer with information exchange, he said.

Another barrier to knowledge transfer is organizations' hesitation to offer incentives and rewards to mature workers for sharing what they know. People are often under duress on the job and are frequently so busy that unless they are given an incentive to transfer knowledge, they simply won't do it, Prusak said.

A third barrier that Prusak sees is the absence of knowledge curriculum in American business schools. Most degrees in business are based on lessons in finance, marketing, and technology. The way that knowledge works in organizations is rarely discussed, even though knowledge and knowledge exchange is the backbone of virtually every organization. Managers and business leaders don't receive training on the topic, which, in turn, feeds the theory that most people don't understand knowledge.

Ironically, another barrier to knowledge transfer may be an organization's lack of knowledge about its workforce. Piktialis said that most companies know how many employees are eligible to retire, but they don't have a grasp on which employees could leave and when. And while the issue piqued companies' interest in the early 2000s, some companies thought they were getting into "murky legal waters" by asking employees when they thought they would retire, she said.

---

20 Piktialis, Diane and Greenes, Kent. The Conference Board. "Bridging the Gaps: How to Transfer Knowledge in Today's Multigenerational Workplace. 2008. p. 4.

Culture and Attitudes

In some organizations, the attitude that one must keep their knowledge to themselves to secure their position must also change before meaningful work can be done. This means creating a more open culture and, in some cases, changing the organizational hierarchy. This can be a major challenge, especially for bureaucratic organizations. We will discuss methods that organizations use to create a knowledge culture in Chapter 10, "Nurturing a Knowledge Culture."

Generational learning preferences and corporate culture and attitudes also pose challenges to capture-and-transfer efforts. However, these are not showstoppers; rather, they are issues that organizations can address and learn to master.

Start with generational differences. In a 2007 article in *Training and Development* magazine, Tammy Erickson said learning is critical to organizations' ability to attract and retain top talent. Generation X and Y workers tend to choose their employer based on what they expect to learn there.

The Technology Hurdle

Grace Robbins, communications director for Robbins-Gioia, says that technology itself can be a barrier to knowledge transfer. While some have turned to technology as a remedy to many organizational woes, Robbins says that technology can be a chasm, rather than a bridge, when transferring knowledge between Boomers and Generations X and Y.

Younger workers are digital natives. Boomers are analog natives, and therefore, digital immigrants. For a first-generation digital citizen, adapting can be difficult. Boomers must take time to learn social network technology that younger generations use so freely. That means adapting to this new way of communicating and sharing so that they deliver information and knowledge in a compelling, relevant way to their younger counterparts.

Although a growing number of Boomers are proficient in the use of social media, many are not, Robbins said. Not knowing, or lacking awareness of new technologies makes one an outsider. Robbins compares it to being at a party, or in a classroom, where one doesn't speak the language.

The fact that government agencies and businesses use social media as a form of branding and sharing deepens the chasm, Robbins said. Organizations and individuals without this capability risk losing ground and being left behind in a new and rapidly growing area.

Learning means something different to Gen X and Y than it meant to Boomers, Erickson said. For Boomers, acquiring new knowledge often meant taking courses and programs for a stretch of time. For the younger generation, learning means people with knowledge take time out of their day to provide constructive tips as needed. Erickson calls this culture a "gift culture."

"The more an organization can create a culture in which people give freely of their time to help others learn, the more they will benefit," she said.

But "giving freely of your time" can be tricky in many organizations. In fact, a perceived lack of time is one of the main reasons why many organizations put off even the most informal capture-and-transfer efforts. Because time is such a precious commodity, formalizing roles and creating a budget for knowledge work are among the first steps toward building a culture that supports capture and transfer.

Going Forward

Knowledge is everywhere in our organizations. In fact, it's so prevalent that we tend to take it for granted, as if it will always be there. But we all know that one day the person with the knowledge that keeps an organization running may not be there. And then what? Organizations need a plan, and that starts with the realization that an organization's knowledge may be at risk of leaving the building. Once a manager or leader comes to this realization, the next step is to assess the knowledge in the organization. Who holds the knowledge the organization needs to stay in business? How many experts are there in relation to the size of the organization? How rare is the expertise, and how much demand is there for it?

There are many questions that managers can ask to help them assess the situation and chart a course. The first step is to look at the organization in a very thorough way. Sometimes, it means looking at an entire industry, which is what we will do in Chapter 4, "Trouble on the Horizon as Boomers Step Away."

4

Trouble on the Horizon as Boomers Step Away

As you can see, knowledge comes in many forms, and in some industries, knowledge loss is a growing threat. Sure, Boomers stepping away from their jobs have given managers reasons to worry. But in some industries, the roots of the problem go much deeper.

For example, rallying younger people to certain jobs is a problem. "Generation Y, the kinder, gentler kids raised by Boomers aren't stepping up to many of the jobs where you're away from home a lot," said Christine Resler, vice president of applied technologies, Smith Technologies, Inc., pinpointing one of the issues plaguing the oil and gas industry as Boomers move toward retirement. "So you see Boomers sticking around in jobs, making good money, but nobody is stepping up to take their place. I see this especially with geologists and senior rig managers and employees."

Another industry, manufacturing, suffers from a similar image problem. Gen Y, in particular, is not attracted to manufacturing. When asked about manufacturing and the prospect of working in this industry, young people tend to stereotypically describe it as an "assembly line." They describe factories as "dark," "dangerous," and "dirty" places and liken manufacturing careers to "serving a life sentence."[1]

---

1 National Association of Manufacturers, The Manufacturing Institute, and Deloitte & Touche LLP. Keeping America Competitive: How a Talent Shortage Threatens U.S. Manufacturing, A White Paper. 2003. p 9.

Negative perceptions and image problems make industries such as utilities, oil and gas producers and marketers, and manufacturing especially vulnerable to impending Boomer retirements. These industries aren't drawing the people who might replace mature workers as they step away. Systemic issues, such as hiring practices and cost-cutting, compound the problem and have created an environment where knowledge gaps could impact operations.

These issues are not unique to energy and manufacturing. Other industries grapple with similar perceptions and challenges. You may even recognize some of these within your own organization. The examples we provide here highlight the reasons why it's important to work through systemic issues, capture Boomer knowledge, find a new cadre of skilled workers, and share what is valuable with them in a way that is meaningful.

Considerations in Attracting New Talent

Is your business cyclical, such that it becomes a problem in recruiting new talent?

Does your business have jobs/roles/functions that today's younger workers potentially might find unappealing, such as the following:

- *Location (away from an urban center)*

- *Excessive amounts of travel/away-from-family time*

- *Working conditions/environment that are a competitive disadvantage*

The Pain Behind the Numbers

The Bureau of Labor Statistics reports that a handful of industries will be most likely to suffer the biggest impact as Boomers begin to leave the workforce. These industries include manufacturing, educational services, public administration, and health services.[2] The Department of Labor's Employment and Training Administration (ETA) has identified the energy industry, comprising oil and gas extraction, utilities, and mining, as a target industry in a series of reports on workforce challenges. Trade associations representing these industries have also done some major number crunching that confirms troubling scenarios lie just ahead.

---

2 Bureau of Labor Statistics, *Monthly Labor Review*, "Gauging the labor force effects of retiring baby-boomers." July, 2000. pp. 20-24.

The oil and gas industries include major producers such as BP, ExxonMobil, and Chevron, oilfield services companies that provide the tools and equipment required in the exploration of oil, including drilling rigs, offshore rigs, and transport equipment, and independent producers. The latter is represented by the Independent Petroleum Association of America (IPAA), and they project that nearly 40 percent of the industry's skilled professionals will reach retirement age during this 2000 to 2010 decade.[3]

In 2009, the Interstate Oil and Gas Compact Commission reported that "the average age of employees working for major operators and service companies is in the range of 46 to 49 years old. With the average retirement age for the industry being 55 years, it is obvious that the industry faces a crisis in the next seven to ten years as more than half of the employee base leaves the work force."[4]

Dave Buczek, a business and technology consultant with deep knowledge in energy, especially the oil and gas sector, noted in a manager's perspective article, "Combating Brain Drain," that the "…impending 'brain drain' will have far-reaching implications for the industry… producers and service companies may not have the manpower to supply the world's growing demand for oil and gas."[5]

Oil and Gas—Boom or Bust

Oil and gas is one example of an industry that is facing a workforce crisis as Boomers begin to step away. It is a boom or bust business complete with head-jerking cycles of price and supply (see Figure 4.1). When prices are high, made so by strong worldwide demand, exploration and production become more cost-effective. Drilling projects spike, and companies seek additional highly skilled workers. Business booms, people stay, and new recruits come in.[6]

When prices drop, so does exploration and production. Companies need fewer people, and more leave the field for other opportunities.

"The cyclical nature of the business scares a lot of people," Resler said.

A 2007 report she supervised stated: "Historically, employees are trained during periods of high and increasing oil prices and laid off during slow periods. Since most workers cannot wait for the next peak period to get their jobs back, they naturally opt for different industries."[7] The industry suffers from cyclical

---

3 Independent Petroleum Association of America, 2008 Oil and Natural Gas Issues Briefing Book.

4 Interstate Oil and Gas Compact Commission: http://www.iogcc.state.ok.us/manpower-shortages. Retrieved 11/9/09.

5 *Journal of Petroleum Technology*. January, 2002.

6 Boyden and Global Energy Management Institute, University of Houston. The Workforce Crisis in the Upstream Oil and Gas Sector. 2007.

7 Ibid. 2007.

trends that make it difficult for companies to retain skilled professionals such as geologists, petroleum engineers, field engineers, and drillers who are "often targeted by talent poachers" from other industries.[8]

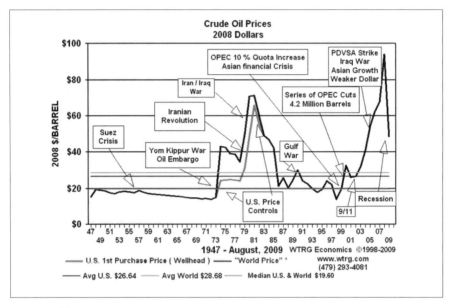

Figure 4.1   *Here is a graph showing the cyclical nature of oil prices since 1947, making worker retention more challenging. (Crude Oil Prices 1947—August, 2009, WTRG Economics, 2009)*

There are other problems as well. There is a perception, especially among Millennials, that the realities of the industry are not conducive to some of the lifestyle factors that are important to this group. Long hours, frequent periods of being away from home for days or even weeks at a time, last-minute scheduling demands, harsh working conditions (for example, being on an oil rig in the Gulf of Mexico during a blustery storm), and a rigid hierarchical reporting structure are realities that make it difficult to recruit Millennials.

The industry has also experienced challenges in recruiting new professionals from college engineering and science programs because of the low number of geoscience graduates. Enrollment in geosciences programs at the college level, and the number of geoscience degrees granted, as seen in Figure 4.2, plummeted after the mid-1980s oil bust and has never resumed pre-bust trends, in part due to the decoupling of enrollments and oil prices. There has been a

8 Boyden and Global Energy Management Institute, University of Houston. The Workforce Crisis in the Upstream Oil and Gas Sector. 2007.

rebound in undergraduate enrollments over the last couple of years, partially driven by a growing interest in issues surrounding energy and environmental topics.[9] A September, 2009, *Newsweek* article noted that oil companies are starting to think about alternative energy investments. Not just as token gestures, such as putting up a few solar panels or sponsoring a green conference, "but as real businesses that might one day turn real profits...."[10]

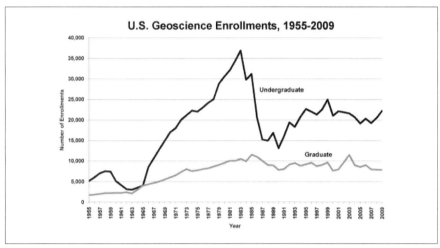

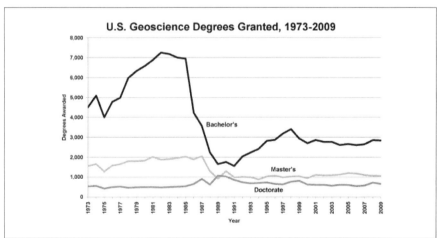

Figure 4.2   *Changes in enrollment in geosciences over the last decades.*

9 Keane, C.M. American Geological Institute. 2009. Geoscience Enrollments Jump Sharply in 2008-2009. Geoscience Currents, No. 23; http://www.agiweb.org/workforce/Currents/Currents-023-Enrollments2009.pdf.

10 Rana Foroohar. "Big Oil Goes Green for Real." *Newsweek,* published September 19, 2009, from the magazine issue dated Sept. 28, 2009.

Given that the majority of geoscience occupations require a Master's degree, there is on average a five-year lag between enrollment and workforce trends. However, the long-term trend of low numbers of enrollments and graduates from geoscience programs has created a critical problem in the geoscience profession. Approximately half of the current geoscience workforce is approaching retirement within 10 to 15 years, and the supply of new geoscience graduates falls short of replacement needs. In the oil and gas industry, the demand for new geoscience graduates exceeds the current and projected supply. Age demographic trends indicate that the number of geoscientists in their early 30s is approximately half of those nearing retirement.[11]

Cost-cutting measures that began in the 1980s when oil prices began to plummet continued through the 1990s and eliminated opportunities for Generation X employees. These employees would have been on track as logical choices for current senior technical and management roles.

The good news is that industry professionals including geoscientists, engineers, project managers, and mid-level and executive management have started making knowledge capture a priority. In a 2009 Oil & Gas Industry Collaboration Survey sponsored by Microsoft Corporation and Accenture, geoscientist, engineer, project manager, and mid-level and executive management respondents said they were aware that older workers were leaving the field. Respondents also expressed concern about capturing these older workers' knowledge and expertise as a way to maintain business continuity.

When asked how prepared their companies are to retain knowledge from workers who are leaving, nearly 40 percent said they were somewhat prepared and 19 percent reported that they were not prepared at all. Almost 50 percent of respondents who said they were not prepared reported that "company management doesn't feel this is a problem."[12]

This same survey shows there are positive developments. Companies are using electronic and written documents as the primary way to capture workers' knowledge, and there is a growing use of social networking, instant messaging, and even some use of wikis and podcasts.[13]

Utilities—A Perfect Storm
Without access to sufficient supplies of affordable oil, gas, nuclear, and green forms of energy that utilities provide, every other sector of American business (to say nothing of our own homes) would quickly be brought to its knees.

---

11 American Geological Institute, Status of the Geoscience Workforce 2009. www.agiweb.org/workforce/reports.html.

12 Microsoft/Accenture. Oil & Gas Industry Collaboration Survey 2009.

13 Ibid. 2009.

The utilities industry plays a critical role in the country's economy and even its national security. Imagine Armed Forces facilities, with their power-dependent weapons computer systems, suddenly frozen because of a utility grid blackout.

But, as with oil and gas, a problem looms: A huge wave of retirements could occur over the next few years, threatening the industry's ability to provide safe, stable, and reliable power.

Ralph Izzo, chairman and CEO of the Public Service Enterprise Group, a New Jersey-based energy company, sounded the alarm in a speech to the Labor and Management Public Affairs Committee (LAMPAC), a cooperative effort among utilities and the International Brotherhood of Electrical Workers (IBEW) in Washington, D.C. "Without exaggeration, the energy industry could face a perfect storm unless we ramp up efforts to prepare the highly skilled workforce of the future," Izzo said. "Powerful currents are heading our way: the wave of Baby Boomers retiring…the lack of skilled replacement workers…growing energy needs…."[14]

Other leaders have expressed similar concerns.

"It is possible to end up with a scenario where some utilities are operating like utilities in third-world countries, said Steven C. Kussmann, president of SK Management, a utility industry consulting firm, in a 2005 article in *Public Power Daily*, a publication of the American Public Power Association.[15] "They won't have a sufficient number of qualified people to operate them. The result will be dangerous working conditions and unreliable power."

Mary Miller, vice president of Human Resources with Edison Electric Institute, an association of electric companies representing 70 percent of the U.S. electric power industry, reported that when they surveyed five key positions representing nearly half of their workforce, they found that 40 to 50 percent were eligible to retire or expected to leave in the next five years.

"Legacy" Jobs–Challenges Over and Above

Do you have jobs/roles/functions that have seen little or no turnover of skilled workers for years or even decades?

Are some jobs/roles/functions mission critical? Is there a job where the employee literally "built" the job?

14 Public Service Enterprise Group (PSEG) Media Center, "The Energy Workforce of the Future." First Annual National Meeting, Labor and Management Public Affairs Committee (LAMPAC) Washington, D.C. June 27, 2008.

15 *Public Power Daily* is a publication of the American Public Power Association.

Tennessee Valley Authority (TVA) is a good example. It is the country's largest public power company and employs over 12,000 people. TVA facilities include a combination of coal-fired plants, hydroelectric dams, nuclear plants, combustion-turbine plants, and 17,000 miles of transmission lines.[16] Following a large increase in staffing during the 1960s and 1970s, TVA went through significant downsizing in the 1980s and 1990s. As a result, the utility has a very mature workforce that is rapidly approaching retirement, according to Jerry Landon of Talent Management at TVA.

The average age of the national workforce is 40, but at TVA the average age of some of its highly specialized and technical employees is 47.[17] This is a concern for the utility company because these employees have knowledge that is critical to the operation and maintenance of TVA's plants and transmission facilities, and their knowledge is not adequately documented. "Many of these employees *literally* built the plants and facilities, which they now operate and maintain," according to TVA.[18]

Experienced workers in this industry often have unique, intuitive, and sometimes undocumented knowledge about obsolete and soon-to-be-replaced equipment. The natural tendency is to shy away from incurring "unnecessary" costs to maintain such equipment. For example, one utility manager described a central service facility that had, while still playing an important role in switching operations, a diminishing future because older equipment was gradually being replaced. A lead technician who was the primary operator of the older equipment was also likely to retire in the near future and did not have a backup technician to support the facility. With no alternate in place, the facility was vulnerable to going down should the lead become unavailable.

The number of people who have trained to become part of the electric power sector workforce has gone up and down over the years, depending on the workforce needs of the industry, macroeconomic conditions, and the attractiveness of alternate career paths, said Miller. After a period of relatively rapid growth in the 1970s, the industry grew more slowly in the 1980s and 1990s.

With deregulation and a more competitive power market, companies increasingly focused on productivity, which enabled managers to reduce hiring levels. Because the industry's demand for new workers slowed significantly in the 1980s and 1990s, companies scaled back internal training programs.

---

16 Knowledge Retention: Preventing Knowledge From Walking Out the Door. An Overview of Processes and Tools at the Tennessee Valley Authority. http://www.tva.gov/knowledgeretention/pdf/overview.pdf. Retrieved 11/17/09.

17 Ibid. 11/17/09.

18 Ibid. 11/17/09.

"There have been a couple of dynamics converging in our industry, including the peaking of Baby Boomers and their eligibility to retire... but several factors are exacerbating the numbers in the energy industry: our workforce is four to five years older than the national average; many of our jobs are more physical, such as line workers and maintenance technicians; and workers typically retire earlier," Miller said. "And there has been a curtailing of hiring in the past due to the dynamics of restructuring: attempts to deregulate energy markets, cost pressures on most companies in this industry, and a lot of mergers and acquisitions activity in the early 90s—all of which contributed to a slowing in the natural pipeline of hiring."

Utilities have also found a significant skills gap, and companies have struggled to identify qualified candidates. Miller also perceives a weakening throughout society of the appreciation for the value of skilled craft work.

Van Ton-Quinlivan, director of Workforce Development at Pacific Gas & Electric (PG&E), notes that predicting retirement is still more of an art than a science.

"With the Boomers departing and also with an aggressive climate change policy affecting our industry, it may create a situation where the demand will be greater than the supply of skilled workers in the future," she said.

Energy utilities are working to avoid a situation where they cannot find workers with the right skills. Some industry leaders have put in place aggressive programs that include strategic workforce planning efforts. Ton-Quinlivan leads a knowledge transfer initiative at PG&E that identifies key areas where critical tacit knowledge is at risk because an experienced worker may leave. The near-term objective is to rank-order the areas of risk to the enterprise. Ton-Quinlivan found that once workers and skills are prioritized, the team will work with supervisors and subject matter experts to mitigate the risk. This will include codifying the knowledge and transferring it to succeeding groups of workers who will be stepping into those roles.

In addition to focusing on knowledge transfer, PG&E, which serves much of California, has launched a workforce development program called PG&E PowerPathway™, which seeks to build capacity in California to produce the skilled workers needed by the utility and energy industry. One goal is to uncover industry-driven needs (the pain shared among multiple employers in attracting skilled workers with the right skills at the right time). Another is to reach deep into high schools and community colleges to develop talent by engaging in public-private partnerships.

The utility industry overall is proactively visiting colleges and technical schools to talk about how select technologies are changing the industry.

According to Ton-Quinlivan, PG&E has taken this concept a step further by creating partnerships with workforce investment boards, colleges, and technical schools to create career pathways that strengthen candidate readiness to compete for future energy jobs.

Still the threat of knowledge loss looms.

Complications in Retaining and Recruiting Talent

Has your business or industry faced restructuring, deregulation, or mergers and acquisitions that complicate your efforts in retaining valued workers or hiring talented new ones?

Have you ever examined how changing societal perceptions of work have an effect on recruiting in your business?

"Workforce development is a safety issue, a reliability issue, a customer care and green issue rolled into one," Izzo said during his June 2008 speech. "Investing in the future of our industry begins with investing in people. If this sounds familiar, it should. Skilled, dedicated, and motivated employees have always been our most important asset and will continue to be."[19]

A 2006 study by Warren Causey, vice president of Sierra Energy Group, the research and analysis division of Energy Central, an information products provider to electric power professionals, suggests that a major disconnect could exist among utility executives and lower level operations and engineering personnel responsible for operating and maintaining critical functions. The study concluded that only 57 percent of all utilities have a strategy in place for managing the impending utility workforce crisis.[20]

Causey's report shows that the industry has started to reduce this disconnect by instituting knowledge capture and transfer efforts. Yet many senior managers remain wary of investing in the time-consuming process of retaining boomer knowledge, in part because it is an unfamiliar practice. However, the Energy Central study, which also surveyed utility employees on workforce planning concepts, found that knowledge transfer was considered critical to daily and ongoing operations.

19 Public Service Enterprise Group (PSEG) Media Center, "The Energy Workforce of the Future." First Annual National Meeting, Labor and Management Public Affairs Committee (LAMPAC) Washington, D.C. June 27, 2008.

20 Energy Central, Research and Analysis Division, The High Cost of Losing Intellectual Capital. May, 2006.

The report suggests that an effective workforce planning process should address these questions:

■ How can organizations assess the amount of knowledge that could be lost?

■ How can organizations capture the knowledge before it leaves?

■ How does employee turnover affect each job function?

Causey does sound a hopeful note that while knowledge transfer alone will not be sufficient to address the loss of many experienced workers, utilities can, and are beginning to, change and improve processes with technology so that incoming employees can carry out the corporate mission. Improving processes and technology for the benefit of incoming employees means that organizations can avoid over-reliance on those who are beginning to step away.

Manufacturing—Partly Cloudy Weather Ahead

While oil and gas and power utilities are major components of America's business infrastructure, it is difficult to imagine an industry that is more central to the success of American business than manufacturing. For nearly all of the twentieth century, manufacturing has been the engine that has moved the United States into global, economic dominance. The industry has also been a source of innovation and productivity that has given Americans an unrivaled standard of living.

Manufacturing, which encompasses aerospace, metalworking, food processing, automotive, and plastics, has an enormous impact on the success of many sectors of the U.S. supply chain. With its appetite for raw materials and prodigious output of goods, manufacturing touches nearly all industries from hospitality to high-tech to retail and health and transportation.

But as with the other two industries, the skies are not without clouds. The Bureau of Labor Statistics reports that the occupational group referred to as *production* is projected to decline by more than a half million jobs from 2006 to 2016. The manufacturing sector employs about 70 percent of workers in all production occupations, but growth in nonmanufacturing sectors, such as employment services, construction, and wholesale trade, will partially offset the manufacturing portion of the decline. [21]

Many of the job losses in production occupations are a result of manufacturers' increased use of automation and rising levels of imports of manufactured goods, both factors that will reduce the need for these kinds of workers over

---

21 Bureau of Labor Statistics, Monthly Labor Review. Occupational Employment Projections to 2016. November, 2007. p. 92.

the next decade. Even though production in the manufacturing sector is anticipated to grow in dollar and annual growth rate terms, employment in the sector is expected to decline significantly from 2006 to 2016.[22]

Manufacturing is among the industries that will suffer the most as managers and highly skilled workers begin to retire, according to the BLS. Manufacturing businesses are in a tough spot because it takes time to train new employees on the increasingly advanced methods of production that are the norm around the globe. The loss of highly skilled Boomers over the next few years may present challenging timing issues for manufacturers. Will the supply of newly trained, skilled workers keep up with worldwide demand as consumers' income grows?

"Manufacturers have competent, knowledgeable people, but as they start retiring, the companies have nowhere to turn for the work these people have been doing because their skills are not easily learned," said Jeff Owens, president and COO of Advanced Technology Services, Inc. (ATS), which provides technical support on production equipment for global manufacturers. "Companies haven't spent the time and energy to develop the next generation to come in behind them."

Adhesive company 3M is one manufacturing leader with a large number of Boomers who are eyeing retirement.

"We are a company of many Boomers," said Brian Ronningnen, manager of human capital planning at 3M. "3M's revenues grew at a fast rate in the late 1970s and early 1980s, and the company hired a lot of people to support that growth. Many of those employees are still with 3M and represent much of the knowledge that drives 3M Innovation. So, generationally speaking, we have a Boomer bubble currently, and our challenge is that a very important part of our workforce could elect to retire over the next several years. Potential retirements in conjunction with a competitive job market could lead to a double-whammy. Therefore, a critical part of our workforce planning and management focuses on retention and knowledge transfer. It's an important part of our plan to retain these employees as a key segment and use our knowledge transfer processes to ensure that what they know is passed on to others before they leave."

The National Association of Manufacturers' advocacy arm, the National Center of the American Workforce, confirms the double whammy.

---

22 Bureau of Labor Statistics, Monthly Labor Review. Occupational Employment Projections to 2016. November, 2007. p. 92.

"One of the biggest challenges in U.S. manufacturing today is the broadening skills gap, which is taking an increasingly negative toll on America's ability to compete in the global economy. This problem will worsen as the Baby Boomers retire from an increasingly high-tech workplace with no skilled employees in the pipeline to replace them."[23]

More than 80 percent of all U.S. manufacturers report that an overall shortage of qualified employees affects their ability to meet customer demands.[24] The report found a moderate to severe shortage of qualified skilled production employees, technicians, and engineers. Organizations have also struggled to fill nontechnical, soft-skills roles in customer service, human resources, and finance.

This shortage of qualified workers, coupled with the loss of the skilled labor force, raises important questions about business performance and economic implications for the manufacturing industry:

- Can the manufacturing industry maintain production that is consistent with global customer demand, or will shortfalls present opportunities for other countries that are ready to fill the void?

- Can the industry meet productivity targets while keeping costs under control and competition at bay while also saving jobs? Reduced productivity as newer workers come up to speed takes a toll on managers' ability to control costs.

- Can the industry acknowledge the real costs spent in recruiting, apprenticeships, and training for this newer generation of skilled workers?

- Can the industry meet customer service and satisfaction demands during the time it takes to complete the replacement of departing Boomers?

Manufacturing has some of the same challenges as we've seen with the energy industries, principally image and education. Millennials are not attracted to manufacturing in the kinds of numbers needed to balance the exodus of Boomers. A troubling picture emerges when industry experts ask young people about embarking on a career in manufacturing. Regardless of their ethnicity, geography, or socio-economic status, young people describe the industry as being one where a worker is like a "slave to the line" or a "robot."[25]

---

23 National Association of Manufacturers. National Center for the American Workforce. Retrieved 12/1/09.

24 National Association of Manufacturers and Deloitte Consulting. Skills Gap Report—A Survey of the American Manufacturing Workforce. 2005.

25 National Association of Manufacturers, The Manufacturing Institute and Deloitte & Touche. Keeping America Competitive—How a Talent Shortage Threatens U.S. Manufacturing. 2003. p. 9.

Gen X and Y also have a skewed perception of what kind of money they could earn in the manufacturing industry. In 2006, the Contra Costa Workforce Development Board, a business-led, public body in the San Francisco Bay Area, conducted a survey[26] to measure the attitudes of high school and community college students regarding manufacturing and found they had an inaccurate picture of what they could earn annually.

"A majority believes that even a highly experienced individual in the manufacturing and refining industry is limited to an income of less than $55,000 annually," the group's report states. "Most of the students have an image of the jobs as 'blue collar,' and believe that most jobs in manufacturing and refining do not require a high level of education."

Regional educational leaders paint a far different picture in literature about programs that prepare students for careers with oil refineries, steel processors, chemical manufacturers, power production and distribution companies, and local water and waste treatment plants. For example, to earn a certificate of achievement in an Electrical and Electronic Technology Program, students must complete courses that cover topics such as physics, semiconductor devices, and instrument calibration. Informational literature describes a high-skill, high-pay career with a starting salary that begins around $70,000 to $90,000 per year with overtime.[27]

The Workforce Development Board's survey also showed that 75 percent of the students had never considered a career in the manufacturing and refining industry. And a majority of the students surveyed believed the sector was a minor employer in Contra Costa County. In reality, in 2005, manufacturing ranked as the fifth largest sector in the county and accounted for about 100,000 regional jobs.[28]

In addition, the perception that offshoring is an inevitable and natural transition compounds the poor image of manufacturing. With more manufacturing jobs leaving the country, Millennials may not see this industry as having an especially bright future. Additionally, a common belief is that a "knowledge-based" economy will replace a manufacturing economy.[29]

---

26 The 2006 Contra Costa Workforce Development Board survey received several hundred responses from high school students and about two hundred responses from community college students, according to the group's public relations representative.

27 Los Medanos College Electrical and Electronic Technician Program brochure. Received September, 2009.

28 Workforce Development Board of Contra Costa County, Manufacturing Survey Executive Summary. 2006.

29 U.S. Department of Labor, Employment and Training Administration. Addressing the Workforce Challenges of America's Advanced Manufacturing Workforce. November, 2005. p. 8.

Education is a concern worth considering, and it is not limited to manufacturing. In 2005, The National Association of Manufacturers and Deloitte Consulting presented a skills gap report that covered the manufacturing industry's short supply of skilled production employees, engineers, and scientists. In the report, NAM and Deloitte referred to "… the frequently voiced concern that the United States is not graduating enough students with technical, engineering and science degrees to meet the current demand for employees with these skills."[30] The report also concluded that the American education system was inadvertently creating a negative stereotype of manufacturing. To a large degree, this stereotype is no longer realistic because of the strong shift toward the use of technology, which shows signs of transforming every aspect of a manufacturing operation, the report said.

There are bright spots. For example, the Manufacturing Institute is focused on advising the educational system on how to move more students through the primary, secondary, and post-secondary pipeline who have interests in advanced production and engineering careers and exhibit skills in these areas. Advanced production methods increasingly require employees at all levels in a company to have a far wider range of skills than in the past, and the Manufacturing Institute wants to make this point clear to young people. For manufacturing, sparking young people's interest is a priority because keeping up with demand depends on a new workforce with a variety of skills.

In addition, competition from developed and developing countries and alliances such as the European Union, BRIC (Brazil, Russia, India, and China), and Southeast Asia are forcing U.S. manufacturers to examine every phase of their operations. Today's competitive landscape has U.S. manufacturers wrestling not only with cost but also with production flexibility and efficiency, as well as product design and quality. Globalization and competition are making manufacturing more dynamic and exciting, a far cry indeed from the "dirty and noisy" reputation that manufacturing seeks to put behind it. These elements are what the industry hopes can be used to recruit the next generation of workers.

The highly skilled manufacturing workforce has low turnover because jobs have proven to be stable, the salary and benefits can be very good, and the Boomer generation workers have classic pension plans (unlike newer employees who contribute to 401K plans). It is not uncommon in manufacturing to see generations of families working side by side or one handing off the tool to the next.

---

30 National Association of Manufacturers and Deloitte Consulting. Skills Gap Report—A Survey of the American Manufacturing Workforce. 2005.

Food for Thought

Oil and gas, utilities, and manufacturers grapple with workforce challenges that may also touch other industries. Here are some questions, gleaned from our research into these industries, that may help you think through workforce challenges in your own organization or industry:

- How does the culture and environment within your organization or industry support or hinder your efforts to attract and retain a well-trained workforce?

- To what extent is senior management prioritizing the aging demographic and its effects? What data can you use to convince them to support a knowledge retention program?

- Are your organization's training programs inactive and in need of a shot in the arm? Could you use a new approach to knowledge sharing?

- What are your future workforce needs and how will you plan for these?

- What are your education and skill expectations for entry-level workers?

- Will the shortfall in the educational system pipeline that affects the industries highlighted in this chapter affect your industry and company? If so, would an internal knowledge sharing program help mitigate this skills shortfall?

- Are your current initiatives designed to prepare qualified, skilled workers to replace your departing Boomers?

The good news is that plant managers and senior executives are recognizing the importance of knowledge retention efforts and seeing these efforts as important to business continuity as Boomers leave. And mature workers want to transfer the knowledge they have accumulated. In the manufacturing industry, mentoring has become the preferred practice, largely because manufacturing workers are action-oriented and comfortable with "showing and doing," according to Owens of ATS.

"With the older generation, on an individual level, there is a strong desire to transfer knowledge to the younger, eager generation," said Owens.

"The older ones have an attitude of 'whatever I can do to help.' When they leave, they don't want to leave the company in the lurch, particularly if they have stock in the company or if their pension comes from the company. They are not looking to damage the company."

The Future in Focus

As you can see, there is trouble on the horizon for the industries we've covered here. The trouble relates to stronger-than-average demographic shifts, volatility, and the changing nature of business and stereotypes that make attracting younger workers more difficult. However, leaders are making strides and taking action to overcome these challenges.

Few companies are likely to escape the effects of Boomer retirements, whether it's tomorrow or in five to ten years. As we move on to the next chapters, we'll look at practical steps that managers can take to capture Boomers' skills, knowledge, and expertise for the next generation of workers. These steps include assessing your workforce and stemming the brain drain before it becomes a serious problem for your company.

Boarding the Knowledge Train

When you think about knowledge capture and transfer programs, imagine two trains running on parallel tracks.[1] The first train represents the immediate issue—impending Boomer retirements—and managers' urgent efforts to capture and transfer Boomer knowledge before they head out the door. The second train represents a long-term, sustainable approach to knowledge retention—the development of a knowledge culture. Both trains are traveling in the same direction, and both are bound for the same place. You may be asking which train you should board first—the Boomer retirement train or the knowledge culture train. The answer is both.

"Even when you aren't facing a wave of retirements, you will still have key individuals that leave the organization from time to time," said Vic Passion, an instructional designer and project management consultant. "That's why organizations make knowledge capture and transfer a part of their culture, so they can preserve knowledge now and in the future."

But if you're trying to get your executive team's attention, presenting them with plans to create a knowledge culture may not be the best approach. If you narrow your focus to capturing and transferring Boomer knowledge, you are more likely to gain executive and stakeholder buy-in, which is critical to the success of your program—both today and tomorrow.

---

1 This analogy provided by Vic Passion.

"We all know that building a culture that values knowledge capture is a best business practice," Passion said. "But the Boomer exodus is a more compelling story to tell executives because it's here and now."

Passion suggested analyzing the Boomer issue and using that analysis to get buy-in and resources to make the knowledge culture happen down the road. Gathering the information you need and getting your program off the ground won't happen overnight, so it's wise to start now. Or, as the Tennessee Valley Authority (TVA), a federally owned power company with a well-known knowledge retention program advises: Start. Somewhere. (See Figure 5.1.)

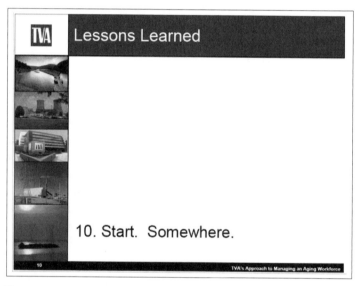

Figure 5.1   *Advice from a Tennessee Valley Authority slide presentation reminds us that we won't go anywhere until we take that first step.*

Planning for Tomorrow

Analyzing your organization and which areas are vulnerable to knowledge loss is a critical first step for creating a knowledge retention program. But what's the next step? This is a common question, and probably best answered by looking at organizations that have navigated the process.

When designing our approach to workforce analysis in this book, we referred to workforce planning models that had been well documented and time-tested by organizations including the County of Fairfax, Virginia, and the State of South Carolina. If you work in private industry, you may be wondering why we would refer to workforce planning guidelines designed by government.

The answer is that the government's workforce is older than its private-sector counterpart,[2] and many government entities have been using workforce planning tools since the late 1990s. This is not always the case with private industry.

While private and public organizations have developed varying models for workforce planning, the processes are all very similar.[3] Generally speaking, workforce planning models analyze the competencies of the current workforce against anticipated needs to identify gaps. Workforce planning models help managers create plans for building the future workforce and evaluation processes to ensure that plans remain valid and meet their objectives.[4] These elements provide managers with a strategic basis for making short- and long-term plans to retain knowledge within an organization.

Workforce planning connects human resource decisions to the organization's strategic plan.[5] Through analysis, workforce planning helps managers understand the areas of their labor force that need to be strengthened. Keep in mind, though, workforce planning is not an exact science.

The process begins with revisiting your organization's strategic plan. If you haven't reviewed it in a while, dust it off and give it a close read. How does your goal to retain knowledge align with your organization's strategic plan? By starting the process with clear strategic objectives, managers can develop a plan to help them meet those objectives.[6] This plan will likely help managers in their quest for budget and resources, as they have now created a link between strategic objectives, the budget, and the human resource efforts required to accomplish organizational goals.[7]

While Human Resources personnel often handle workforce planning, the process must relate to other planning efforts to be successful.[8] Kristin Resta, senior human resources consultant with the Fairfax County Department of Human Resources, said she often advises agencies within her county to look far and wide when launching workforce planning efforts. While her recommendations apply to county government, the private sector could benefit from her advice to be as thorough as possible.

---

2 The Center for Organizational Research, a division of Linkage, Inc. The Aging and Retiring Government Workforce. 2003. p. 3.

3 United States Department of Health and Human Services. Workforce Planning Resource Guide. November, 1999. p. 2. Retrieved 10/2/09.

4 United States Department of Health and Human Services. Workforce Planning Resource Guide. November, 1999. p. 2. Retrieved 10/2/09.

5 County of Fairfax, Virginia, Department of Human Resources. Strategic Workforce Planning. August, 2003. p. 4.

6 County of Fairfax, Virginia, Department of Human Resources. Strategic Workforce Planning. August, 2003. p. 7.

7 This concept represented here: County of Fairfax, Virginia, Department of Human Resources. Strategic Workforce Planning. August, 2003. p. 7.

8 County of Fairfax, Virginia, Department of Human Resources. Strategic Workforce Planning. August, 2003. p. 7.

"We usually recommend managers look at their department's strategic plan and the county's strategic plan," said Resta. "We tell them to look at the budget process, new programs and services, and what is happening with succession planning and retirement. This way, they are looking at many planning efforts at the same time they are working on workforce planning."

Some experts have said that merging workforce planning and knowledge transfer efforts can be difficult, even unlikely, in heavily siloed organizations where knowledge transfer is a Knowledge Management or operations function and workforce planning is a Human Resources function. But some groups, such as the State of South Carolina Office of Human Resources, have successfully blended workforce planning and knowledge transfer efforts across agency and county lines.

For Sam Wilkins, director of South Carolina's Office of Human Resources (OHR), knowledge transfer is a key piece of workforce planning—one simply cannot exist without the other. Wilkins, who oversees the human resources activities of more than 80 state agencies, also knows something about silos. Each South Carolina agency, from the Arts Commission to the Department of Transportation, is broken into divisions. For example, the Department of Transportation may have a highway, administration, and bridge division, and separate units within those divisions that focus on interstates or roads. And the state's agencies are not all structured exactly the same; some have a handful of divisions, while others have many more.

In 2000, OHR officials reviewed their statewide workforce demographics and found that 29 percent of the workforce would be eligible to retire or enter into a retention incentive program within five years. Many of these employees worked in key leadership roles, leading the OHR to encourage the state's agencies to develop succession plans, knowledge transfer approaches, and other workforce planning strategies.[9]

OHR brought the state's HR directors together and used workforce demographics to present a snapshot of each agency's staffing issues. When OHR officials initially introduced workforce planning as a way to plan for the future, they were met with blank stares, Wilkins said.

"When we first talked about workforce planning, it seemed like such a big task," Wilkins remembered. "The HR directors' eyes glazed over. No one really knew where to start."

Wilkins had sound advice for the group: Start small. Take bites of the elephant; don't try to swallow it whole.

---

9 Office of Human Resources, South Carolina Budget and Control Board. South Carolina Workforce Plan. 2009.

Taking bites of the elephant meant that each agency's HR director would first review the data Wilkins had collected. Next, they analyzed their agency's workforce even further, focusing first on employees who had enrolled in a deferred retirement, or DROP, program.[10] Employees enrolled in the DROP program had worked for the state for 28 years, and were entitled to full retirement, but had opted to work for up to five more years.

Then the directors looked at employees who were eligible to retire but had not enrolled in the DROP program. Theoretically, these employees could retire at any time.

Directors then looked at which employees were critical to agency and unit operations. How would a key employee's retirement impact the unit? How would their retirement impact the agency as a whole?

Once the directors had identified retirement-eligible employees and the impact their retirements might have on respective agencies and units, they were able to gain a better understanding of future needs and perform a gap analysis.

By giving the directors some initial data and encouraging them to work methodically, Wilkins promoted a sense of possibility, and helped dispel the frustration that could crush a project before it even started.

"What I gave them initially were basic workforce demographics," Wilkins said. "Then they looked at where they were vulnerable and how they would address those vulnerabilities. Really, the more you drill down, the better decisions you will make."

Other groups have commented on the benefits of a well-researched, targeted approach to workforce planning. In a 2003 report, the Center for Organizational Research noted that the 12 organizations it profiled fared better when they zeroed in on the most strategic trouble spots and selectively addressed them.

The Business Case for Knowledge Retention

Drilling down, targeted approach…

This is all well and good, but what's the business case for building a knowledge retention program? Why should your organization invest in analyzing your workforce and developing a knowledge retention program?

Plenty of organizational leaders have asked themselves these questions, and the truth is many have responded by putting their knowledge management

---

10 South Carolina's deferred retirement program allows employees to continue to work for a specified amount of time after they retire and begin drawing their pensions.

woes aside during the economic slowdown that began in 2007. However, pushing the issue under the rug doesn't mean it has been resolved. As the workforce continues to age and change, experts predict more organizations will renew their concerns over losing valuable knowledge and look for new ways to retain intellectual capital. When it's time to address the issue again, managers will benefit from first building a strong business case to present to executive leadership.

It's important to acknowledge that transferring knowledge takes time and effort.[11] Address this simple fact from the beginning. And, while knowledge retention programs typically help companies work better, faster, and more efficiently, these programs certainly are not without cost.[12] However, before you focus exclusively on costs, take a look at how your organization could benefit from a knowledge retention program.

But first, a caveat.

In their 2008 report, Bridging the Gap, Diane Piktialis and Kent Greenes suggested that benefits from a knowledge transfer program "must be understood as *potential* benefits to organizations, since actual value isn't realized until knowledge is actually applied. The metrics here are slippery, because the process of application, unlike the process of transfer, is less easily controllable and quantifiable."[13] Piktialis and Greenes suggested that transferring knowledge from one person to another is only the beginning. The hard part is managing and monitoring how receivers apply knowledge to make a tangible difference in the way they work.

Piktialis and Greenes said that, assuming the knowledge is applied, the potential benefits resulting from knowledge transfer range from a change in productivity to increased speed adapting to change to new profit and growth. Still, it's important to factor costs into the equation.[14] Focusing on costs will help you target the specific knowledge you want to capture, understand why, create a realistic budget, and motivate employees by acknowledging its importance to the organization, Piktialis explained.

For Kathy Krumpe, president of MBT Business Solutions, the business case is a manager's big sales pitch to upper management. And, as with any sales effort, it's important to know your audience well, and what they expect from your research and presentation.

---

11 This concept represented here: Piktialis, Diane and Greenes, Kent. The Conference Board. Bridging the Gaps: How to Transfer Knowledge in Today's Multigenerational Workplace. 2008. p. 13.

12 Ibid. p. 13.

13 Ibid. p. 13.

14 Ibid. p. 13.

"It's how you begin to turn theory into reality," Krumpe said of the business case for a knowledge retention program. "It's where you answer the question, 'What does knowledge transfer mean for my company?' You have to be able to talk about what it's going to cost and what the company is going to get out of it."

When focusing on what the company will get out of the effort, brainstorm ideas based on key areas of the business. Think about how the organization could benefit from business continuity as veteran workers step away from the workforce. For example, effective knowledge capture and transfer will mean that valued knowledge exists in more places than one person's head. Knowledge retention efforts could also provide a seamless customer experience as the next generation of workers adapts what they've learned from their Boomer counterparts. And efficient workers mean fewer hours to accomplish tasks.

Additionally, some organizations that implement knowledge retention programs report reduced turnover among staff. Remember Scripps Health, the hospital system that implemented a nurse mentoring program? Their program reduced turnover rates from 20.3 percent in 2005 to 12.1 percent in 2008 because new nurses felt more supported and less overwhelmed on the job. Where have *you* noticed heavy turnover within your organization? Could a knowledge retention program be the answer?

Cultural considerations are also important. Knowledge retention programs have been known to increase morale, expand social networks, and enhance the learning environment in the workplace.

Craft a business case using the results of your brainstorming session and research into your organization's pain points (it's what keeps leaders up at nights). Generally speaking, a strong business case includes:[15]

- Executive summary that defines knowledge retention programs and provides details on why this is the right time to pursue this issue.

- Description of the business opportunity. How will the organization benefit from retaining Boomer knowledge?

- Description of how a knowledge retention program maps to strategic goals and objectives.

- Discussion of what the competition, or comparable organizations, has done to prepare for Boomers leaving the workforce.

---

15 Most content gathered during interview with Kathy Krumpe.

- Discussion of industry trends.

- Alternative knowledge retention solutions. Alternatives could be an established mentor program, where the organization adds jobs as Scripps Health did, versus a volunteer mentor program. What happens if the company opts to do nothing?

- Analysis of the cost of alternatives. What are the team's recommendations?

- Description of the governance model for the program. Who is responsible for the program's success? How will you measure success?

- Discussion of how the organization will determine return on investment (ROI) for the program. Will it be through reduced turnover? Increased productivity? Be sure to include a discussion of how long it will take the organization to reach "payback" on the program.

- Statement about next steps, which includes a preliminary project plan with proposed resources and timeline.

Calculate Return on Investment

There are many different ways to calculate ROI. Here's an easy formula that provides management with a ratio: (Benefit-Cost)/Cost = ROI.

Source: Kenneth H. Silber, Ph.D. Calculating Return on Investment, Version 4.0, April 3, 2002. www.silberperformance.com

Of course, executives will want to know how much the program will cost. This may be the first piece of information they look for. One method for calculating cost is to look at what it costs to do nothing, said Passion. That means calculating the cost of turnover and the cost to train newcomers and replace experienced resources when they leave. Compare these numbers with the cost of the knowledge retention program. When considering costs of the knowledge retention program, think of who might be involved in the program now, and over the long-term, and what the human capital costs might be. Also, consider line items such as office space and IT costs.

Chalyce Nollsch, of Robbins-Gioia, echoed Piktialis and Greenes' assertion that metrics for knowledge work are slippery. Nollsch suggested that managers clearly define what they need to accomplish with the program and build a measurement based on that requirement. For example, when Nollsch was developing the Knowledge Management department's business case for a revamped Intranet system, she focused on staff requirements for accessing subject matter experts within the company. Historically, staff had found it difficult to find the experts they needed, mostly because the staff was dispersed across the country. If an individual didn't immediately know which expert to go to, he or she performed a random search on the company's database. Searches didn't always pan out, and people were frustrated when they couldn't find people who could help them.

Wish List Rating

When drafting your business case, Chalyce Nollsch, an information architect and project manager with Robbins-Gioia, a program and project management consulting firm, suggested categorizing the company's pain points and developing lists of "must-haves," or highest priorities, along with "should-haves" and "could-haves." The should-haves are items that are important but not show-stoppers, and the could-haves are items that would be great to have but not imperative.

Nollsch's team focused on this organizational pain point when drafting their business case. Their goal was to build a system that connected people to people and enhanced knowledge sharing. So they based their measurement of success around these goals and presented them in their business case.

Building a Project Charter

Now that we've discussed the business case for knowledge retention, let's go back to Sam Wilkins at South Carolina's OHR. When Wilkins spoke to the state's HR directors that afternoon in 2001 and presented them with preliminary workforce data, he painted a picture of workforce issues that could impact South Carolina's future. While there may have been some initial reticence from directors, Wilkins' findings helped ensure that the group would join his push to find solutions to the issues he presented.

Many managers agree that gathering preliminary data and presenting an overview, or Project Charter, is a great way to rally support and gain executive buy-in for a knowledge retention program. Some managers suggest drafting a Project Charter in tandem with your business case. That is, present your business case first, and follow up with a Project Charter that restates the problem and provides details on scope, milestones, roles, and responsibilities.

"You have to have some level of executive support behind your project, and a Project Charter can help you with that," said Nollsch. "And you can also use it to gain support from everyone else once you do have the executive support you need."

Elements of a Project Charter

Managers use a Project Charter to define the problem, propose a solution, discuss associated costs, and paint a picture of success and how they will measure it, said Meryl Natchez, founder of TechProse, a corporate communications consulting firm in Lafayette, California. While the length of the document depends on the complexity of the organization's workforce issues, a Project Charter should always be concise and straightforward, she insisted. Natchez also recommended that managers summarize key points in one page that precedes the Project Overview. This single page is known as the Executive Summary, and Natchez always writes this content at the end, after she has completed the rest of her document.

"There are people who will read only the one page that summarizes the issue," Natchez said. "Back up the points you make in the summary in the pages that follow. And remember, the more complex your organization, the more elaborate the supporting material will need to be. However, even in the largest global enterprise, you should be able to state the problem and proposed solution simply in a one-page Executive Summary."

You may be tempted to do an exhaustive analysis at this stage. Resist this urge. This is not a place for extensive analysis, Natchez said. In the Project Charter, you are painting with a broad brush, allowing people to generally agree on what you are trying to accomplish. You are also backing up your business case with additional, compelling reasons for why your organization should develop a knowledge retention program before Boomers leave.

"It may be easier to get general agreement at this stage than it will be to get everyone to agree on all the details of how you will implement your solution," Natchez said. "At the same time, you don't want the general agreement to be too vague. You want it to be specific enough so you can test your ideas and proposal against it. You want your audience to be able to look at your Project Charter and ask, 'Does this indeed meet our objectives?'"

Ideally, executives will see the value of your plan and get behind it, providing you with the time and resources you need to perform a larger, more in-depth analysis of your workforce and design, develop, and implement a knowledge retention program.

Who's Your Audience?

Before you get started, take a moment and think about your audience. Are your executives formal or informal? Do they appreciate brevity? Or do they tend to want more detail? Take some time to answer these questions before you start to draft your Project Charter.

During this phase, it's important to remember what is known as the data rule:[16] Gathering accurate data is essential to addressing the challenges of an aging and soon-to-retire workforce, the Center for Organizational Research reports. Accurate data allows you to plan effectively, identify areas that need immediate attention, persuade senior executives, and encourage individuals to take action.[17] When collecting data for your analysis, use the strongest, most accurate data you can find.

You can access a project charter template designed by the Texas Department of Information Resources on the Cengage Learning Web site at www.courseptr.com/downloads. You can easily adapt this template to your organization's needs. We take the template apart here and provide some additional details on completing each section. Before you get started, keep this in mind: Workforce planning, analysis, and knowledge capture and transfer are not exact sciences. And one size does not fit all—every organization will have different needs and require varying levels of research and data to gain executive buy-in and move forward.

Generally speaking, a project charter should include the following information:[18]

- Project Overview

- Project Authority and Milestones

- Project Organization

- Glossary

- Revision History

- Appendices

- Approval and Sign-off Page

---

16 The Center for Organizational Research, a division of Linkage, Inc. The Aging and Retiring Government Workforce. 2003. p. 5.

17 The Center for Organizational Research, a division of Linkage, Inc. The Aging and Retiring Government Workforce. 2003. p. 5.

18 Based on the Project Charter template developed by the Texas Department of Information Resources. Version 1.4. May 30, 2009.

A Few Words on Design

Think about the last time you received a document to read. Did the design draw you in and make you want to read, or at least skim, the pages? Or did walls of text on every page make you want to stuff the document down a manhole?

Because many document writers are not page designers, much of the work we read on the job is visually complex and not easy on the eyes. Unfortunately, poorly designed documents have a way of getting put off. Worse, poor design contributes to a reader's lack of understanding, a sad circumstance that can hurt well-conceived plans.

When writing your project charter, or any document, remember that readers are a diverse and fickle bunch. Most will give a document a cursory look, flipping the pages to gauge how long it will take them to get through it.[19] Some start on page one and read to the end. Others may find a detail that hooks them somewhere in the document, read that section, and return to page one later.[20]

With this in mind, keep your visual arrangement simple and remember the four basic principles of design:[21]

- **Proximity:** Pull related items together to give readers visual cues about the organization of the page. Using this rule can be as easy as creating tables or other graphics that bring related items close together.

- **Alignment:** Infuse your design with purpose! Avoid placing items on the page in a haphazard way (or in a way that makes sense only to you). Design the page so the reader can make a connection among design elements.

- **Repetition:** Humans respond to repetition in music, story, and design. Remember this tip and repeat some element of the design throughout the document. Repetition could be as simple as using a bold font on all subheadings and a distinct bullet style for lists, or placing page numbers in the same position on every page.

---

19 White, Jan V. *Graphic Design for the Electronic Age*. Watson-Guptill Publications. New York. 1988. p 3.

20 White, Jan V. *Graphic Design for the Electronic Age*. Watson-Guptill Publications. New York. 1988. p 4.

21 This list based on lessons taught here: Williams, Robin. *The Non-Designer's Design Book*. Second Edition. Peachpit Press, Berkeley. 2004.

- **Contrast:** Tell your reader that you are shifting gears by making items that are not the same, such as headings and regular text, visually different. For example, use a 14-point bold font for headings and a 10- or 12-point plain font for text. When creating bulleted lists, vary the bullet color from the text that follows it.

Following the principles above, remember to break up walls of text with graphics and tables whenever possible. Your reader will thank you.

Section I. Project Overview

Let's start with the Project Overview. This section outlines the problem, provides preliminary data to illustrate workforce issues, and describes what you hope to achieve by implementing a knowledge retention program. Break this section into smaller pieces with clear headings, giving the reader signposts that guide them through your document. A typical Project Overview could unfold this way:

1.1 Problem Statement

Here, define the business problem within your organization or department using basic workforce demographics. Examples of workforce demographics that show emerging business problems could include:

- Total number of employees
- Total number of full-time and part-time employees
- Average age
- Average years of service or work
- Description of roles

Consider depicting some of this information in a graphic format, especially if you have gathered data that spans several years. For example, create a graph that shows the number of employees by age bracket (see Figure 5.2).

Reduce, Reuse, Recycle

When drafting your Project Charter, look for ways to reuse some of the content you presented in your business case. Your Project Charter also gives you an opportunity to fine-tune items, such as milestones, that you introduced in the business case.

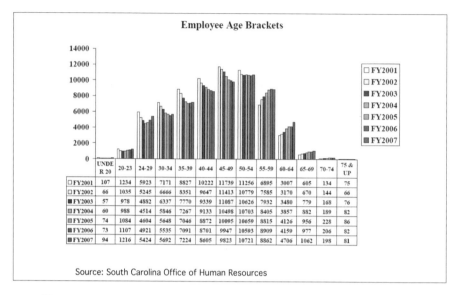

Employee Age Brackets

	UNDER 20	20-23	24-29	30-34	35-39	40-44	45-49	50-54	55-59	60-64	65-69	70-74	75 & UP
FY2001	107	1234	5923	7171	8827	10222	11739	11256	6895	3007	605	134	75
FY2002	66	1035	5245	6666	8351	9647	11413	10779	7585	3170	670	144	66
FY2003	57	978	4882	6337	7770	9339	11087	10626	7932	3480	779	168	76
FY2004	60	988	4514	5846	7267	9133	10498	10703	8405	3857	882	189	82
FY2005	74	1084	4604	5648	7046	8872	10095	10659	8815	4126	956	228	86
FY2006	73	1107	4921	5535	7091	8701	9947	10593	8909	4159	977	206	82
FY2007	94	1216	5424	5692	7224	8605	9823	10721	8862	4706	1062	198	81

Source: South Carolina Office of Human Resources

Figure 5.2   *In its 2009 Workforce Plan, the State of South Carolina Office of Human Resources used charts such as this one to illustrate trends.*

1.2 Project Description

In this section, describe your knowledge retention program and provide a general definition of the analysis methods you would use to provide an in-depth view of your workforce. For example, if you believe completing a demand forecast will help you define your organization's work in the future and how that work will be performed,[22] discuss this here. We cover demand forecasts later in this chapter.

If you have previous experience with knowledge capture-and-transfer methods, discuss the methods you believe would be most effective within your organization. If you are navigating uncharted territory, let executives know that the purpose of your analysis is to investigate and discern the methods that would be most effective.

1.3 Project Goals and Objectives

Here, describe the business goals and objectives of your proposed knowledge retention program. It's important to also touch on how you expect the results of your analysis to help you tailor a knowledge retention program to your organization.

---

22 The County of Fairfax, Virginia's Strategic Workforce Planning Guide defines demand forecasts in this way. August, 2003. p. 13.

Business goals and objectives for your knowledge transfer program could include:[23]

- Preparing the organization for future staffing changes.

- Strengthening areas of the organization where less experienced workers are struggling.

- Raising awareness among employees that sharing knowledge is important to the future of the company.

1.4 Project Scope

Remember Wilkins' advice, and take bites of the elephant. Keep your program's initial scope small.

"Look for something that's manageable," said Passion. "Look for an area where you know you can be successful."

Jerry Landon, knowledge retention program manager with the TVA, also encourages managers to start small and even pilot knowledge retention efforts.

"Demonstrate value with some quick wins, and then expand," he said.

The transit agency we introduced in Chapter 1, "When Boomer Brains Walk," took this approach. They started with a pilot e-learning and mobile learning program that covered one aspect of their infrastructure, rather than trying to take on too much at once. Within a year, they were ready to move on to the next area that would benefit from a similar knowledge capture-and-transfer effort.

When drafting your project scope section, be sure to give a clear picture of the boundaries so executives know what to expect. Vic Passion recommends that managers discuss what's within—as well as what's outside—the program's scope. To streamline your document when listing what's included and what's excluded, consider using tables like the ones in Figure 5.3.

1.5 Project Metrics

Managers find ways to measure the success of their projects before their projects even push off the runway. For knowledge transfer, key metrics are what the person leaving knows and what the person staying needs to know. We provide an overview of metrics here, and cover specific types of metrics in Chapter 9, "A Long View of Evaluation."

---

23 Most content gathered during interview with Vic Passion.

Project Includes

Project Excludes

Source: The Texas Department of Information Resources

Figure 5.3 *The scope establishes the boundaries of a project; using tables like these makes it easy for readers to see what's in and what's out.*

Natchez suggested quantifying these metrics in an objective way. For example, when Natchez planned her exit from TechProse, she sat down and thought about what she did for the company that no one else knew how to do. Those tasks included proposal writing and editing. Natchez then followed two steps to create her metric for knowledge transfer.

Step 1: Write a description of the skills required to write and edit a proposal. What kind of background and characteristics does a person need to successfully complete this task?

Step 2: Look around the company. Does anyone currently employed with the company meet the criteria you have described? If not, make the appropriate hire.

"From there, you create a series of checkpoints to ensure you have effectively transferred the knowledge," Natchez said. For proposal writing, Natchez created four metrics, each building on one another:

- Can the new person take over the template and get it ready to pour in the content?

- Can the new person draft specific sections of the proposal based on work completed while working closely with Natchez?

- Can the new person fill in the appropriate boilerplate for each type of proposal?

- Can the new person write new sections with minimal support?

Natchez knew her knowledge transfer effort had been successful when the new person could draft an entire proposal without her assistance. This process took about 18 months.

"It wasn't a quick process," Natchez said of transferring knowledge in proposal writing, as well as in the areas of project estimating and marketing. "But this is a multi-stage process, transferring complex skills and knowledge when a key executive is leaving. On the other end of the spectrum, there are some simple processes that can be more easily transferred. For example, with some technical procedures, if you thoroughly document or record a procedure, a new hire with the appropriate technical background can easily follow it and accomplish the task. It's like a recipe—if they follow it step-by-step, they will be successful."

One handy metric that proves very valuable in the corporate world is time and the amount of time it takes to perform a task. Let's go back to Natchez' proposal writing example. Natchez knew when she hired a new person that it would take them a while to perform the task as quickly as she could. She used time as another metric to track how well the new hire was absorbing her knowledge.

For technical procedures, for example, as when you have your car repaired, there are already existing metrics about how long the repair should take. Then the question becomes: Can the new employee perform the task accurately in the allotted period?

It's almost impossible to track metrics if you haven't defined tasks, timing, and quality measures, Natchez said. Once you have these, they become the performance measures for knowledge transfer.

Keep in mind, sometimes measuring a knowledge retention program's effectiveness can be difficult, but that doesn't mean the program isn't valuable. Take Sabre Holdings, the company that created the SabreTown online community for its global staff and later discovered the program also served as a knowledge management tool. In 2009, several years after Sabre launched SabreTown, managers still hadn't spent a whole lot of time measuring its effectiveness, said Erik Johnson, general manager of cubeless.

"We tried at one point to look at finance measures," Johnson said. "And we were able to find some level of people who came forward and said [SabreTown] helped them and saved them time. But we've been unable to create an aggregate, across-the-board measure."

Johnson looked at it this way: 70 percent of Sabre's employees used it at least once a month. The company knows it's important, but how do you measure that *knowing*? It's like your email, Johnson said. You know you can't live without it, but how does a company measure the ROI on their email system?

Johnson recalled the time a European company visited Sabre's Dallas headquarters shortly after SabreTown had been launched. Prior to their guests' arrival, Sabre executives considered hiring an Italian translator to accompany them when they showed their guests around and discussed their products. The cost to hire a translator was $3,000. Someone suggested putting a note on SabreTown asking if anyone spoke Italian well enough to help executives communicate with their guests. A short time later, a 12-year Sabre employee answered the query. He not only spoke Italian, but he grew up in Italy! This meant he could do so much more than translate; he could speak in a fluent way about Sabre because he had worked there for many years, and he could identify with Sabre's guest in a very culturally aware and connecting way.

Needless to say, Sabre won the business.

"This is why it's so hard to quantify the value of SabreTown," Johnson said. "We saved $3,000 on a translator, and we won the business. There is no way to know if we would have won the business if we had used an outside translator. There just is no way to measure the bigger picture."

Johnson's example is a reminder that as much as we want to measure everything, we can't always do this successfully. In other words, when you're talking about knowledge, sometimes you just have to keep an open mind.

1.6 Assumptions and Critical Success Factors

When thinking about your knowledge retention program, you assume certain resources, people, even circumstances will be in place. Discuss those elements here. The easiest way to present assumptions is to lead with a sentence that says something like, "The team bases this project charter on the following assumptions," and then follow with a bullet list of items.

"You might assume that specific resources will be available to assist with the effort, or that you will have access to software," Passion said. "Or you might assume that the project will have funding for a length of time."

Be thorough. When coming up with your list of assumptions, ask yourself what you need to get the job done, and then make the assumption you will have it.

When listing critical success factors, describe what you need for your analysis and knowledge retention program to be a success. Here are a few examples: Your analysis will be a success if you can interview 50 percent of all line managers. Your knowledge retention program will be a success if Internal Communications lets you promote the effort in the company newsletter. What factors will influence their success?

Be clear, Landon recommended, and emphasize what will make or break your program, whether it's funding, resources, or access to team members.

1.7 Constraints

It's important to know in advance what factors might create challenges for your knowledge retention program and to discuss them up front. Typical constraints include budget, time, and resources. Another constraint might be scheduling. In fact, schedule always seems to be a constraint, Passion said.

For example, if a key employee has announced she will retire in six months, and you need at least that long to bring her replacement up to speed, the difficult schedule is a constraint for the entire effort. Discuss constraints openly; choosing to downplay them at this early stage could lead to uncomfortable surprises later.

Typical constraints include competing priorities, such as another project being pursued or launched at the same time, Passion said. Constraints can also lurk in IT. For example, you may find your organization doesn't have the number of software licenses it needs to cover all the staff you will need for this effort. When constraints such as these rear their head, have a few solutions in your pocket to keep them from interrupting your progress.

Section 2. Project Authority and Milestones

In this section, define project sponsors who will serve as allies to your knowledge retention program. These sponsors have the authority to make decisions about the project and should be among those you invite to review and approve the Project Charter.

If you're uncertain about whom the project sponsor and authority might be, ask your supervisor for recommendations. Or ask yourself these questions:

- Who stands to gain the most from this effort?
- Who has the budget to sponsor this effort?

Passion suggested these two questions should go hand-in-hand. If someone in your organization stands to gain from the effort but they have no budget to support it, consider bringing them onboard as an advocate.

2.1 Funding Authority

Provide an estimate of how much you expect your knowledge retention program, which will include an in-depth analysis, to cost. If you plan to use vendors or consultants for any part of the effort, discuss their contribution here and provide their rates and costs.

Then discuss the funding source for the program.

2.2 Project Oversight Authority

Here, describe who will have management control of the project and what their relationship to your organization is.

Also describe groups that will have external oversight.[24] This could include union groups or external legal counsel.

2.3 Project Milestones

Write a narrative that describes your milestones. You may also create a simple chart (see Figure 5.4) for easy skimming that lists the major milestones of your proposed analysis and program and dates for delivery.

Milestone/Deliverable	Planned Completion Date
Source: Texas Department of Information Resources	

Figure 5.4   *This simple chart tells readers when you expect to complete and deliver major milestones.*

Section 3. Project Organization

It's just as important to carefully define your project team as it is to define your project goals and objectives. Give this section plenty of thought, and consider people you *expect* to be on your team as well as those you would *like* to be on your team.

Don't rule out a potential team member just because they aren't an obvious match. For example, when Nollsch of Robbins-Gioia was planning a social network analysis as a part of the company's Intranet revamp project, she became aware that an intern for the company was keenly interested in this kind of analysis. Nollsch invited her to join the team and made her a major player from start to finish.

Essentially, this is a lesson in keeping an open mind.

3.1 Project Structure

In this section, describe the project team and the reporting structure you envision. Include an organization chart that illustrates the flow of authority and responsibility.

---

24 Texas Department of Information Resources. Project Charter Instructions. May, 2008. p. 3

Depending on the size of your organization and its structure, you may want to consider building a Knowledge Council once you gain executive buy-in. Knowledge Councils go by many different names, but their objective is largely the same: bring relevant department leaders together to ensure every group is represented as you analyze the workforce and develop a knowledge retention program. We will discuss Knowledge Councils later in this chapter, but consider adding your ideas around this concept to your Project Charter.

3.2 Roles and Responsibilities

Here, summarize team members' roles and responsibilities, including external subject matter experts and vendors you may want to engage. Your summary of individual responsibilities should include project checkpoints and deliverables that will require approval.[25] Including this information removes the ambiguity around who is responsible for completing tasks and checking in.

If you are thinking about creating a Knowledge Council, describe the responsibilities of this group as well. Also consider creating a Contact Register that identifies each team member and their role, and that provides contact information.[26]

Who Does What?

A RACI matrix (see Figure 5.5) is an easy way to list tasks and the parties responsible for completing them. Create a matrix and list each task or deliverable and each person on your team. Put the appropriate letter in the cell to designate whether team members are responsible or accountable for a task or deliverable, or if they will be consulted or informed about a task or deliverable.

> *R stands for Responsible*
>
> *A stands for Accountable*
>
> *C stands for Consult*
>
> *I stands for Inform*

	Jane	Paul	Gary
Collect Workforce Demographics	RA	I	C
Brainstorm Knowledge Council Roles	C	RA	I
Research Mentoring Programs	I	C	RA

Figure 5.5 *A brief RACI matrix is illustrated.*

25 Texas Department of Information Resources. Project Charter Instructions. May, 2008. p. 4

26 Based on Project Charter Instructions. Texas Department of Information Resources. May, 2008. p. 5.

3.3 Project Facilities and Resources

Here, discuss the facilities and resources you will need, such as office space, computer equipment, badges for visitors and vendors, and other tools that will support the program. Also consider identifying which team members are responsible for securing specific items.[27] When drafting this section, some items may seem obvious, but consider mentioning them anyway. Don't assume you will have access to facilities and resources because they may already be accounted for by other managers and other projects.

Additional Sections to Include

Now that you have presented your ideas, named the sponsors and project team, and discussed roles and responsibilities, you are ready to wrap up your Project Charter. Include a Points of Contact page that provides the reader with contact information for the primary and secondary contact for the project.

If you have used terms or acronyms that executives may not be familiar with, include a glossary that defines these terms. Add this section to avoid alienating readers, even if it only contains a few items.

A revision history (see Figure 5.6) is also an excellent addition, and keeps track of the kinds of changes that were made and by whom. Some document writers put the revision history in the front of the document; others prefer to have it at the end before the appendices.

Revision History			
Version	Date	Name	Description of Change

Figure 5.6 *A revision history tracks changes made to the Project Charter and can be helpful when multiple reviewers are involved.*

An approval page is the finishing touch to your Project Charter. Your title page (the page that follows the cover) at the beginning of your Project Charter can double as an approval page—just add a signature table like the one in Figure 5.7.

---

27 Texas Department of Information Resources. Project Charter Instructions. May, 2008. p. 5.

When executives or sponsors sign off on the Project Charter, it indicates they understand the purpose and content of the document. It is also an important reminder to you and to others who read the charter that they are behind your project.

[Agency/Organization Name]			
[Project Name]			
Version: [Version Number] Revision Date: [Date]			
Approver Name	Title	Signature	Date

Source: Texas Department of Information Resources, Project Charter Template

Figure 5.7   *Make your Project Charter easy to approve. Add a formal place for executives to sign off.*

The Law and Analysis

For some, creating a Project Charter for a workforce analysis and knowledge retention program is an ambitious task; many employers never get past merely thinking about these aspects of their business. This is because many managers believe they must ask people who may be nearing retirement what their plans are, and this topic seems too sensitive to broach. In fact, when it comes to gathering information from mature employees about their retirement plans, many managers' reactions can be summed up in two words: risk averse.

"A number of managers shy away from discussing retirement," said Susan Murphy, association manager of the National Human Resources Association headquartered in New Hampshire. "They're afraid they'll open the door to an age discrimination lawsuit, so they just don't ask. However, if their organization is focused on open performance discussions, career planning, and succession planning, the likelihood of encountering a discrimination claim is decreased."

Some companies, such as the TVA, a federally owned power company, have successfully discussed mature employees' plans with them and gathered the data they needed to act. Their secret? Carefully communicate *why* they are collecting this information.[28]

TVA launched its lauded and well-documented effort to learn more about its aging workforce in 1999, said Jerry Landon.

---

28 The Center for Organizational Research, a division of Linkage, Inc. The Aging and Retiring Government Workforce. 2003. p. 92.

"Our workforce planners knew the age distribution of our employees," he said. "We had more employees in their sixties and seventies than in their twenties, and there was a big bubble moving toward retirement."

TVA had the data they needed, but they didn't have a firm grasp on what mature employees were planning to do. A federal corporation, TVA offered employees a generous retirement plan and age 55 was what many employees considered "full retirement" age, Landon said. Because of their workforce demographics, TVA wanted to start recruiting and filling its labor pipeline because apprentices would require at least a few years to learn the skills needed to replace retiring workers, and the clock was ticking. But many questions remained unanswered. What were longtime employees approaching retirement planning to do? When were they going to make a move?

TVA worked with its unions and asked them for their support in planning the power company's future. Then TVA leaders did something few employees do: They surveyed all their employees and asked them when they planned to leave TVA for retirement or other reasons.

TVA reports that in 2007, nearly 80 percent of employees completed the questionnaire when asked.

The company's approach was based on three principles, Landon said.

- The questionnaire was completely voluntary.

- Employees could change their mind and redo the questionnaire whenever they wanted.

- TVA did not use the questionnaire to make decisions about people, only about the future of the company.

Once the questionnaire was complete, TVA used an At-Risk Assessment (see Figure 5.8) to rate the criticality of the position and consider the risk associated with losing each particular employee's knowledge. This helped TVA gauge where knowledge retention efforts were most needed.

For those high-risk positions, the next step was to interview employees to learn more about their job's specific knowledge content.[29] Interview questions were designed to identify explicit, implicit, and tacit knowledge. Interviews included four kinds of questions:[30]

---

29 Knowledge Retention: Preventing Knowledge from Walking Out the Door. An Overview of Process and Tools at the Tennessee Valley Authority. www.tva.gov/knowledgeretention. Retrieved 10/19/09.

30 Knowledge Retention: Preventing Knowledge from Walking Out the Door. An Overview of Process and Tools at the Tennessee Valley Authority. www.tva.gov/knowledgeretention. Retrieved 10/19/09.

- General questions, such as: "What knowledge will TVA miss most when you leave?" These questions elicited responses that identified higher-order kinds of knowledge, such as complex problem solving or deep understanding of a piece of equipment.

- Task questions, such as how to perform specific tests or operate equipment.

- Fact or information questions that focused on what the employee knew. These questions helped TVA generate content such as contact lists, maps, and manuals.

- Pattern recognition questions that elicited information about lessons learned and insights into common problems with equipment and processes.

The TVA's At-Risk Assessment   Establishing Guidelines

Retirement	X	Position Risk	=	Total Attrition
Factor		Factor		Factor

Retirement Factor —The projected retirement dates in the workforce planning system (based upon employee estimates or on age and tenure data):

- 5 - Projected retirement date within 1 year
- 4 - Projected retirement date within 1 to 2 years
- 3 - Projected retirement date within 2 to 3 years
- 2 - Projected retirement date within 3 to 5 years
- 1 - Projected retirement date is > 5 years

Position Risk Factor—Manager's/supervisor's estimate of difficulty or effort required to replace the position incumbent:

- 5 - Critical and unique knowledge and skills. Mission-critical knowledge/skills with the potential for significant reliability or safety impacts. TVA- or site-specific knowledge. Knowledge undocumented. Requires 3-5 years of training and experience. No ready replacements available.
- 4 - Critical knowledge and skills. Mission-critical knowledge/skills. Some limited duplication exists at other plants/sites and/or some documentation exists. Requires 2-4 years of focused training and experience.
- 3 - Important, systematized knowledge and skills. Documentation exists and/or other personnel on-site possess the knowledge/skills. Recruits generally available and can be trained in 1 to 2 years.
- 2 - Proceduralized or non-mission critical knowledge and skills. Clear, up-to-date procedures exist. Training programs are current and effective and can be completed in less than one year.
- 1 - Common knowledge and skills. External hires possessing the knowledge/skill are readily available and require.

Total Attrition Factor—Estimated effort and urgency necessary to effectively manage the attrition.

- (20 and higher) High Priority - Immediate action needed. Specific replacement action plans with due dates will be developed to include: method of replacement, knowledge management assessment, specific training required, on-the-job training/ shadowing with incumbent.
- (16-19 points) Priority - Staffing plans should be established to address method and timing of replacement, recruitment efforts, training, shadowing with current incumbent.
- (10-15 points) High Importance- Look ahead on how the position will be filled/ work will be accomplished. College recruiting, training programs, process improvements, reinvestment.
- (1-9 points) Important - Recognize the functions of the position and determine the replacement need.

Figure 5.8   *TVA's At-Risk Assessment helped managers set priorities for capturing critical knowledge.*

The approach has worked so well that in 2009 Landon reported that TVA had largely stopped using the questionnaire and interview process. Some divisions still used it, but essentially, the process was the vehicle for incorporating knowledge sharing into TVA's organizational culture. Now that knowledge sharing is part of the culture, TVA focuses on *all* critical jobs, regardless of whether employees are close to retirement, Landon said.

"It was very reasonable to focus on those most immediate risks posed by retirements," Landon said. "But ultimately, we needed to focus on capturing and sharing all critical knowledge."

One mission accomplished. Now, moving on to the next one....

Testing the Waters

Managers who believe it's time to start learning more about employee retirement plans are wise to proceed in a thoughtful manner. Even companies with the best of intentions sometimes find themselves breaking the law. Attorney Deborah Weinstein is president of The Weinstein Firm in Philadelphia— her firm focuses on providing legal and consulting services on workforce issues. Weinstein also co-authored Putting Experience to Work—A Guide to Navigating Legal and Management Issues Related to a Mature Workforce[31] and teaches employment law at The Wharton School. This experience has provided Weinstein with a long list of examples of managers who crossed the line into unlawful territory.

Some examples are more surprising than others.

First, there are the companies that hold retirement events and invite only mature workers, giving them the opportunity to speak to experts about financial planning, investments, and retirement in general. While seemingly benign and well-meaning, employees and legal counsel could interpret the act of inviting *only* mature workers as classifying and segregating[32] individuals on the basis of age.

Weinstein cites the Age Discrimination in Employment Act of 1967 and explained: "This kind of event is only offered to older workers on the assumption they will be retiring," Weinstein said. "This is classifying and unlawful. It doesn't hurt these workers, but the assumption that people are going to retire is dangerous because it can lead to others treating those workers differently.

---

31 This practical guide published by The Conference Board. 2007.
32 This interpretation made using Section 623 [Section 4.a.2] of the Age Discrimination in Employment Act of 1967.

It also sends a message to older workers that they are expected to leave. People are working into their 60s and 70s, and we anticipate that will continue."

By "treating older workers differently," Weinstein suggested that managers might see an employee at a retirement event, assume they were on their way out, and subsequently deprive them of training or other workplace enrichment. "What's the point in training them on the new system?" managers may think. "They are obviously planning to retire soon."

These assumptions also feed negative stereotypes that older workers will remain on the job for a shorter time than younger workers. However, statistics show the opposite is true.[33]

Weinstein added that hosting a retirement event isn't unlawful in itself. But to stay on the right side of the law, employers must invite *all* employees, regardless of age. In fact, consistency is the answer to many issues concerning the aging workforce. Just as employers avoid legal pitfalls by inviting the entire organization to retirement-themed events, they can avoid trouble by asking *everyone* to discuss their plans for the future.

Mind you, asking someone when they plan to retire is not something managers should do willy-nilly, Weinstein said.

"I think that if people are asked in the context of succession planning or career planning by the person who is in charge of that aspect of the business, it is a legitimate thing to do," Weinstein said. "There has to be a legitimate business reason to know."

Perhaps it seems silly to ask a 25-year-old when they plan to retire, but these kinds of questions can be framed in a way that elicits a conversation about career and personal goals at all levels of the organization. And creating career plans for all employees may have the added benefit of reducing turnover among the younger generations, Weinstein said.

Of course, a longtime Boomer worker eyeing retirement is likely to respond differently to questions about career goals than a Generation X or Y worker with fewer years of tenure.

Shell Martinez Refinery in Martinez, California, is one organization that asks all its employees to discuss career aspirations during yearly meetings with managers and supervisors. The information gained during these meetings helps the company better understand the goals of its workforce, which informs operations, training, and human resources objectives companywide, said Michael Hinchcliff, manager of Human Resources for Shell Martinez Refinery.

---

33 On September 26, 2008, the Bureau of Labor Statistics reported in an economic news release that median tenure for employees age 55 to 64 was 9.9 years in January, 2008, almost four times the tenure (2.7 years) for workers age 25 to 34.

The company uses Individual Development Plans (IDPs) that document employee goals two and five years into the future. According to Hinchcliff, approximately one-third of the Shell Martinez Refinery will be eligible to retire between 2013 and 2015. Figure 5.9 presents a sample IDP used by the South Carolina OHR. Like Shell, the South Carolina OHR uses these plans to get an idea of employees' short-, mid-, and long-range plans.

Individual Development Plan (IDP)

Name _____

Date_____

Department _____ Supervisor

_____

Goals	Competencies What will be learned?	Desired Outcome How will success be evaluated?	Actions What steps will be taken?	Resources What is needed (training, people, library, etc.)	Time Frame to Complete
Short-range Critical within present position (1 year)					
Mid-range Important for growth with present or future position (2 years)					
Long-range Helpful for achieving career goals (3 years)					

Source: State of South Carolina Office of Human Resources

Figure 5.9 *South Carolina OHR developed this Individual Development Plan (IDP) template for supervisors and employees to develop and implement together. Working through a document such as this gives employees an opportunity to share career and personal plans and goals with their supervisors.*

"Obviously, when you talk with someone who is getting toward the end of their career, you get comments like, 'This is probably my last role,'" Hinchcliff said. "Or, because Shell is a global company, you might hear something like, 'I don't want to go overseas anymore.' You don't have to blatantly ask people when they plan to retire. Normally, you can get the gist by how they respond during their annual sit-down with their supervisor. And a pretty high percentage of people will tell you they are leaving in a few years."

When Shell managers and supervisors learn from these conversations that an employee is getting ready to retire, they consider how critical the role is and if succession planning and knowledge transfer are in order. For roles that require knowledge transfer, Shell uses a proprietary process known as Retention of Critical Knowledge, also known as "the ROCK process." During this process, facilitators conduct in-depth interviews with key individuals to capture their knowledge. The process takes several days and has proven to be a successful method for capturing knowledge, Hinchcliff said.

Essentially, Shell has combined the annual performance review with succession planning processes, which yields telling information from employees, into the company's analysis process. Using this method, Shell hears from all its employees, not just the ones who may be nearing retirement. All employees have annual performance reviews, which include career planning conversations and development plans. The ROCK process is used for people leaving roles who are deemed "critical," Hinchcliff said.

Survey *Every* Employee

Playing devil's advocate, Attorney Deborah Weinstein suggested that Boomers aren't the only employees with valuable knowledge, making it even more important to survey all employees on their plans for the future. She gave a powerful example of how treating people differently can limit an individual's potential in a company.

Imagine that you are in charge of looking at your organization's workforce and that you need to assess who will be available for an important, upcoming project. Are you going to walk around the office and ask all the women of child-bearing age if they plan to become pregnant during the course of the project? Few managers would consider this appropriate. Why? Because the act of asking women this question segregates—and potentially limits—a group of people based on stereotypes and assumptions.

The law is an important driver, and can help companies prepare for the future and implement policies that treat all workers with respect and fairness, Weinstein said.

"Absent the law, companies would be doing all kinds of things they shouldn't be doing," Weinstein said. "If you were a Boomer, you wouldn't be happy about it."

She adds that managers need to be cognizant of the environment in which employees' career plans are discussed; employees will likely withhold information if they believe they might suffer for their honesty.

"Questions about the future can only be asked in an environment and culture where people are not afraid to say, 'I want to leave in three years,'" Weinstein said. "If they were to answer this way, what would that mean for them? Does it mean they are off the track for this training or that promotion?"

"Everybody has a crystal ball, and not everybody is going to be right," Hinchcliff said of expert efforts to predict when Boomers will leave and what the effects might be. The best a company can do is to have a system in place to regularly look at its workforce and respond effectively when employees are leaving or changing roles, especially those who have critical knowledge.

Communications Makes an Appearance

We'll use Weinstein's comments about a safe environment for sharing as a jumping-off point to discuss the role that communications play in any knowledge transfer program. Consider the scenario: You receive executive sign-off on your Project Charter and begin to analyze your workforce. You decide not to discuss the purpose of your analysis—or that it will be the basis of a knowledge retention program—with the larger group. You figure you will simply discuss the new program once you're closer to the design phase.

Word gets out that you are looking for workforce gaps, but the staff never hears about your plan to help the organization capture and transfer valuable knowledge. The staff sees you and your team working on something, but they don't really know what, so they become uncomfortable and suspicious.

Part of your analysis includes calling each employee into your office to discuss their short-, mid-, and long-range plans. You don't tell them ahead of time that these questions will become part of their yearly review from here on. Instead, you leave all the details out, but expect cooperation.

You arrive at the first interview session anxious to hear from your staff, but you encounter a somewhat hesitant, even tentative response to your questions. "What's happening here?" you ask yourself. "Why is everyone being so guarded, so resistant?"

The short answer is nobody, aside from the team working with you, understands what you are doing. You haven't communicated the goals and objectives of your analysis and nobody knows a thing about the ensuing knowledge retention program. You haven't intentionally kept it a secret; you simply haven't felt you had enough to share.[34] But your silence has stoked employees' fears, and now, everyone is resisting you even though no one knows what you are planning.

---

34 This concept represented here: Larkin, TJ, Ph.D and Larkin, Sandar. "The Secrecy Trap: Keeping Employees in the Dark Can Doom a Company's Plans for Major Change." *Communication World*. Nov-Dec, 2008. p. 23.

Even at this early stage, before managers have formal buy-in and certainly once they do, they should be thinking about communications, Passion said. Keep it on the back burner, but keep it warm.

The reason is an in-depth analysis of your workforce and a new knowledge transfer program will likely lead to changes in organizational processes and the way employees do their jobs. Communications can go a long way to help employees feel they are part of the new process, and therefore part of the team.

"Once you get sign-off on your charter and your project kicks off, you will want to begin communicating about your program immediately so people don't fill in the silence with rumors," Passion said.

Rumors tend to fly when people don't understand what's behind managers' actions—for example, why they are taking certain employees aside and not others, or why there's a flurry of activity. The reason may be legitimate—perhaps a manager is gauging interest in a new mentorship program—but if employees can't see the big picture, they are likely to become anxious and resistant.

People resist change for many reasons. They may not understand what's behind the change, or they may simply be nervous about how the changes will affect their jobs, their lives, and their futures.[35] To gain buy-in from employees, you must make them a part of the process, and you must be ready to listen to their concerns and their ideas.[36] Change management[37] experts recommend that managers speak to every level of the organization about what is driving the change,[38] in this case, an in-depth analysis of the workforce and subsequent knowledge transfer program. By the time these conversations are over, every member of the staff should understand how their jobs might be different before, during, and after the analysis is complete and once the knowledge transfer program is put in place. In addition, if you are uncertain about some aspects of your program, communicate this to your staff.[39]

---

35 These concepts represented here: Gotsill, Gina and Natchez, Meryl. "From Resistance to Acceptance: How to Implement Change Management." *Training & Development*. November, 2007. pp. 24-27.

36 These concepts represented here: Gotsill, Gina and Natchez, Meryl. "From Resistance to Acceptance: How to Implement Change Management." *Training & Development*. November, 2007. pp. 24-27.

37 In their piece "From Resistance to Acceptance: How to Implement Change Management," Gina Gotsill and Meryl Natchez defined change management as a process that "focuses on people and how they resist, cope with, and ultimately accept change in the workplace."

38 This concept represented here: Gotsill, Gina and Natchez, Meryl. "From Resistance to Acceptance: How to Implement Change Management." *Training & Development*. November, 2007. pp. 24-27.

39 This concept represented here: Larkin, TJ, Ph.D and Larkin, Sandar. "The Secrecy Trap: Keeping Employees in the Dark Can Doom a Company's Plans for Major Change." *Communication World*. Nov.-Dec., 2008. p. 23.

Methods for Communicating in the Early Stages

Your communications, and therefore your communications plan, will evolve over the life of your program. At this early stage, you may still be getting your ducks in a row and preparing for when you will get the executive buy-in you need to move forward. Still, at this time, it is wise to begin thinking about the people—executives and sponsors—who matter most to the program. What will you need from them once the program is underway?

Communications Step-by-Step

Use communications to guide your program from the very beginning. In the early stages, your communications should be focused on building awareness.

You may also consider coaching executives on the messages they will communicate about the program once you gain buy-in. Depending on the size of the program and the organization, you may want to use an outside consultant to coach executives, as they may be more neutral and not as mired in office politics. Be prepared to design a general communications plan and an executive communications plan. Also, plan to meet with your executives on a regular basis to ensure that they are building awareness of the effort.

It's essential that executives support the effort and communicate that support to the organization, according to Passion. There are many ways to do this. Executives could discuss the program during regular office meetings or engage individuals in water-cooler conversations about the program. Because of their position, executives can help build excitement about initiatives, and one of the most powerful ways to do this is simply by talking about it, Passion said.

You may also need executives' help with bringing people around who may be resisting the effort, especially if these individuals are in positions of influence.

Once you gain executive buy-in, use timely, practical, and inspirational messages to help ensure the continued cooperation from staff.[40] Here are some ideas for communications at this stage:

■ Create an internal advertising campaign that announces your group's plans to analyze the workforce. The campaign could include flyers, emails, or brief presentations during staff meetings. When designing the campaign, be sure to include as many details as possible about how the in-depth analysis will guide the creation of a knowledge capture-and-transfer plan.

---

40 Gotsill, Gina and Natchez, Meryl. "From Resistance to Acceptance: How to Implement Change Management." *Training & Development*. November, 2007. p. 26.

- Hold a kick-off event for your team and invite staff to visit the event toward the end to ask questions. Or invite staff to drop questions in a box prior to the kick-off. Set aside time during the event to answer questions and invite staff to attend this portion of the event.

- Create a monthly or quarterly email newsletter that gives staff updates on the progress your team has made.

- If your organization tends to lean toward the informal and fun, consider creating a knowledge retention program mascot and slogan. A small consulting firm did this during a major change within the company and found it was a great way to energize the team and help staff visualize the change. The communications team decided on the mascot and slogan, but gave staff the opportunity to name the mascot. They offered a basket of prizes to the person who contributed the winning name, which drove interest and friendly competition among the group.

We will discuss communications throughout the rest of the book, but it's important to begin thinking about these concepts now.

Building a Knowledge Council

If more than a few departments will benefit from your analysis and knowledge retention program, consider creating a Knowledge Council. Timing on assembling the Knowledge Council depends on the organization. Because these groups are generally cross-functional teams, some organizations wait to have executive buy-in before they begin recruiting members. Others may opt to loosely assemble their group first as a way to get input for their business case, Project Charter, or other appeals for executive buy-in.

During the late 1990s, when the Pratt & Whitney Rocketdyne Knowledge Management department was beginning to plot its course, the group tapped executives from major organizations in the company to join a Knowledge Management Council, said Chief Knowledge Officer Kiho Sohn.

"This way, Knowledge Management had a connection to all of the major groups in our company," Sohn said. "We had a Knowledge Management functional team with representatives from IT, HR, Manufacturing, Quality, and a few other areas responsible for developing KM processes, tools, and enablers. The Knowledge Management Council members identified needs in each area and the KM team tried to develop solutions based on what they reported to us. The council members also acted as KM delegates, promoting KM capabilities to their respective organizations."

Nollsch from Robbins-Gioia thinks of her team's council, known as the Intranet Excellence Council, as a governing board that provides direction and authority. Nollsch's team created their council by approaching leaders whose departments would benefit from knowledge management and Intranet-revamp efforts, and asking them if they would like to participate.

The response was overwhelmingly positive, Nollsch said. She added that in most cases, council members were flattered to have been selected to represent the views and needs of their department or division, and all were anxious to have their opinions heard.

For Nollsch, creating a council to oversee knowledge management-related efforts has value. First, a diverse group of employees representing a project gives it some clout and visibility. Second, council members go back to their groups and serve as spokespersons for the project, which encourages buy-in from employees. And finally, the act of listening to the ultimate consumers of the project ensured that the final deliverable would meet the group's self-identified needs.

"It's a good way to get grassroots support," Nollsch said. "You probably want to wait to form a council until you get sign-off on your charter, but once you have that, the earlier you can get people involved, the better off you will be."

Getting the Most from Your Knowledge Council

When creating Robbins-Gioia's Intranet Excellence Council, Chalyce Nollsch and her team approached company leaders and asked them to nominate individuals within their departments. The goal was to leverage front-line employees for feedback.

Nollsch and her team also created a sketch of what they'd like the council member role to look like. This is a good idea for anyone assembling a Knowledge Council. What will you ask them to do? Will they be in charge of vetting technical information related to the program and making recommendations? Or will they authorize the proposals you and your team make? Nollsch suggests managers define council members' roles before assembling them for the first meeting. Once you have sketched out their roles, consider creating a document that provides specifics on what you expect. Hand it out at your first meeting and set aside time to answer questions. Robbins-Gioia incorporated the sketch of council members' roles into the Governance Policy for the project.

South Carolina OHR's council, known as Workforce Planning Champions, has been going strong since 2001. The OHR launched the group shortly after it began its big push to develop planning strategies for agencies across the state in the late 1990s. The approach made sense: ask each of the state's 80 agencies to appoint a person to the group, and bring them together quarterly to discuss best practices, successes, challenges, and lessons learned. The quarterly meetings also encouraged networking among the agencies' leaders, Wilkins said.

The council has enjoyed some successes over the years, according to Wilkins.

"Some agencies have put in place leadership programs designed to share information among employees in the organization, and those kinds of things come out at the meetings," he said. "Some of our organizations are fairly complex, and you may have one unit that has no idea what other parts of the agency do."

Council members also work through challenges, which in the past have included the logistics of succession planning and the legal ramifications of pre-selecting a candidate for a position. Discussions among the council members led to the creation of a formalized pool of qualified candidates, which agencies turn to when leadership positions open up.

More than a Snapshot

Now it's time to begin looking at your workforce. Very, very closely. With each analysis method, you will build on the workforce data you compiled for your Project Charter.

As we mentioned earlier in this chapter, we use workforce planning models as a foundation for our analysis of the organization. The methods we describe here—Demand Forecast, Supply Analysis, and Gap Analysis—will help you analyze your present workforce, identify the competencies needed to achieve future goals, and compare present and future workforce competencies.[41]

When these analysis efforts are complete, you should be able to move forward with design and development of a knowledge transfer program tailored to your organization. But remember, workforce planning is not an exact science, and even the most effective workforce planners confess to learning its concepts—as well as knowledge retention practices—through trial and error. The State of South Carolina OHR says it best: "Projections are not predictions… and even your best projections will not be precise!"

---

41 United States Department of Health and Human Services. Workforce Planning Guide. November 1999.

Demand Forecast—The "What" and the "How"

This step helps you analyze the type of workforce needed to accomplish future goals of the organization. You will analyze two elements of the workforce here: First, you will look at *what* work the organization will perform in the future. Then you will look at *how* the work will be performed. That means you will look at workforce changes driven by changing work *and* changing processes.[42] Two basic questions[43] to ask when starting a Demand Forecast are: How will jobs change as a result of new products, services, or new technology? How will these changes affect workflows?

For example, say your company has a long history of providing paper-based manuals, but your clients have said they want online support materials in the future. You already have a group of technical writers who are well-versed in delivering printed content; now you need to look into the future to determine where and when you will need new skill sets to meet your clients' needs.

Questions that will propel demand forecasting could be broken into three sections[44] and include:

1. What changes do you anticipate over the next two to five years regarding:

    ■ Generations of workers that you anticipate joining the organization

    ■ Strategic and operational goals and objectives

    ■ Organizational structure

    ■ Outsourcing

    ■ Budget

    ■ Labor force availability and the organization's attitudes toward using remote resources

    ■ Skills and competencies

    ■ New technology

    ■ New policies, procedures, and processes

    ■ New laws or regulations

    ■ Use of interns or volunteer help

---

42 This concept represented here: United States Department of Health and Human Services. Workforce Planning Guide. November, 1999.

43 Based on questions discussed here: County of Fairfax, Virginia, Department of Human Resources. Strategic Workforce Planning. August, 2003. pp. 13-14.

44 Based on questions suggested here: County of Fairfax, Virginia, Department of Human Resources. Strategic Workforce Planning. August, 2003. pp. 13-14. Also based on conversations with Vic Passion.

2. How will these changes affect:
   - Where work is performed
   - What work is performed
   - Amount of work
   - Skills needed to perform work
   - Supervisor-to-employee ratios

3. What does the future look like in terms of:
   - Number of full-time and part-time employees
   - Skills needed at each level of expertise
   - Critical knowledge, skills, and abilities (KSAs)
   - Number of supervisors
   - Number and types of teams

Once you have determined what work will need to be performed and how it will be accomplished, proceed to identify the knowledge, skills, and abilities needed to accomplish this work.[45]

With a demand forecast, you will be able to predict, for example, the percentage of your workforce that may be retiring over the next several years. You will also be able to assess whether the skills of the people you will be losing to retirement will still be relevant, and, if so, to what degree they will be necessary in your organization. Essentially, you will be creating a future workforce profile[46] that helps to uncover what positions will be needed in the future to run your organization.

Supply Analysis—See Today, Project Tomorrow

This step will provide data on existing staff, and also help you project your future workforce supply in terms of staff numbers.[47] You'll start by looking at your current workforce, that is, number of employees, competencies, salary levels, age, and education.[48] Keep in mind, your organization may not have documented competencies. If it doesn't, consider focusing on job descriptions that list skills for various jobs or functions.

---

45 County of Fairfax, Virginia, Department of Human Resources. Strategic Workforce Planning. Virginia. August, 2003. p. 13.

46 These concepts represented here: County of Fairfax, Virginia, Department of Human Resources. Strategic Workforce Planning. Virginia. August, 2003. p. 14.

47 These concepts represented here: County of Fairfax, Virginia, Department of Human Resources. Strategic Workforce Planning. Virginia. August, 2003. p. 15.

48 These concepts represented here: County of Fairfax, Virginia, Department of Human Resources. Strategic Workforce Planning. Virginia. August, 2003. p. 15.

Look at turnover statistics if these are available. If you have data or insights into the number of potential retirements or eligibility, bring these into the equation, as well. Then project this profile out a few years and imagine if no management action were taken to replace those employees who might retire.[49] How does the future look from this vantage point?

Look as deeply as you can into the future by using trend data for additional insight. For example, is the turnover rate changing over time? What factors influence turnover? Kristin Resta of Fairfax County's Department of Human Resources said that trend data could be drawn from the organization and from the industry as a whole. Examples of trend data her group looked at included retention issues with certain jobs and hard-to-find skills.

Turnover can have huge knowledge transfer implications because as individuals leave, they take their knowledge with them and may not pass it along to the worker that replaced them. That's why predicting turnover is a big part of workforce planning, according to Brian Ronningen, Human Capital Planning Manager of Talent Solutions at 3M, the multi-national adhesives company. By analyzing its workforce, 3M has been able to pinpoint areas of the business that are susceptible to turnover and begin to look for ways to reduce it, or conversely, prepare for it.

Turnover is one of the variables to consider when creating your projections for the size of your future workforce. The ability to know where, and gradually why, turnover happens will serve an organization well as it integrates its workforce planning and knowledge transfer processes. Set a goal to more closely study turnover, and keep track of what you learn. Data from exit interviews can be especially helpful here, and highlight specific factors that influence turnover within your organization.

Gap Analysis—Comparing Demand and Supply

A Gap Analysis compares the findings of your Demand Forecast with those of your Supply Analysis. You now know what work will be performed, how it will be performed, and the demand that you will have for various knowledge, skills, and abilities.

Your Supply Analysis has shown you what your current workforce looks like and what your future workforce will likely need to look like. Where are your gaps? By analyzing what you have and what you need, you will identify areas where demand exceeds supply, and vice versa. You may find that if all the retirement-eligible employees leave a vulnerable business unit within three years, you will need to promote a minimum number of employees from within

---

49 These concepts represented here: County of Fairfax, Virginia, Department of Human Resources. Strategic Workforce Planning. Virginia. August, 2003. p. 15.

and have recruiting processes in place in the event you lose those replacements to turnover. In this situation, a likely question to come out of the Gap Analysis is this: Whether you promote from within or recruit new hires, how will you ensure they have the critical knowledge, skills, and abilities they need to accomplish the work of the current, more experienced workforce?[50]

Once you've discovered the gaps between demand (future needs and projected workload) and supply (workforce and competencies), you're ready to prioritize what areas your organization will focus on first.[51]

Rethinking Succession Planning

Oh boy, that important go-to guy over in production just announced he's retiring in 30 days, and management hasn't identified a qualified person to take over. So much to know, so much knowledge to transfer.

Many managers have heard about succession planning, but often, this process is only used to ensure business continuity when executives step away. Here's an idea: Why not take this same process and apply it to your key roles, positions, and functions as experienced Boomers begin to retire? The same steps used in succession planning with executives should work just as effectively when applied to Boomers and the Gen X and Millennial groups who could step up, at any level in the organization.

Familiar steps in the succession planning process include:

- Linking long-term corporate objectives and strategies with shorter-term workforce planning.

- Focusing on critical roles that are essential to business continuity and potentially vulnerable as key players leave.

- Identifying the talent pool from which potential successors can be identified.

- Designing and developing a realistic succession strategy.

- Implementing the strategy by working with executives and successors.

- Monitoring and evaluating the progression of the succession plan.

---

50 This question inspired by the United States Department of Health and Human Services Workforce Planning Guide (November, 1999), which states that workforce planning is about getting "the right number of people with the right skills, experiences, and competencies in the right jobs at the right time."

51 This concept represented here: County of Fairfax, Virginia, Department of Human Resources. Strategic Workforce Planning. Virginia. August, 2003. p. 16.

This process is often coordinated by HR and talent management, but we encourage business unit and line managers, those leaders who are in the best position to know who may be up and coming, to get involved early in the succession planning process. And we're talking about any key role, be it manager, specialist, technician or operator, where losing the employee could jeopardize service and operations.

The differences between the familiar succession planning approach and its application to Boomers, Gen X, and Millennials include:

- Making certain executive leadership is involved and committed because succession planning for any non-senior executive role may be unfamiliar to these leaders.

- Accounting for learning style differences for the veteran and the successor to determine how best to transfer knowledge.

- Determining the willingness of the departing employee to share the key skills, knowledge, and experiences that need to be transferred to avoid a continuity gap.

- Finding out if your organization already has a succession management component to the HR/WFP system, one that can make this planning process much easier.

Now is the time to identify Gen X and Y employees who may be qualified to succeed valuable workers. Map your succession plan to strategic and business unit goals, and think of this method as akin to baseball's farm system where developing talent is always the top priority.

Audience Analysis—A Profile of Recipients

Audience Analysis is a close companion of Gap Analysis. While Gap Analysis identifies areas where staff numbers or competencies in the current workforce will not meet future needs,[52] Audience Analysis looks at the people on the receiving end of knowledge transfer efforts. Basically, you find the holes in your workforce, and then you look more closely at the population that needs to receive knowledge.

---

52 This concept represented here: United States Department of Health and Human Services. Workforce Planning Guide. November, 1999.

Don't cut corners here. Start with basic characteristics, such as:

- Age
- Education
- Gender
- Culture (This term can refer to many aspects of a person's background, and can include work environment.)
- Title
- Years of experience

Then go deeper, looking at generational factors and how these might influence the way your audience will learn best. Is your audience team-oriented, or will you need to consider one-on-one mentorships? Do they respond to just-in-time, technology-driven learning environments? Or do they tend to drag their feet when given full control of when and where they receive knowledge? By answering these questions, you will gain a better sense of what your audience needs and how much structure you will need to provide.

What's the Good Word?

The audience analysis phase could also include speaking to recipients and getting their feedback on how they would prefer to receive knowledge.[53] *Try posing the question to your intended audience using an email survey form, or by passing around an anonymous suggestion box during a regular meeting. Asking your audience what they want increases participation and engagement and often provides valuable insight into which methods could work best. See? Your job is getting easier already!*

Supplements to Workforce Planning Analysis

Typical workforce planning analysis methods include Demand Forecasts, Supply Analysis, and Gap Analysis, all of which will help you look at today's workforce and tomorrow's needs. But some organizations, such as Boeing, use extensive staff surveying tools to bolster workforce demographics.

---

53 In Bridging the Gap: How to Transfer Knowledge in Today's Multigenerational Workplace, Diane Piktialis and Kent Greenes encourage organizations to involve younger employees in the process of selecting a knowledge transfer method.

It's All About the Audience

While this example of audience analysis is derived from a training case study and not a knowledge retention program, it provides a strong example of the benefits that come from looking closely at your audience:

A $5 billion distributor implemented a new application that gave its customers the ability to place orders online. This was a costly step for the company because many of the sales staff were unfamiliar with wireless technology, and preferred the time-honored, paper-based process. The company needed to train its sales force on the new application and contacted TechProse, a San Francisco Bay Area consulting firm (and the authors' employer), for help.

The consulting firm first analyzed the company staff who would receive training on the new application. They considered the staff's current use of technology, as well as previous technology implementations that had been successful. They also spoke to managers and learned that the resistance they had encountered to the new application was mostly along generational lines. Newer, more tech-savvy employees welcomed the new, electronic process while longtime workers expressed their disdain.

The consulting team investigated the reasons behind the change from paper to wireless. They found a slow order process compounded by lost and incomplete orders, an imbalance of productivity among the staff, and low retention rates among the sales team. This was measured by orders placed per day and per week for each salesperson and by employee turnover.

After conducting the audience analysis, the consulting firm recommended hands-on, instructor-led training for the sales team. They also recommended creating two sets of training: one set for the younger sales people who were comfortable with technology and embraced the change from paper to wireless, and another set for older sales people who were opposed to the new system. This two-pronged, customized approach provided intensive training that introduced the sales team to the new processes and allowed for supervised practice in a training sandbox[54] database. This approach also gave the consulting firm plenty of time to address resistance among the sales staff and promote the benefits of the new system. Once salespeople could see how the system improved their earning power, resistance dissipated, and training began in earnest.

---

54 The term "sandbox" is used in training circles to describe a demonstration space where users can experiment without affecting the larger application.

First, a little background. At Boeing, the average age of the workforce is about 45. The company's large Boomer population, coupled with higher attrition rates among employees with 0 to 5 years of tenure, is an area of concern for the company, said Dianna Peterson, director of strategic workforce planning. (The group of more recent hires, known simply as "0 to 5's," is mostly comprised of Generation Y employees, Peterson said.)

"We know we have a large Boomer population that is eligible to retire, and we have higher attrition among 0 to 5's," Peterson said. "But the 0 to 5's, that's our pipeline. So we had to ask ourselves how we were going to keep the knowledge of the Boomers while also retaining the 0 to 5 population. This has led to a lot of work with surveying employees at both ends of the spectrum. That's how we started to really understand the language of the generations. Through exit interviews, we found out why people were leaving. Then we asked, 'Why do we only survey people when they leave?' That led to us doing a survey on why people stay. Then we wanted to know what engages people. We looked at all the surveys, and we found that employees want challenging work—it's really that simple. And this leads us right back to leaders. A good leader can have a huge impact on why people stay or leave. In the absence of good leaders, employees need a good mentor."

Conducting surveys like these give organizations insight into those who are leaving and those who are joining the ranks. Because you will need to fill gaps with people who are new to the department or organization, it makes sense to understand the trends that affect their desire to stay and grow with your group. By surveying employees, you find out what employees want from their work environment, what engages them, and why they leave. This information can be used in many ways to improve processes and procedures, and it can also be used to guide knowledge transfer efforts when the time comes.

Peterson's comments provide a window into this theory. Say you notice that a large number of Gen Y workers surveyed report they would like exceptional mentors to help with challenging tasks. Now, imagine one of your Boomer employees is leaving the organization, and you must split up his tasks among one or more less experienced employees. When designing your knowledge transfer approach, you already know from surveys that Gen Ys tend to appreciate mentor-mentee relationships. This knowledge could save you time and money as you look for ways to transfer the Boomer employee's knowledge to the workers who will replace her.

Making a habit of surveying employees and tracking their responses can inform knowledge transfer plans now and in the future. Interviews can also prove helpful, Passion said. It may be tempting to refer only to quantitative data when analyzing your workforce and knowledge gaps, but anecdotal evidence can help you tell a compelling story by providing the people side.

Why Not Ask Them Why They Stay?

Rather than reserving surveys for when employees leave, Boeing surveys employees throughout their careers and crafts programs around what they say they need. Here are a few sample questions from their "Why do you stay?" survey that encourages employees to provide narrative and insights:

> *I stay at Boeing because there are opportunities in my job for professional growth and learning.*
>
> *I stay at Boeing because there are opportunities to be assigned new and challenging work.*
>
> *I stay at Boeing because my work assignments are meaningful to me.*

One Consultant's Approach to Assessing Knowledge at Risk

Gail Trugman-Nikol, owner of Long Island, New York-based Unique Business Solutions, Inc., has a few approaches for finding out which employees have knowledge a business can't live without. She starts by asking the CEO what keeps them up at night. One medical lab CEO responded that there were eight employees on his staff of 400 who played a critical role, yet no documentation existed to help the business carry on in their absence.

"If one of them were to get hit by a bus tomorrow, we may as well stop what we're doing," he told Trugman-Nikol.

In addition to plainly asking executives about their pain points, Trugman-Nikol analyzes businesses using their organizational chart and job descriptions. If they don't have these key pieces of documentation— and many businesses don't—she develops them from scratch, working with managers to learn how the organization works and what tasks people are responsible for. The information she gleans from managers helps her work with the employee, creating a job description for each role. Essentially, job descriptions describe the tasks and duties employees must complete and the attitudes they are expected to espouse as part of the team.

Job descriptions include:

- A company conformance statement (a section of the job description that states the mission of the company)
- Business purpose and objectives
- List of essential duties and how they map to business objectives
- Qualifications, minimum education, certifications
- Preferences, or "nice-to-haves," such as advanced degrees or fluency in additional languages

Once she understands the hierarchy and the roles, Trugman-Nikol develops a workflow process analysis document. This document shows each process from beginning to end and all the departments a single process might flow through. Looking at the workflow process, it's easier to see which employees are the cornerstones of the organization. From there, Trugman-Nikol often creates documentation that makes employees' implicit knowledge explicit and accessible.

Trugman-Nikol said her penchant for asking unusual questions helps her draw out critical knowledge from an employee's head. When creating documentation for an Executive Assistant for Sales (one of the eight roles that kept the medical lab CEO awake at night), she asked the employee what would happen if, for example, Box No. 26 was filled out incorrectly or not at all. The employee answered that if anything went wrong with that particular box, the client would not be able to send the company their specimen. Essentially, the business would be lost.

"How would you convey the urgency of filling in this box correctly to a new hire?" Trugman-Nikol asked. The employee paused. "Oh yeah," she said. "That's a very good point."

Social Network Analysis—Who Talks to Whom?

When you hear the term "social network," you probably think of networking and exchanging information via Facebook, Twitter, LinkedIn, and sophisticated corporate Intranet sites. But the online communities you belong to in your business and professional lives are not the only forms of social networks. In fact, while social networking usually refers to technology and the applications that connect us, social networks are simply who talks to whom in an organization. Therefore, social network analysis, or network analysis, is the study of these networks and how they influence and shape organizations, according to Heather Walter, communications professor at the University of Akron.

Some organizations use social network analysis to identify knowledge at risk and illustrate how Boomers leaving the organization could impact operations. This analysis can skim the surface and look at individual departments or take an in-depth look at an organization. (A small sampling of a unit or department could be included in your Project Charter.)

Here's an example of how organizations can use social network analysis to guide their knowledge retention program.

In 2007, Chalyce Nollsch and her knowledge management team at Robbins-Gioia were in the midst of revamping the company's Intranet when they decided to do a mini-social network analysis of the 25-person Human Resources department. Their analysis consisted of a Collective Knowledge Analysis Survey (see Figure 5.10), used to locate hidden pockets of expertise within the company. The survey also helped them understand how employees interacted with each other and how the organization's structure contributed to their success on the job.

The team's goal was to capture tacit knowledge within the 650-person project management consulting firm, starting with one department. Nollsch's objective was to eventually look at the entire organization, but she needed to create a sample first to show executives the benefits of social network analysis and what she could uncover.

Using an intern as a resource, the Knowledge Management department created the survey questions, deployed the survey to the HR department, and then compiled and plotted the results using a free software tool (see Figure 5.11). The diagram she created, known as a *sociogram*, depicted connections between individuals throughout the company. Free software tools provided a low-cost way to map network data. Additional tools were available for purchase and allowed for measurement and analysis.

"The analysis we did provided a visual of where people went for knowledge," Nollsch said. "It also showed us where the bottlenecks were. Looking at the results, you definitely see there are pockets of knowledge within the company, and you ask yourself, 'Where would we be if this person left?'"

While plenty of software tools exist to help organizations conduct Social Network Analysis, this form of analysis can be done manually as well. George Barnett, a communication professor at the University of California, Davis, says manually performing social network analysis of a group larger than about 20 people would be very hard, because it is simply too difficult to capture all the connections between people and to illustrate how strong those connections are.

Sample Collective Knowledge Analysis Survey

Please provide the following information about yourself:

Name and title:

To whom do you report to:

Department and primary function:

Section 1: Individuals You Seek

Identify five individuals who provide you with information to do your work, or help you think through complex problems. These may or may not be people you communicate with on a regular basis but should work within the company.

For each individual you chose, answer the following questions:

1. What is each individual's area(s) of expertise that you see when completing tasks. What knowledge assets or skills do you seek from them?

2. The knowledge possessed by these individuals can be found and accessed:

a. On an information-sharing system within the company

b. From other team or department members

c. In paper-based documents or the individual's computer

d. Only in the individual's head

3. How often do you see out each of the above individuals?

a. Once a day

b. Once a week

c. Once a month

d. Other_____

4. Please indicate the organization in which each person works:

a. Within same department

b. Outside department, inside business unit

c. Outside business unit, but within company

5. In general, how accessible is each individual when you need information or advice?

Section 2: Individuals Who Seek You

Name five individuals who you provide information to and who would consider you an important part of their problem-solving and task-completion process.

What are some of your areas of expertise or skills that allow you to contribute to the company in terms of your own deliverables on projects or tasks? What are the skills and knowledge that you possess that allow you to effectively fulfill your role in the company?

End of survey

Figure 5.10   *This is an abbreviated Sample Collective Knowledge Analysis Survey. A more complete version is available on the Cengage Learning Web site at www.courseptr.com/downloads.* Source: Robbins-Gioia

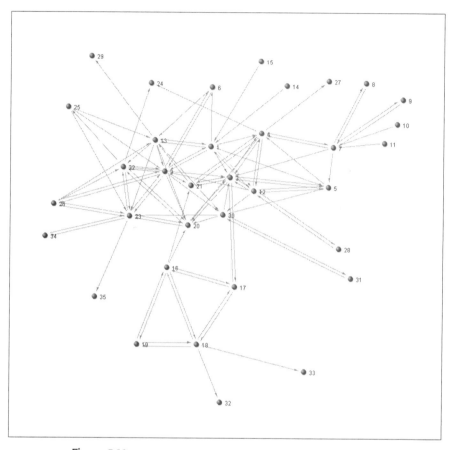

Figure 5.11   *The sociogram of Robbins-Gioia Social Network Analysis of its Human Resources Department.*

Barnett adds that social network analysis does more than just show who talks to whom in an organization; it also provides insight into an organization's structure. While some people may say their organizational chart depicts organizational structure, Barnett argues that organizational charts simply show the flow of authority and responsibility. On the other hand, sociograms produced by social network analysis show who is communicating and exchanging information with whom within any given area of an organization. These connections give much more detail about how an organization is structured.

Barnett also advises organizations to look at the probability of interaction within an organization as a way to project knowledge gaps. He bases this on the tendency of people to communicate with other people they are similar to.

As the old saying goes, "Birds of a feather tend to flock together." To accomplish this form of social network analysis, Barnett suggests that organizations look at individual characteristics and areas of knowledge such as hobbies, where people went to school, what they studied, and past employers. Using this data, he creates a two-dimensional network structure that is based on those characteristics and the likelihood that people who are similar will interact. The structure is a spatial model, allowing Barnett and his clients to see the open spaces, or gaps, in the organization's collective knowledge.

An Eye on Technology

Technology can play a role in just about every knowledge retention method. With this in mind, consider the technology aspects of your program as you assess your workforce. Here are some questions to consider as you analyze the technology component of your knowledge retention program:

■ Will everyone have access to a computer for the purpose of participating in a knowledge retention program?

■ What kinds of machines will your audience use and what kind of bandwidth do they have? Don't forget to consider the diverse requirements of global participants.

■ Do these machines have appropriate capabilities if you decide on a knowledge retention method that includes audio and video elements?

■ Will others sitting nearby be disturbed by an audio or video component? If so, will space be set aside where your audience can participate in the program without disturbing others? If not, will headsets be an option?

■ Will the audience need to use the Internet to participate in the knowledge retention program? If so, does the organization have any restrictions on access?

■ For global audiences, will a technology solution in one country work elsewhere?

The Goal of Planning and Analysis

As you can see, preparing your organization for the future begins with careful planning and analysis. When your analysis is complete, you should have a much better idea of the impact of potential retirements and specific skills and knowledge your organization needs to retain.[55] You should come away from this phase with a detailed assessment of the current situation and recommendations for the future.[56] These elements will help you define the knowledge capture-and-transfer methods you will use and will inform the design and development of your knowledge retention program.

It's not uncommon for organizations to scrimp on the time spent on analysis. That's because managers sometimes think they know what kind of knowledge transfer program their organization needs before they review organizational strategy and workforce data.[57] It's a common problem that's often compounded by budget problems and management pressure to keep costs down. When money is tight, it's tempting to cut out the planning and analysis phase and build a program on anecdotal evidence alone, but this doesn't always yield the best results.

The purpose of analysis is to collect enough data and information to make informed decisions. In a world where several generations are working side by-side and Boomers are bucking previous retirement trends, managers are wise to incorporate planning and analysis into their knowledge transfer plans.

As you will learn in the chapters that follow, there are many ways to capture and transfer knowledge. Organizations have used methods ranging from Communities of Practice to mentoring to job aids to story programs. Some strategies will work better than others in your organization. The challenge for managers is to develop practices that are appropriate for *their* unique organization and *their* audience. Documenting your needs and goals, and the roles and responsibilities of your team will help. So, too, will careful analysis.

---

55 This concept represented here: Ball, Ken. "Prepping Your Company for the Baby Boomer Exodus." *Continuity Insights*. Nov.-Dec., 2008.

56 Ibid. 2008.

57 This concept represented here: American Society for Training and Development. Basics of Instructional Systems Development. Issue 803. March, 1988.

6

Knowledge Retention by Design

Now that you've analyzed your workforce, you may be looking at the data and thinking, "OK, now what?" It's a very good question. How do you use the results of your analysis to design and develop a program that captures and transfers Boomer knowledge, and as a second, more long-term goal, plants the seeds of a knowledge culture in your organization?

Welcome to the design phase. During this phase, you'll use workforce data to further define the expected outcomes of your knowledge retention program. You'll zero in on the holder of the knowledge, the recipient, the knowledge you want to capture and transfer, and the method and technology you want to use.

Let's stop and talk about technology for a moment. Really, any of the knowledge transfer methods covered here—mentoring, social networking, communities of practice, storytelling, and After Action Reviews—could have a technology component, even if it's as minor as an online surveying tool. During the design phase, consider whether you'll need a customized technology solution or something off-the-shelf, or if you'll use a blend of the two. In any of these cases, you will first need to identify your needs and then document functional and technical requirements. Then research whether your organization has the technology already in place. If your organization lacks the technology to support your program, work with other leaders to make these elements a reality.

During design, you'll also outline the structure of your program, which will include everything from what knowledge capture and transfer methods you will use to who will participate in the program.

Keep in mind, some of these knowledge transfer methods may already exist in your organization. You may simply need to formalize them or rethink the organization's previous approach. But first, let's think about how this process needs to relate to other efforts to be successful. Don't abandon this lesson now that your analysis is complete; continue to involve stakeholders during the design phase, as they all bring something important to the process. For example, you'll need buy-in from the C-suite to ensure alignment between your knowledge retention program and organizational strategy. On the other hand, Human Resources and business line managers will be involved on a more tactical level, and will likely work together to coordinate design efforts. These managers are closest to the workforce because they are in a good position to work with Boomer employees and their Gen X and Y counterparts to retain the knowledge that is critical to business continuity.

How We Developed This Chapter

Typically, the design phase is considered to be the main planning stage of a project. However, some of the steps we cover in this chapter will go beyond design and into development and piloting, implementation, and evaluation. While this chapter focuses on design, our goal is to provide a complete overview of a solution and show how solution design can impact the phases that follow. We will cover development, implementation, and evaluation in future sections and chapters, providing you with additional insight into each phase of our knowledge retention methodology.

What Kind of Knowledge to Transfer?

Now, let's take a closer look at the kind of knowledge you want to capture and transfer. Is it more intuitive and complex, like Meryl Natchez' knowledge of proposal writing and editing, described in Chapter 5, "Boarding the Knowledge Train?" Or is it more procedural, like Gail Trugman-Nikol's example of completing online forms for the biomedical company? Remember knowledge management consultant Pamela Holloway's definition of knowledge from Chapter 3, "Knowledge in the Workplace." Knowledge has many layers, and revealing the types of knowledge people use in the workplace is like peeling an onion, she said. Keep this analogy in mind during the design phase to help ensure you don't leave out valuable knowledge.

Now consider the complexity of the job, role, or function.

"If it's a routine or manual job, knowledge capture may be as simple as creating an operations manual," said Sam Wilkins of the South Carolina Office of Human Resources. "If it's a position that requires analysis or networking, or if the incumbent worker is the go-to person in the organization, perhaps the replacement worker should do some cross-training, and walk with the more experienced worker before they leave. The more complex the job, the more complicated the knowledge transfer tools will be. Generally speaking, this is the rule."

Communications During the Design Phase

While you may be busily looking over the data from your analysis and designing your knowledge retention program, it's important to continue to build awareness. Ask managers and executives to talk about the initiative during staff meetings or around the water cooler, even if it's just a brief mention that the effort is moving forward, said Vic Passion, an instructional designer and project manager.

"If they don't mention it regularly, people lose focus. They begin to believe the initiative is not happening, or that it's not important."

Follow the Needs of Your Audience

Once you have a handle on the role and the kind of knowledge you want to retain, consult the results of your gap and audience analysis, your employee surveys, and any other workforce data you have. Ask yourself these questions:

- Who are the recipients of the knowledge you want to capture and transfer?
- What are their characteristics and preferences?
- What knowledge do they need to be successful?

You may have covered some of these elements in your Project Charter in the project definition and project metrics sections. Refer to these pages and, if necessary, borrow language from them for memos, communications, and other correspondence. Recycling and refreshing content you have already perfected saves time. No sense in reinventing the wheel.

The next step is to look at the different knowledge capture and transfer methods and pick the one that best suits your organization and your audience. For some managers, this is the fun part. Why? Because now it becomes real, and you can begin to envision how your workforce will benefit from your efforts.

Once the analysis of your workforce is complete, it becomes very exciting to start building a framework.

There are many different ways to approach knowledge retention, and yet, there is no right way. You may also want to mix and match methods to fit your audiences' needs at various stages of their learning. Here's an example: Instructional designer Vic Passion suggests that at first glance, some methods, such as job shadowing and mentoring, seem very similar. However, there are some differences between these two methods, and their unique characteristics can be leveraged at different phases of the knowledge retention process. Job shadowing, which is often used in the restaurant industry to train new servers, is a passive form of knowledge transfer. In these job shadowing situations, the recipient watches the knower as she performs various tasks, but engages in very little of her own hands-on activity. Often, learners are required to shadow a more experienced worker for a few days or weeks—just long enough to understand the best and most efficient ways to perform the job. Then the learner is on her own, using the more experienced worker's example as a guide.

In many mentoring relationships, however, the mentee performs the job and receives feedback from a more-experienced mentor. The mentor-mentee[1] rela tionship works best when the mentee has a good base of knowledge; ideally, their mentor's feedback and guidance help the mentee grow in his new role.

Passion says managers could consider using job shadowing at the beginning of the transfer process, when a more passive approach is required, and follow up with mentoring to encourage feedback and interaction. For example, for sales roles, managers may not want to ask a new salesperson to interact directly with a client until they have observed a sales call and have a good understanding of the company's sales process.

"Job shadowing is a good method to use when they are soaking everything in," Passion said. "Gradually, you increase their independence and that could be when you introduce mentoring."

The Method Behind Mentoring

Here's a bit of irony: The same 1980s corporate downsizing that helped shape Gen X's cynical view of the workplace is partly responsible for the field of mentoring as many of us know it today. According to Wharton management professor Peter Cappelli, a generation ago, bosses knew how to be mentors, and they were expected to help subordinates move through the organization.

---

1 Some mentoring experts prefer to use the term "protégé" instead of mentee. We use both terms interchangeably throughout this chapter.

Learning by Doing

In 2009, AnswerLab, a San Francisco-based user experience research company, created a series of high-tech tutorials for new hires to use during their first week on the job. The company based the tutorials on various scenarios from past projects and made the modules highly visual to appeal to technology-savvy new hires. Amy Buckner, a founder of AnswerLab, said that experienced team members created the modules as a way to provide some initial guidance to new hires and make it easier for them to hit the ground running once the training period was over.

The reaction from new hires surprised company leaders, said Amy Buckner, AnswerLab president.

"They didn't want to come into the office for two days out of the week just to watch a tutorial," she said. "They told us they wanted to immediately begin working on a real project and use the tutorials as a supplement to what they learned on the job."

Company leaders obliged, and decided to incorporate the tutorials into a larger, on-the-job support rather than making them the primary training method.

In hindsight, new hires' reaction to the AnswerLab tutorials made perfect sense, Buckner said. Founded in 2004, AnswerLab helps clients improve their Web sites, mobile applications, and software development initiatives through usability testing, ethnography, surveys, and behavioral analysis. A growing company, AnswerLab's workforce is comprised almost entirely of Generation X and Y managers and employees, and its organizational culture is steeped in a go-getter attitude that is palpable even to the casual visitor.

"Here, people want to figure things out for themselves," Buckner said. "They want to be able to get help and support, but only when they need it."

AnswerLab's experience is a vivid reminder that many Generation X and Y employees want to learn by doing. They also want to be trusted to work on their own, although they tend to welcome feedback and support as they learn. These are important characteristics for managers to consider as they begin to design knowledge capture-and-transfer programs for this independent and ambitious audience.

"They knew what employees needed to do and they knew how to give employees a chance to accomplish things," Cappelli said in a 2007 article published by *Knowledge@Wharton*, the Wharton School of the University of Pennsylvania's business journal. "Mentors were assessed based on the number of subordinates who got promoted and how the subordinates moved along in their careers."

The supervisor-subordinate mentoring model eventually fell away when corporations began cutting jobs during the 1980s, Cappelli said in the article. Following the upheaval, bosses continued to mentor as much as they could, but soon after, organizations began to embrace the idea that mentors could be someone an employee didn't necessarily work with directly.

Flash forward a few decades. Today, there are many examples of mentoring in organizations. Some relationships are forged by mentees, while others are initiated by mentors.

Some workers are even moving away from having just one mentor, and are nurturing Developmental Networks,[2] or groups of people who show an interest in their development and career growth. Terri Scandura, a researcher and professor at the University of Miami, said the developmental networking model of mentoring will be particularly relevant to Gen Y workers, as this group regularly seeks out feedback from a variety of sources. And studies show this group does not expect to spend their career with one organization, so creating a network of mentors will make sense for them.

Many Reasons to Choose Mentoring

As Baby Boomers near retirement age, managers are launching mentoring programs as a way to both develop high-potential workers and transfer valuable institutional knowledge.

"There are many drivers for organizations to create mentoring programs," says Margo Murray, a researcher, designer, and evaluator of mentoring programs and author of *Beyond the Myths and Magic of Mentoring*. "It can be to support succession planning, the assimilation of new hires, and as a way to promote diversity and cross-skilling."

Murray says that in her experience, mentoring is probably the only reliable way to transfer tacit knowledge, which is generally not documented or taught in online courses or in the classroom.

---

2 M.C. Higgins and K.E. Kram developed the concept of developmental networks, according to footnotes here: Kram, Kathy E and Higgins, Monica C. "A New Mindset on Mentoring: Creating Developmental Networks at Work." MIT Sloan Management Review. April 15, 2009.

"That's because experienced and skilled people, whether they're in a profession or craft, don't verbalize some of the tacit knowledge they have," Murray said. "But the kind of knowledge they pass on isn't limited to tacit. A good mentor will transfer all kinds of mastery that could not possibly be learned in other formats."

Murray recalled working with a national manufacturer whose subject matter expert was asked to review documentation for running a major piece of equipment.

"The documentation was flawed, the expert said, because it didn't include critical information on *why* some decisions were made when using the equipment. In this situation, a less-experienced user could compromise the safety of the entire plant if they didn't understand the background behind certain procedures. Here, a mentor-protégé relationship could fill in the gaps left by documentation and online and classroom training," Murray said.

Mentoring programs are also effective when less-experienced workers need coaching on the nuances of client relationships. Here's an example:

An insurance firm faced losing some of its strongest salespeople to retirement. Leaders of the company were understandably nervous and didn't believe the younger, less experienced sales force would be able to provide their longtime clients with the level of service they had come to expect. The company knew they needed to take time to develop the new sales force and instill in them the customer service standards that were the foundation of the company. They also needed to educate them on how to nurture relationships with their longtime clients. After many years in the business, the longtime salespeople knew all their clients quirks and needs; the company could not allow this knowledge to walk out the door when individuals retired.

Company leaders and the Human Resources director mobilized and designed a mentoring program that paired the company's longtime salespeople with less experienced workers. They knew that transferring deep sales knowledge was not going to happen overnight, so they began working on the program shortly after they heard rumblings that longtime salespeople were planning to retire. They also knew that it would be impossible to have a mentoring program on-site during work hours, as interruptions were frequent and would distract mentors and mentees from their critical mission of knowledge sharing. So, rather than ask mentors and mentees to meet after hours, the company asked them to set aside two hours once a month to take a long lunch off-site. Mentors and mentees were enthusiastic about the plan. After all, who doesn't like to take a long lunch once in a while?

"The design of our mentoring program was based on the knowledge that people become consumed with their workload while they are at work," said Janet Michael, the HR director. "They accept interruptions to address issues and those issues take priority. We realized that on the surface, mentoring doesn't seem like a priority when compared to the day-to-day issues. Mentoring is viewed as something that can always be pushed aside, but the more we do that, the more trouble we will be in over the long run."

The company knew that if mentors and mentees put the lunch appointments on the calendar once a month, they could dedicate the time necessary for knowledge transfer. And the lunch dates provided a more casual environment for the mentees.

"Sitting at a restaurant off-site, an employee may feel more comfortable talking about the areas where they are struggling," Michael said. "The conference room or the mentor's office may feel more formal, and the employee may clam up."

Making Time for Mentoring

Managers who have watched well-intentioned efforts fall to the wayside know that making time is a critical piece of the knowledge transfer puzzle. For best results, managers should consider the time element when they design a mentoring program.

The length and frequency of the mentor/mentee relationship should depend on the kind of knowledge that is being transferred. Let knowledge transfer be the constant and time be the variable, Murray advises.

"For example, if you're transferring higher level leadership skills, and the two can only meet once a month, the relationship could last for a year or two," she said. "If it is more job-specific, say, for a sales person, and if the mentor can ride along on a sales call, do some pre-coaching and debriefing, then that relationship may only last a few months if they can meet a few times a week. There are many variables to the length of a mentoring relationship."

The relationship should be a just-in-time arrangement for either or both the mentor and the protégé, Murray said. This means the protégé may tap the mentor's knowledge or skill coaching when they need it.

The Nature of the Informal Mentoring Relationship

The relationship between mentor and mentee is based on chemistry, the mentee's interest in gaining new knowledge, and the mentor's desire to pass along knowledge and expertise collected during a long career. Mentoring is one of the most diverse practices used for knowledge transfer, and there are many different styles and methods. We'll focus on informal mentoring, formal mentoring, and reverse mentoring.

Let's start with informal mentoring. While they do not represent any one organization, BZ Smith and Colleen Dolan are a good example of informal mentoring. Smith is a prominent storyteller who has been spinning yarns and organizing community arts events since the late 1970s. After years of organizing literacy projects, storytelling tours, and community events in Tuolumne County, California, and across the country, she was growing concerned over who would step into her shoes when she retired.

Then, in 2008, Colleen Dolan, a 24-year-old college student with a background in theater arts and a degree in Community Development, approached her and shared an interest in becoming a professional storyteller. Having grown up in neighboring Calaveras County, Dolan had known of Smith for most of her life. Smith was delighted to hear from Dolan—and relieved.

"After a while, you want someone to take over," said Smith. "You ask the next generation how you can partner because you want to pass along this little pearl of wisdom. You also want to step away with confidence that the important work you started will continue."

Dolan entered into the mentoring relationship having extensive experience being a mentor herself. As a teenager, she participated in a two-year youth mentoring program and worked closely with a younger girl in her community. Dolan draws parallels between her experiences as a mentor and her experiences as a mentee.

"During the youth mentor program, we talked a lot about how knowledge, behavior, and skills are transferred to others," Dolan said. "We talked about how it's usually a much more informal process—at least that's how it was for us. In the youth mentoring program, our mentoring relationship was about establishing trust and spending quality time together. That's what happened with BZ, too. We have long conversations, we meet, we share stories. I watch her when she tells her stories, and she gives me feedback when I tell mine. I am just starting to notice the method behind how she tells stories, and she is slowly giving me more complex assignments, like giving me longer stories to tell and putting me in front of different audiences than I have experienced before. It's very subtle, and very much like the youth program in that trust and friendship were established first."

In her role as mentor, Smith has invited the young storyteller to join her on stage during her performances. She has also blogged about her protégé, which has drawn attention to Dolan's skills and abilities. People in the community have started to contact Dolan, inviting her to participate in and lead storytelling programs and events, Smith said.

The pair is approaching their relationship as an apprenticeship, with Smith sharing more than just the nuances of storytelling. After more than 30 years in community arts, Smith knows there is much more to being a storyteller than creating stories and engaging audiences. An artist must also organize her resources in order to bring storytelling events to the community. The practical and financial side of being an artist and supporting oneself through art and storytelling are also vital parts of the pair's curriculum, Smith said.

After reading this story, some managers may ask what makes this an informal arrangement. After all, Smith and Dolan have their goals, they have outlined their objectives, and they are both seeing results. Here's the answer: While Smith and Dolan certainly seem to be making progress—Smith with knowledge transfer and Dolan with knowledge capture—their mentoring arrangement is not tied to any one organization's goals or strategic plan. And Smith and Dolan conduct the relationship on their own with little or no input from outside sources that could support, validate, or measure their success. These are some of the factors that make it an informal mentoring arrangement.

Adding Structure to Informal Mentoring

Lois Zachary, an expert in mentor-mentee relationships and president of Leadership Development Services said that informal mentoring relationships in organizations vary greatly.[3] These relationships range from casual conversations, to "flash mentoring" (conversations and information sharing taking place on an as-needed basis), to more structured and formalized relationships.[4] Often, these relationships fly under the radar in organizations and don't receive much attention or support.

There are many ways organizations can support and give credence to informal mentoring, according to Zachary. Here are a few suggestions:

- *Provide an informal mentoring toolkit[5] to mentors and mentees that includes guidelines for successfully navigating each phase of the mentoring relationship. (We cover Zachary's four phases later in this chapter.) Depending on what workers need, the toolkit could also include tips on how to ask for feedback.*

- *Provide a worksheet that helps mentees think through and identify what they hope to get out of the mentoring relationship.*

- *Host networking forums[6] where mentors and mentees can meet and discuss forging an informal mentoring arrangement.*

---

3 Zachary, Lois. "Filling in the Blanks." Training and Development. May, 2009. Retrieved 12/8/2009.
4 Ibid. Retrieved 12/8/2009.
5 Ibid. Retrieved 12/8/2009.
6 Ibid. Retrieved 12/8/2009.

■ *Provide a list of people who are willing to be informal mentors. Include a blurb about each person's expertise, why they want to mentor, and their previous mentoring experience.*

Providing structure and support for informal mentoring can help to strengthen arrangements that already exist and spark new mentoring relationships among staff, without instituting a formal program that pairs mentors and mentees and measures progress. These tools will also make mentees aware that preparing for any mentoring relationship through self-survey and reflection will help them set appropriate expectations, so they can get the most out of mentoring.

Informal Versus Formal Mentoring

While organizations tend to want to measure efforts that contribute to learning and development and the bottom line, there is research that supports informal, spontaneous mentoring relationships such as Smith and Dolan's. In two select studies,[7] researchers found that mentors and mentees lean toward informal mentoring and prefer not to make the process "too formal." Other studies have found that individuals in mentoring relationships prefer to let the process evolve naturally.[8] They also prefer to select their own mentors and mentees instead of having someone in their organization design their mentoring relationship.[9]

In many cases, the reasons behind this preference are the spontaneous nature of chemistry between people and their tendency to learn more from those whom they admire and respect, said Scandura. However, when organizations keep mentoring relationships informal, only those assertive and savvy members of the team tend to find mentors, she said.

"While informal mentoring relationships are known to be effective, not everyone has access to career development, emotional support, and insight into the organization with an informal model," she said. "You can't be sure that everyone has what they need to be successful."

---

7 Chao, Walz and Gardner. "Formal and informal mentorship: A comparison of mentoring functions and contrasts with nonmentored counterparts." *Personnel Psychology*, 1993 45: pp. 1-16; and Noe, R.A. "An investigation of successful assigned mentoring relationships." Personnel Psychology. 1988 41: pp. 457-479.

8 Scandura, T.A., Siegel, P.H. "Mentoring as organizational learning during a corporate merger." Paper presented at the 1995 National Academy of Management meetings. Vancouver, Canada. 1995.

9 Ibid. 1995.

Who Makes a Good Mentor?

When designing the nurse mentor program at Scripps Health, Cindy Steckel combed through employment and performance reviews of everyone who applied for the role. She looked for comments about applicants' leadership, communication, and mentoring abilities, and looked for words like "expert," "mentor," "preceptor," and "teacher." Then she and her team validated what people had said about the applicant to help ensure they were hiring the right person for the role.

As you may recall, Scripps added jobs to create their program; this was not a volunteer effort. Still, some of the same characteristics apply whether the mentor was solely responsible for mentoring or adding it to their regular duties.

In every case, good communication skills and the ability to provide guidance were among the hallmarks of an effective mentor. But the list doesn't stop there. Here are a few characteristics that mentoring expert Lois Zachary suggests organizations and mentees use to define who will make a good mentor:

- Time and willingness to participate in the relationship and share knowledge

- Expert knowledge of the organization and area being mentored

- Patience

- Interest in other people's development

- A belief in the power of development

- Demonstrated skill in giving constructive feedback

Margo Murray also suggests that status, prestige, and personal power are important mentor characteristics.[10] In her book, *Beyond the Myths and Magic of Mentoring*, she suggested that a mentor's status may not be important "when the relationship was invisible to others." However, when the mentoring process was public and designed to prepare the protégé for increased responsibility, the mentor must have some prestige within the organization and know how to share it with the protégé.

---

10 Murray, Margo, *Beyond the Myths and Magic of Mentoring: How to Facilitate and Effective Mentoring Process.* Jossey-Bass. 2001. p. 121.

When it's time to recruit mentors, Murray suggested that program planners look across the organization, not just at the highest levels, and use volunteers and nominations by executives and protégés.[11] Be sure to specify what you are looking for in your mentors before you make a request for volunteers or nominations.

For example, if your workforce assessment reveals that an entire class of employees could benefit from mentoring, you may want to consider designing a formal mentoring program. This way, each employee in this group will have access to mentoring and to the support a formal program can offer.

Additionally, it's important to note that being a mentor is closely linked to leadership development, Scandura said. When organizations use an informal model, would-be mentors may not have the opportunity to develop leadership skills and share valuable knowledge, simply because mentees are not approaching them for guidance.

Making Mentoring Work

As you can see, there are benefits to both informal and formal mentoring arrangements for knowledge capture and transfer. However, in both situations the key to a successful relationship is a good mentor-mentee match. When a good match happens naturally and informally, the protégé finds someone they admire who can fill in the knowledge gaps they have assessed in themselves. In return, the mentor sees something special in the protégé and feels inspired to share what they know. In an informal arrangement, the relationship evolves on its own and doesn't need a lot of propping up. As with Smith and Dolan, the pair is accountable only to themselves.

With formal mentoring programs, organizational leaders pair mentors and mentees as a way to advance organizational goals, transfer knowledge and skills, and promote career and professional development of its staff. This often means mentors and mentees are accountable to a coordinator or manager who oversees and supports their relationship. Managers who have taken the time to assess their workforce and zero in on knowledge gaps may prefer a more structured approach such as this one. However, when managers become involved in matching mentors and mentees, they must be aware that a good match is crucial, and consider this when designing their formal mentoring program.

---

11 Murray, Margo, *Beyond the Myths and Magic of Mentoring: How to Facilitate and Effective Mentoring Process.* Jossey-Bass. 2001. p. 121.

Dr. Rachel Permuth-Levine, director of employee wellness at the National Heart, Lung, and Blood Institute (NHLBI), knows the value of a good match. After enjoying productive relationships as a mentee and a mentor, Dr. Permuth-Levine, who also helps lead the institute's Office of Strategic and Innovative Programs, decided to provide matching assistance through the formal program she designed for her institute's extramural staff.[12] While mentees in the NHLBI program can choose their own mentors, Dr. Permuth-Levine and her co-lead Angela Mark are often asked for help finding a match. They take this work very seriously, Dr. Permuth-Levine said, and put in the time necessary to find the best matches among the 1,500-employee NHLBI. They also search for mentors within the National Institutes of Health (NIH), a 30,000-employee federal agency that houses the NHLBI.

"We don't take it lightly," Dr. Permuth-Levine said of her small team's role in finding good matches. "It can take a long time, because our matches are not computer-generated like some organizations are. We often use our own networks to find the right people to work together."

Mentees can add comments to the mentoring program database and specify what they are looking for in a mentor, but many people opt to come in and talk with Dr. Permuth-Levine and Mark. The two elicit as much information as they can about preferences. Questions run the gamut and could include the following:

- Is it important that your mentor work in the same area as you do?
- Do you want to move to a different area of NHLBI?
- Do you want to learn a different academic content area?
- Do you want to network outside of the institute?
- Is the ethnicity of your mentor important to you?
- Is it important that your mentor also be a parent?

Dr. Permuth-Levine also asks mentees about their career goals, which can include conversations about mentees' future plans outside the organization. These are frank, closed-door, confidential discussions, she said, and help participants feel comfortable with her as an administrator of the program.

Dr. Permuth-Levine used a similar approach when asking mentors if they wanted to participate in the program. She said most people were happy to be invited to mentor, but are often concerned about the time commitment.

---

12 At NHLBI, extramural staff include science administrators and peer review and grant and contract management staff.

Dr. Permuth-Levine speaks honestly about the amount of time mentors can expect to spend in the program. Mentors usually sign on once they know the details.

Should Supervisors Serve as Mentors?

In her role as wellness director, Dr. Permuth-Levine interacts with many people across the organization. She designed, developed, and piloted the program in response to comments she heard about individuals seeking additional support and guidance. With the mentoring program, Dr. Permuth-Levine hoped to make the NHLBI a better place to work. She also hoped that a mentoring program would facilitate knowledge transfer at all levels and provide an opportunity for more experienced leaders to share institutional knowledge.

From the beginning of the program in 2008, Dr. Permuth-Levine set the bar high and required mentees to meet with their mentors at least once a month and attend various seminars. At the end of the nine-month program, which runs from March through December, mentees graduated and were invited to return the following year.

With the NHLBI program, supervisors cannot serve as mentors to their direct reports. Dr. Permuth-Levine requires supervisors to approve mentors' and mentees' participation in the program because mentors take time away from work to meet. But aside from their initial approval, supervisors do not have any oversight into mentors' and mentees' work together.

Other organizations have used a similar approach. While there are certainly supervisor/direct-report relationships that may respond well to formal mentoring, it can also lead to conflict. Often, mentees may be nervous about revealing what they don't know to their direct supervisors, which can start a mentor-mentee relationship off on the wrong foot. Mentees must feel safe asking questions of their mentors if the relationship is to flourish.

There are other reasons why some organizations prohibit supervisors from serving as formal mentors to their direct reports. For example, if supervisors and direct reports experience conflict in their relationship, this may lead to difficulties with performance appraisals.[13] Additionally, supervisors may have too much control over mentee assignments and career-enhancing development opportunities, which could lead to a power struggle if the relationship goes sour.[14]

---

13 Scandura, Terri A. "Dysfunctional Mentoring Relationships and Outcomes." Journal of Management. 1998. p. 450.

14 Ibid. p. 452.

Managers should consider these kinds of scenarios when designing formal mentoring programs. While conflicts and mismatches do occur, the mentee should not be concerned that ending the mentoring relationship will result in drama with their boss.

Added Bonus: Reverse Mentoring

Reverse mentoring has been gaining attention, especially as organizations recognize the differences workers of varying age groups bring to the table. However, some employees and managers could argue that there is nothing new about reverse mentoring; in fact, these mutually beneficial relationships have long existed in organizations where workers span the generations. In these organizations, reverse mentoring is known as a practice that increases productivity, promotes knowledge sharing, and encourages camaraderie.

Reverse mentoring, like informal mentoring, can happen anywhere in an organization. However, there are ways to facilitate reverse mentoring where it will be most beneficial. As with any knowledge sharing effort, organizations that assess their workforce and tie reverse mentoring efforts to organizational goals will reap the greatest rewards. And, by assessing your workforce first, you will be able to identify workers who have the most to teach one another.

Once you have indentified these individuals, ask them to join you in a conversation about reverse mentoring and share your ideas on how their partnership could benefit the organization.[15] Discuss goals and objectives for the reversed mentoring relationship and ask the pair what they hope to gain from the relationship as well.[16] Ask the pair some standard questions: How will they measure success? How often will they report back to management regarding their progress? Work with the pair to create a timeline for how long they will work together. Will they meet every week for a month? Six months? And, remember to set aside time for the pair to work together and learn from one another. Making the relationship a priority will help ensure it doesn't get lost in the shuffle of everyday work and commitments.

---

15 This concept represented here: Piktialis, Diane. How "Reverse Mentoring" Can Make Your Organization More Effective. Encore Careers (www.encore.org). Retrieved 12/24/09.

16 Ibid. Retrieved 12/24/09.

Setting Goals and Objectives for Formal Mentoring

Creating well-defined goals and objectives for a formal mentoring program is an important step toward designing your program. During the design phase, look at the results of your analysis to help you come up with a list to guide you.

Sample mentoring program goals could be similar to any of the following:

- Mentees will be more confident when addressing clients.

- Mentees will feel well-supported and want to stay with the organization.

- Mentors will exhibit improved leadership abilities.

- Mentors will begin to share knowledge that is important to business continuity.

Objectives should be measurable. The following objectives give you an idea of the level of detail to consider when crafting your own:

- After the first three months of the program, mentees will be able to lead a presentation for executives.

- By the end of the program, mentees will be able to complete sales forecasting in half as much time as they did before being mentored.

- By the end of the program, mentors will suggest several areas where their mentee needs additional training.

Reflecting on your list of goals and objectives can also help you scope the duration of the program and the best times to check in with pairs on their progress.

Use Training to Set the Stage

When leaders articulate the program's goals and objectives, all parties involved —including mentors, mentees, supervising managers, and support staff— should know what is expected of them.

An outline helps set expectations from the beginning. So does training for mentors and mentees. Experts agree that managers responsible for designing and developing a formal mentoring program are wise to include training for mentors and mentees in their design plans.

"Training means understanding what the goals of the relationship are," Scandura said. "When I train mentors and mentees, I sometimes train them together using a role play model. I also have trained them separately, and then brought them together to discuss what is expected of each person. By training mentors and mentees, you aren't just throwing them into the relationship. Everyone understands what their role will be."

At Scripps Health, top-level nursing leaders hold a week-long orientation for nurse mentors before they join the rest of the team on the hospital floor. During the orientation, these top-level nurses cover topics such as how to mentor people who are your peers and how to communicate with physicians. They also discuss the role of the nurse mentor and how to blend adult learning principles into the practice of mentoring. At the end of the orientation, program leaders solicit feedback from the group on how the orientation could be improved. The team is constantly tweaking the orientation, Steckel said.

"We used to do a whole morning on different generations and adult learning principles that was much more textbook-oriented, but people just didn't engage," Steckel said. "The feedback was they preferred the back-and-forth interaction. We have also brought current mentors in to talk with new mentors and discuss challenging elements of the role. That was very well-received because it's so practical and helpful."

The Scripps Health nurse mentor program is far from static. When Steckel describes the program, it's easy to envision a cycle with four main steps:

1. New mentors attend orientation and provide feedback on content.
2. New mentors join colleagues on the hospital floor.
3. Mentors and mentees provide feedback on the program.
4. Steckel and her team tweak the orientation and the program to meet the needs of the audience.

Steckel says the program works best when mentors let nurses care for patients and show them what they know. The mentor then steps in and talks them through the process, sharing their own experiences with similar cases. The program does *not* work if mentors are troubleshooting the situation or simply providing nurses with an extra pair of hands, Steckel said. This point is communicated during orientation so mentors know how to conduct themselves on the floor and how they can provide the most value to mentees and the organization as a whole.

Many people do not realize they should receive training before starting a mentoring relationship. For Dr. Permuth-Levine, training has been part of her program from the beginning. Conducted by mentoring expert Brad Johnson, NHLBI's mentoring training lasts about two hours. Not only does training help pairs set expectations, but it also energizes them and gets everyone excited to start the program.

Four Steps to Mentoring Success

Mentoring expert Lois Zachary designs and delivers training for mentors and mentees that focuses on what she describes as the four phases of the mentoring relationship.[17] These phases are:

- **Prepare:** During this phase, mentors and mentees prepare for the relationship through training, self-survey, and coaching. Zachary recommends mentors and mentees prepare separately first; they prepare for the relationship during their initial meeting.

- **Negotiate**: This phase includes defining learning goals and success criteria, establishing protocols for addressing issues in the relationship, and creating a work plan for learning goals. During this phase, mentors and mentees should also discuss how they prefer to communicate and how often they will meet.

- **Enable**: This is the longest phase of Zachary's four-phase method, and is the period during which most of the work is accomplished.

- **Come to closure**: During this phase, mentors and mentees integrate what they have learned, celebrate their successes, redefine their relationship, and move on. This phase can pose challenges, especially when mentors and mentees hang on, not wanting to offend the other by ending the relationship. More commonly, in formal mentoring arrangements, the specified end date of the relationship arrives without incident, Zachary wrote in *Mentoring & Protégé*.[18] However, to gain optimum value from the relationship, mentors and mentees should take time to evaluate their relationship and review their goals.

During the training, Johnson provides mentors and mentees with guidelines around topics that include:

- Actively listening and participating during meetings
- How often to meet; where and when pairs will get together
- Confidentiality among pairs
- Admitting when you make mistakes and having a sense of humor

---

17 Lois Zachary discussed the four phases during interviews. The four phases are covered in detail in Zachary's book, *The Organization's Guide: Creating a Mentoring Culture*. Jossey-Bass, an imprint of Wiley & Sons. 2005.

18 Zachary, Lois, "Mentoring Relationships: 7 Tips for Coming to Closure." *Mentoring & Protégé*. Vol. 9, No. 4. Fall, 1999.

Table 6.1 provides additional, specific areas to cover during mentor and mentee training.

Table 6.1   Specific Topics to Cover During Mentor/Mentee Training

Mentee	Mentor
Be proactive.	Affirm your mentee.
Be respectful of your mentor's time; don't assume you can drop by.	Set expectations for meetings.
Communicate clearly.	Listen to what your mentee wants from their career.
Start every meeting with an agenda.	Model the behavior you are encouraging.

Covering these topics and others discussed in this section can help mentors and mentees start their relationship on the right foot. Mentee training—in addition to mentor training—is especially valuable because it reinforces the fact that mentees must drive the relationship if they expect it to flourish, Scandura said. Training can include lessons on how to create an agenda for each meeting and how to be proactive and organized for the duration of the relationship.

Helping Mentees Articulate Their Needs

Scandura suggests that mentees should articulate their needs even in situations where the organization is pairing them with a more experienced colleague for the purpose of knowledge transfer. In other words, it's always important for mentees to spell out their needs, whether they are entering an informal or formal mentoring arrangement. By articulating what they want to get out of the relationship, mentees also provide their supervisors with valuable information, Scandura said.

"What they think they should be learning may not match what the organization wants them to learn, and this needs to be negotiated," Scandura said. "I think the process of articulating your developmental needs also helps calibrate expectations. This is especially important with Gen X and Y because they tend to want to be promoted very quickly."

Scandura said that even if the organization has different things in mind for the mentee, their answer to the mentee's proposed developmental goals may not necessarily be no, but rather "not now."

"This can be difficult when you're working with Gen Y," Scandura said about the "not now" factor. "They want to learn and grow very quickly, so it's best to know what they want and what the organization needs so you can set an appropriate time for them to engage."

Development plans (see Figure 6.1) can help protégés articulate their goals and take responsibility for their own progress. In her book *Beyond the Myths and Magic of Mentoring*, Murray advises that before the protégés can complete their development plans, the organization must first establish how much time they can dedicate to mentoring activities. Once this has been decided, Murray suggests the protégé create a plan[19] that includes the following:

■ **Career goal:** Written in terms of the outcome, rather than the process

■ **Development objective:** Skills or experience that mentees hope to gain

■ **Action steps:** Sequential steps for achieving the development objective

■ **Target dates:** For each action step, set a date for completion

■ **Resources:** People, funds, or other items needed to meet goals and objectives

Having a development plan in place is among the Critical Success Factors that Murray has documented during her research and experience. Critical Success Factors for Facilitated Mentoring Processes are:[20]

■ Identify need, goal, opportunity, readiness

■ Planning and design

■ Communication

■ Matching, agreements

■ Orientations/training

■ Development plans = healthy relationships

■ Evaluation

---

19 Murray, Margo. *Beyond the Myths and Magic of Mentoring*. Jossey-Bass. 2001. p. 141.

20 Source: Margo Murray, MMHA The Managers' Mentors, Inc. Used with Permission.

Sample Mentee Development Plan

Name:
Date:
Career Goal:
Development objective:

Action Steps	Target Dates	Resources Required	Status and Progress Comments

With whom will I share the accomplishment of this goal?

Source: Career Planning Workbook. Copyright 1995, MMHA The Managers' Mentors, Inc. Used with permission

Figure 6.1   *Development plans provide mentees with a way to keep track of their goals and accomplishments.*

Social Networks and Social Media

Now let's discuss a different form of knowledge transfer—one that introduces technology and social networking tools. As you may know from your personal and professional use of social media, social networks can help break down barriers that may exist among generations, leveling the playing field and making knowledge and information far more accessible.

There are many technologies that support social networks:

- **Blogs:** Short for "web log," a blog is a Web site that features regular posts on a particular subject, corporate brand, or general topics of interest. Blogs can also serve as an individual's online diary. Posts are displayed in reverse chronological order (most recent first), and can combine text, images, videos, links to other blogs, and Web pages. Organizations use blogs for internal and external purposes to keep readers and users informed and to generate interest and buzz around their brand.

- **Wikis:** A collection of Web pages that anyone can edit, organizations use wikis as a collaboration tool to help organize and prioritize information. Some organizations also use wikis as a way to cut down on back-and-forth emails related to projects; stakeholders simply use the project wiki to share information and resources and post updates.

- **Forums:** These online discussion groups give individuals a place to post comments and questions about a topic of interest. Forums can become lively centers of back-and-forth conversation and debate, and often become the go-to place for employees.

- **Micromessaging or microblogging applications:** Like Twitter, micro-messaging applications allow users to send quick questions, updates, and news to colleagues and friends.

Motorola Paves the Way

Some social networks also include communities of practice. Global communications company Motorola is an excellent example of an organization that offers its workforce tools that support formal and informal communities of practice and social networks to enable collaboration and knowledge sharing.

Motorola was an early adopter of collaborative tools, and in 1996 launched an enterprise-wide document repository and collaboration suite based on tools from OpenText corporation. Since then, the company has witnessed the evolution in collaborative technologies and has continued to grow and evolve its toolset as users needs, behaviors, and expectations change.

Appropriately named *Compass,* Motorola's early document repository served the needs of most internal communities of practice. As technology and user behavior evolved, Motorola found more teams using forums and threaded discussions[21] that enabled them to interact and ask each other questions, while also serving as repositories for shared knowledge. As Motorola expanded the system's capabilities, groups of employees began to depend on a community of internal business user volunteers, called Compass Knowledge Champions, whom Motorola had trained to help others take advantage of its collaborative toolset.

In 2005, Motorola introduced a significant upgrade to the Compass toolset that included new features such as blogs, wikis, and discussion groups. The upgraded toolset also included a formal community of practice capability, which could combine these features into an integrated workspace.

---

21 A threaded discussion is an online conversation in which messages are grouped. Definition based on content found here: http://en.wikipedia.org/wiki/Threaded_discussion. Retrieved 1/28/10.

"Our IT strategy team looked at the demographics of who would be joining the company and upcoming needs for asynchronous learning," said Art Paton, senior learning consultant at Motorola. "They decided we needed to have these tools in place."

The flexibility of the new tools gave Motorola room to grow their collaborative capabilities and was a logical step as the company looked to the future of Web 2.0 and asynchronous learning. According to Motorola, adoption of the tools was dramatic and viral and primarily driven by the Compass Knowledge Champion community itself. Users quickly took advantage of the self-service tools in expected and unexpected ways. For example, the company was surprised to find that project teams began using blogs as the preferred tool to share project status updates.

Motorola IT leaders released the new tools to support informal communities and at the same time approached Paton and his team to ask if they thought enabling formal knowledge communities should be a part of Motorola University. Paton and his team agreed, and soon after, Paton asked IT for a report that showed how many communities had formed since the new OpenText tools had been released. The results surprised Paton and others at Motorola. After just a few months, users had created nearly 2,400 communities—quite a high number when leaders considered that IT had barely promoted the new tools or trained users. Out of the 2,400 communities, nearly 250 persisted and were active, Paton said.

"With new tools there are always a lot of people who try it and then abandon it. This is natural," Paton said. "The numbers we found revealed a few things. First, there was a strong underlying need for these functions. People are not going to take time out of their day to use something unless it is something they need. So, we decided to create a knowledge communities resource office and bring together the leaders of the communities and work out the best ways to run them."

After interviewing community leaders to learn more about their needs, Paton and his team built a support system for these groups and their leaders. This included creating resources and operating models for communities and support and coaching for leaders on how to entice participants to join, contribute, and stay in the group.

Additionally, leaders noted that two types of communities were emerging at Motorola: Phase 1 types meet for a fixed amount of time and tend to solve an existing problem or learn a new tool or method. Phase 2 communities investigate what is needed on a continuous basis. These teams often attract senior leader support and persist over long periods of time.

Motorola attributes the success of its communities of practice to committed and passionate leadership, broad contributions from members, and lively debate and discussion when developing new methods, processes, or tools. The organization also launched its own internal micromessaging system, similar to Twitter, known as Motmot. The service allows the Motorola workforce to share short 512-character notices with friends and colleagues, ask quick questions of the Motorola online community, or post and receive breaking news alerts via the Internet, RSS feeds, and other instant messaging services.

In 2010, just four years after Motorola discovered its burgeoning cache of communities, Paton reported the following usage statistics at the organization:

- 8,688 blogs

- 8,763 wikis

- 6,000 Motmot accounts

- 4,154 forums

- 2,626 FAQs (with 23,143 answers)

- 1,736 communities

This is a far cry from the boring, static Intranets found in many organizations, for example, the systems that were intended to bring employees together, but that no one uses or updates. As you can see, Motorola has created a vibrant, changing place, a locale, where workers can go to collaborate and receive and share information and knowledge. In fact, in organizations with bustling social networks, workers come to rely on the tools to quickly find the answers they need to get the job done.

Cerner Corp. Creates New Connections

Robert Campbell, Chief Learning Officer of Cerner Corp., a Kansas City-based company that offers health care IT services, has numerous examples of how social media can facilitate knowledge sharing among departments, organizations, and generations. In 2009, Cerner rolled out uCern, a home-grown social media platform that connects associates and clients via discussion groups, blogs, and user-generated video. In many cases, uCern breaks down hierarchies within the organization, and gives users access to people they would never have connected with otherwise, Campbell said. Such was the case when a Cerner corporate lawyer, who hadn't participated much in uCern, posted a request for a basic definition he needed to include in a contract. Across the organization, a content developer saw the posting and quickly responded with an answer.

"Is this what you need?" she asked.

Within a few minutes, the lawyer responded that yes, the content was perfect.

Campbell looks at this example and sees more than just a quick answer to a question. He sees connections that would never have been made without social media tools. Prior to posting his query, the lawyer rarely, if ever, used uCern, and had never interacted with the content developer, who likewise had never interacted with him.

There are many stories like Campbell's in the workforce today—stories of how social networks level the playing field in an organization, tear down hierarchies, and connect employees that may not have otherwise crossed paths.

Crossing the Generation Gap Barrier

The generations have varying comfort levels communicating and connecting via social networks: Gen X grew up with it and uses it seamlessly; Gen Y were early adopters of the first wave of social media applications; and some Boomers have embraced it with the zeal of a 20-something. Statistics back up what we have all observed: In a 2009 poll[22] by Harris Interactive, surveyors found that 74 percent of adults ages 18 to 34 had a Facebook or MySpace account, while only 24 percent of adults ages 55 and over had an account.

The Harris poll also found there is an educational difference in people's usage of social media. Forty percent of people with a high school degree or less have a Facebook or MySpace account, while 55 percent of those with some college and 52 percent of those with at least a college degree use these social media channels.

The personal use of social media sites is dramatically changing how people connect, communicate, and sustain relationships with each other, Justin Dumont, director of marketing and product strategy development with Five Star Development said during a 2009 presentation[23] on social media and knowledge sharing. Although the external use of social media is more prevalent than internal use, more organizations are reporting use of social networking tools, or they are at least catching on. During Dumont's presentation, attendees from organizations ranging from health care systems to real estate groups reported using internal social networks to share information and knowledge.

---

22 This poll was conducted online within the United States among 2,220 adults ages eighteen and over. http://www.marketingcharts.com/interactive/half-of-americans-dont-use-twitter-myspace-facebook-8775/. Retrieved 1/5/10.

23 Dumont delivered his talk "Using Social Media as a Learning and Knowledge-Sharing Tool" at the American Society of Training and Development's Golden Gate Chapter meeting on November 10, 2009.

Organizations at the meeting tended to start with something small and manageable, but kept their eyes on the stars. For example, one manager with a Northern California real estate developer and property owner said the company had taken its first step with an internal database that maintenance teams used to search for parts. Teams also used an internal blog to seek out expertise on how to troubleshoot and fix equipment and appliances at the company's various properties. The company's ultimate goal was a social network for all its multifamily properties, the manager said at the meeting. She added that having such a network in place would promote contact among residents, and that could be a good thing.

During his presentation, Dumont pointed out several challenges that have long haunted learning and development professionals:

■ It is difficult to know what happens before and after formal learning.

■ There is limited time and resources to fill all the learning gaps that exist.

■ It is difficult to know who is responsible for formal and informal learning content.

Social media tools reverse the old paradigm and help provide solutions to these challenges, Dumont said. Before social networking, learners received much of their information from subject matter experts through various training methods. Once the training was over, knowledge gaps sometimes remained. With social networking, relationships with people help fill the learning gaps. That means employees can learn as needed from trusted sources within the organization.

In addition, social media tools give employees immediate access to information and encourage shared participation, thus making learners producers of content and not just consumers, Dumont said. And, as you can see from some of the other examples in this section, social networks can also connect people across many geographies, roles, and generations.

Creating a Social Media Network for Everyone

So how do you create a social network that everyone, from Veterans to Boomers to Generations X and Y, is comfortable participating in? For Sabre Holdings, designing their community was more of an iterative process from the beginning, and that same process continues, said Erik Johnson, general manager of Sabre Holding's cubeless.

"We identified the purpose of the system and the different kinds of people who would be using it, then began building out the functionality, starting with the profile," Johnson said. "We get new ideas on how organizations can and want to use social media from just about every conversation we have about the platform and document those ideas within our development queue system."

Johnson and his team discuss and prioritize new development features and rebuild existing functionality based on input from the innovation lab staff and with the council Sabre has set up to govern the community. New iterations of the system are built every two weeks, and they have a new release each month.

Johnson and his team build and test new functionality in their test environment, and then, when it's ready, they release the new functionality, making it available to users in cubeless communities.

While Johnson and his team have fine-tuned this iterative process, the group is always learning.

"There truly are no experts in enterprise social media or social networking," said Johnson. "We are learning day by day how companies can use it. The more you can learn from others, the better."

In the spirit of learning, here are some basic guidelines for designing a social networking community.[24]

Resist the Technology Temptation

Too often, organizations launch an implementation because they've discovered a cool new tool, and they want to put it to work. Resist the temptation to create a social network based on technology alone, or because others are doing it and you think it's what your organization "should be doing." Sabre Holdings, which has connected its workforce through its SabreTown social network, advises organizations to focus first on the purpose of the network, then on the people, and finally, on the technology.

Make It Fun

Social networking tools scare a lot of people, and generally speaking, participation is voluntary. That's why it's important to make the system simple and fun to use, Johnson said.

"It has to be easy to use," Johnson said. "Once it gets to IT, it gets functionality creep and soon you have a system that few people understand. It's important to remember that there are a lot of people in any organization with extremely deep knowledge who are afraid of a computer. The more complex you make the network, the more likely it is they won't use it."

---

24 Erik Johnson discussed these general guidelines during interviews and correspondence with the authors.

Make It Personal

The social network should help the organization accomplish its business goals, but allow personal conversations, too, Johnson advised. This is part of making it fun! SabreTown made its social network personal by including a profile component that lets employees give plenty of detail about who they are, what they do, and what they are passionate about. But the profile has another benefit—it helps the SabreTown relevance engine locate the best person to answer questions posted in the system. Employee profiles, personal and loaded with fun questions, are one of the pillars of SabreTown. They are fun, and they are important; so, that means in SabreTown, it's important to have fun.

Employees can also post their photo in SabreTown for an additional personal touch. In fact, Johnson and his team realized early on that a photo was the key to getting employees to complete a profile.

"We realized that people who didn't have a picture to upload were less likely to work on their profile and be engaged in the system," Johnson said. "So we set up a camera in the cafeteria and took pictures of people to upload to the system. This way, everyone had a photo of themselves and an interest in developing their profile."

It's the Employees' Community

Johnson recommends that organizations creating a social network should resist the temptation to turn it into another corporate communication vehicle.

"We didn't want it to seem top-down or hierarchical," Johnson said of his team's conversations during the design and development phases. "We already have a document repository, which is very top-down and the official corporate communications vehicle of the organization. We were, and still are, careful about making SabreTown the place where employees can talk among themselves. This way, it's a place where we break down barriers as far as titles and hierarchies are concerned."

Motorola's Art Paton had a similar experience as he watched his company's knowledge communities and social network evolve. Motorola's communities emerged as a grassroots effort with little or no executive sponsorship, he said. In fact, during its early days, a leading performance association visited Motorola and predicted the company's communities and blossoming social network would fail. The reason was that there were no corporate-level strategies, no executive leadership, and the communities were not linked to certain business objectives. Motorola forged ahead nevertheless. Today, some of the company's communities are linked to strategic business objectives; however, Paton remains firm on what role executives should play.

"There is a place for grassroots efforts and there is also a place for senior sponsorship," Paton says. "We were careful to say at the beginning that these were grassroots efforts that could be killed by senior leaders who tried to take them over and drive them under a different agenda. Even today, their role is to encourage communities and speak about how they work, but to essentially stay out of the way. We told them early on, 'it's not your role to go in and take over.' This can be difficult for senior leaders because they are about leadership and presence, but the way we were promoting it was a come-as-you-are, zero depth pool party. This means there could be no barriers to entry or exit, and you did not have to be an expert or someone special to participate. We encouraged the grass roots side so people would at least try it out. Then we showed them the value of communities, and now we have them starting up all over the company and providing critical benefits in all functions."

Expertise Isn't Always Where You Expect It to Be

We've all experienced the frustration of looking for assistance, expertise, or information where we think it should be and coming back empty-handed. Johnson suggests that organizations create a social network system that helps users locate expertise where it actually exists. SabreTown's relevance engine, which Sabre built and now licenses to other companies, is an example of how a system can use profiles and other data to help users find what they need.

"It's not enough to put a system up and expect users to find experts for themselves," Johnson said. "There can be so much complexity around finding the right information and people—whatever the organization can do to help people identify the expertise they need…that's a big part of the game."

People are very willing to help each other, Johnson said. However, most of the time, they just don't know where and how they can help. When the system proactively helps users find what they need, timely answers are within reach.

Seed the Community with Valuable Content

When starting a social network, post content and comments that would be similar to what you hope to see others post.

"Often, when you start something like this, there are going to be people who join and begin using it immediately," Passion said. "But some will be puzzled over how they should use it. By seeding the community with good content, you are illustrating for them what to do. They see your vision. They also see the possibilities."

In the spirit of helping people along, consider posting Q&As for people visiting the site for the first time.

Lead by Example

This guideline could go hand-in-hand with seeding the community. Johnson recommends development and launch teams and senior executives lead by example, which could mean posting valuable content, asking questions, and sparking conversations for others to see.

Acting in this way shows the rest of the organization that executives are pushing for success. However, there is a fine line between leading by example and getting in the way of the social network's progress. Sometimes, the rest of the organization won't play if they know executives are watching, some experts say.

Make It Transparent

Let everyone see all content, Johnson said, and create accountability by prohibiting workers from making anonymous posts. This helps promote proper behavior. And remember, communities become very good at self-regulating and self-policing, many experts say. Etienne Wenger, an authority on knowledge communities of all kinds, recalled covering a community of patients who suffered with a rare blood disease. The community talked about everything from feeling isolated to offering useful tips and posing questions. It was a very practical group, where members actively learned from one another.

One day, a member posted a joke that wasn't wholly inappropriate, but wasn't relevant to the topic or tone of the group.

"The community really reacted to it," Wenger said. "People responded with posts that said, 'Hey, this really isn't the place for that kind of thing.' It was interesting—almost as if the community had its own immune system."

Communities of Practice

Wenger's example of the community of patients provides a perfect introduction to a deeper discussion on communities of practice,[25] or CoPs. Organizations such as Motorola use CoPs, also called *knowledge communities*, to share knowledge among groups. And, while CoPs often use elements of social networking, they are built around a specific topic, project, or problem. Social networks, on the other hand, can be a group of people that is simply exchanging ideas and knowledge around an array of topics, said Jacob McNulty of Orbital RPM, a consulting firm that specializes in social business strategies.

---

25 Jean Lave and Etienne Wenger are credited with coining the term "communities of practice."

Groups can range in size from a handful of members to more than a thousand. Often, communities of practice consist of a core group and many peripheral members.[26]

In some organizations, a community of practice is a group of people who get together on a regular basis to brainstorm ideas. In others, it is a social network that collaborates online, hosting blogs, wikis, forums…the list goes on. Communication methods run the gamut from purely virtual to a mix of face-to-face and online meetings. And, while "communities of practice" and "knowledge communities" may sound cutting-edge, there is nothing new about people getting together to talk about their common interests and common problems.

"Communities of practice have been around for as long as human beings have learned together," Etienne Wenger wrote in a 2006 white paper.[27] "At home, at work, at school, in our hobbies, we all belong to communities of practice, a number of them usually."

Here are a few scenarios for which communities of practice may be a good fit for an organization:

- You notice a group of employees that share a common problem or interest in a topic and need support in order to stay organized and continue to share knowledge. However, CoPs are not only sparked by managers or organizational leaders. Some of the best communities of practice arise in response to members' needs, Wenger said.

- Your organization supports multiple competencies, and you need a cross-functional way to share best practices.

- Your organization competes in a field that moves very fast, and you need a way for staff to help each other solve problems and keep up with the field.[28]

Keeping CoPs Open

Wenger said that while the value of CoPs can be their ability to cut across silos, they can become closed and club-like. Tips for avoiding these kinds of problems could include bringing in newcomers who are interested in the topic and attending conferences and other networking events.

---

26 Wenger, Etienne. Communities of Practice, A Brief Introduction. June, 2006.

27 Wenger, Etienne. Communities of Practice, A Brief Introduction. June, 2006.

28 Etienne Wenger provided the context of this example.

Members of CoPs may meet in a few different learning environments:

- **Synchronous:** This means "at the same time." Examples of synchronous learning could be a classroom event, webinar, or teleconference.

- **Asynchronous:** This means "not at the same time." Asynchronous participation could include the use of discussion boards or wikis, which enable interaction even if participants are not online at the same time.

CoPs are a good place for Gens X and Y to capture Boomer knowledge and share their own. They also provide a forum for them to get to know more experienced practitioners who can help them develop their skills.

Employees who have access to communities of practice also report these groups make them feel supported and valued—an added benefit to the organization. At Fluor, an Irving, Texas-based engineering, procurement, construction, maintenance, and project management company, employees have praised the organization's 48 communities of practice and knowledge sharing culture, saying they remind new *and* experienced employees that no one is on their own on projects.

"There is always someone available to help with a problem within the corporation that you can contact," one employee wrote in the company's yearly knowledge management survey.

Fluor's CoPs have also helped newcomers come up to speed quickly by putting them in touch with subject matter experts across the organization. John McQuary, vice president of Knowledge Management and Technology Strategies, recalls hearing about a new employee who was working on a Fluor job site when a client contractor confronted him with a complex question about a procedure. The young man, who had recently graduated from college, had only been with the company a few months, but he knew about Fluor's knowledge management system, which houses its knowledge communities. He promised the client he would have an answer by the end of the day, and then got on his bicycle and rode back to the office where he posted the clients' question to the appropriate knowledge community. Within a few hours, he had received responses to the clients' query, and he was able to return—as promised—with an answer by the end of the day.

Mapping CoPs to Business Goals

Fluor has linked communities of practice to business success since it launched its formal knowledge management strategy in 1999, McQuary said. Fluor operates in five segments: Energy and Chemicals, Industrial and Infrastructure,

Government, Global Services, and Power. Projects include designing and building manufacturing facilities, refineries, pharmaceutical facilities, power plants, and telecommunication and transportation infrastructures.[29]

During the 1990s, Fluor responded to a highly competitive global marketplace and opened offices in countries across the world to keep wages manageable. In 2000, the company began linking its global offices through its newly developed knowledge management system, Knowledge OnLine. Today, as in the past, Fluor often has several different offices working on pieces of the same project, which requires consistent business processes, tools, and collaboration, according to Fluor. And, with more than 600 clients in 85 countries,[30] Fluor employees need to be able to tap into the company's expertise anywhere in the world.

"With offices all over the world, some in very remote locations, we knew we needed to share knowledge in a much bigger way," McQuary said. "We aligned our knowledge management system and KnowledgeOnLine with the company's strategic direction, and provided a way for people in every location to tap into the knowledge base."

Fluor also recognizes that despite the arrival of thousands of newly hired employees, Boomers hold much of the company's technical expertise. The company's knowledge management strategy, which includes its communities of practice, a robust mentoring program, and a knowledge loss risk assessment process,[31] provides the backbone that supports knowledge capture, knowledge sharing, and staff development, McQuary said.

In 2009, McQuary reported that Fluor's 48 communities of practice cover all major functional groups, business lines, and a handful of support services. Communities of practice rarely meet face-to-face; however, knowledge managers—the leaders who oversee each community—get together about every other year. Nearly 100 percent of the workforce is involved in one or more communities where they share knowledge globally, enable work process, and help to quickly bring newcomers up to speed. Most of the communities have more than 1,000 members, McQuary said.

Fluor encourages knowledge sharing across the organization. Any employee can join one or more communities, and can post a question—or answer a question—to any community in the Knowledge OnLine system. All responses are captured within the system for future access and reuse.

---

29 Source: Fluor internal document.

30 Source: Fluor internal document.

31 Fluor uses a knowledge loss-risk assessment process based on the Tennessee Valley Authority's knowledge risk assessment process to help estimate the effort needed to mitigate knowledge loss, according to John McQuary. We discuss TVA's knowledge loss risk assessment in Chapter 5.

Communities of practice provide leadership opportunities as well, McQuary said. For example, every community needs a community leader and a knowledge manager. And Fluor integrates knowledge-sharing objectives into every aspect of an employees' career from start to finish. For example, Fluor's New Hire Orientation immediately introduces new employees to knowledge communities and familiarizes them on where they can go to find critical knowledge for their function. As employees move through their career at Fluor, the company uses participation in communities as a measure in their annual performance review, which helps to ensure that knowledge management and knowledge sharing remain a high priority at every level.

No Two Communities Are Alike

Fluor is a good example of how organizations build knowledge communities to align with organizational goals. The company's community deployment process is rigorous and consistent, and includes a readiness assessment that evaluates whether or not the community is aligned with business objectives and strategy.

However, not all knowledge communities are formed in this way. Some emerge spontaneously, without much input or oversight from anyone outside the immediate group. Such was the case with NexGen, a community of practice designed by young financial planners affiliated with the Financial Planning Association (FPA), a trade group representing 25,000 members.

Working in firms across the country, the young planners shared a few common denominators. All were in their twenties and early thirties and relatively new to the industry. All faced common challenges, such as how to start your own financial planning firm, how to find new client relationships, and how to develop these relationships. And all were searching for a place to ask questions and share knowledge. The result was NexGen, a community of practice that started rather spontaneously as a Yahoo! group, said Jude Boudreaux, an early member and president of the group in 2009.

"NexGen was a response to the realities of the financial planning community, mainly that the majority of the industry is made up of older professionals," Boudreaux said.

Many of the older planners got into the business through life insurance and stock channels, Boudreaux said. On the other hand, many new planners have financial planning degrees and different expectations when they enter the business. New planners are not expected to come into the business and start finding clients; rather, they are expected to serve the firm's existing client base and eventually grow into other roles. That's why they needed NexGen—to help them find the answers to questions that someone in their same situation would know the answers to.

The different experience among age groups and generations led NexGen founders to set the age limit for membership at 36, Boudreaux said. A cohesive group that communicates mostly online, NexGen had 250 members in 2009. The group regularly fields questions ranging from how to make an IRA contribution to how to start your own financial planning firm, Boudreax said. While Boomers are not allowed to participate in the community's online discussion, the members occasionally seek Boomer ideas and advice through discussions at the firms where they are employed. Members then share what they have learned with others in the NexGen community.

Founded in 2005, the NexGen community also launched a conference that brings members together to meet, network, and discuss topics of interest and concern. The annual conference, which is part of the larger FPA conference, also gives members an opportunity to attend meetings and talks with more experienced professionals (Boomers) who share personal experiences and provide their perspective on the future of the industry.

While NexGen isn't a part of any single business, it does receive some support from the FPA, Boudreaux says.

Designing a Community of Practice

As you can see, every organization and group approaches communities of practice in a different way. Some organizations create and support these groups as part of a knowledge management strategy, promoting their use and linking participation to performance appraisals. In other cases, small groups forge communities of practice as a way of meeting their personal and professional needs, and may only be linked to an organization in a cursory way. Even in situations where communities of practice sprout forth in a spontaneous way, the community has a purpose, and that purpose is tied to the group's goals, objectives, and interests.

In their 2005 white paper,[32] Darren Cambridge, Soren Kaplan, and Vicki Suter describe purpose as paramount to the success of a community of practice. The purpose of the community must drive all design choices and must be clearly defined, they wrote.

"The purpose of a community is essentially its reason for being—why it exists in the first place, including the essential value that it provides to its stakeholders and members," Kaplan said. "The objectives are one level down —specific things that the community focuses on achieving as a way to help realize its overall purpose."

---

32 Cambridge, Darren, Kaplan, Soren, and Suter, Vicki. Community of Practice Design Guide. http://net.educause.edu/ir/library/pdf/NLI0531.pdf. 2005. Retrieved 12/09.

Cambridge, Kaplan, and Suter categorize the purposes of a community into these areas of activity:[33]

- Develop relationships
- Learn about the topic and collaborate with others
- Carry out tasks and projects
- Create new knowledge

Use your business case, project charter, and the results of your workforce analysis to define the community of practice you'd like to design. Once you have defined the community's purpose, you are ready to move forward. Create a purpose statement and set it aside. It will come in handy later.

There are five basic steps for creating a community of practice.[34] In fact, these steps can apply to most, if not all, knowledge transfer methods. They are:

- Identify the audience
- Design and plan
- Pilot
- Go-live
- Expand and sustain

Let's look more closely at each phase.

Identify the Audience

Use what you have learned from your workforce assessment and other analyses to help you identify the community's audience. Your CoP may have a range of participants, including facilitators or community managers, subject matter experts, and novices. Still, it's important to identify who the community will actually benefit and who it is for.

"The first order of the day is to find potential members who may be interested in coming together," Wenger said. "Ask what some specific problems might be that the community could focus on."

---

33 Cambridge, Darren, Kaplan, Soren, and Suter, Vicki. Community of Practice Design Guide. 2005. p. 2.

34 The authors based these steps on interviews and on the following research: Cambridge, Darren, Kaplan, Soren, and Suter, Vicki. Community of Practice Design Guide. 2005. Piktialis, Diane and Greenes, Kent. The Conference Board. Bridging the Gaps: How to Transfer Knowledge in Today's Multigenerational Workplace. 2008.

Consider This Scenario

A utility company faced the loss of knowledge as valued employees approached retirement age. To prepare itself, the company assessed its workforce and identified employees in key construction and maintenance roles who were at risk of leaving. They also identified less-experienced workers who would logically move into these roles once vacated. The utility considered designing and developing a community of practice as a way to help less-experienced employees develop competence in vital areas. The audience would be longtime employees, who were experts at completing key maintenance and construction tasks, and less-experienced workers who needed guidance, support, and a place where they felt comfortable asking questions and sharing knowledge. But the generational piece could not be the focus. The utility needed to pinpoint some specific problems and topic areas to rally employees around.

As the picture of your audience begins to gel, map the community's purpose to your organization's business goals. By completing this task, you will likely begin to unveil areas of interest, as well as resources that will support the group.

Once you have identified your audience, reach out to the group and let them know you are designing a community of practice to capture and transfer knowledge on the topic in question. Let them know you are thinking of them, and that you would like them to be a part of the community.

Design and Plan

During the Design and Plan phase, you'll create guidelines for how the community will work. Consider the following elements as you move forward:

- **Objectives:** What learning objectives do you have for the community? Your objectives should specify what you hope participants will be able to accomplish as members of the community.

- **Metrics:** Tie the objectives to metrics. How will you know the community is achieving its goals? For example, one company may measure community performance as progress toward meeting business objectives.

  Statistical measurements associated with this effort could include response time to answer questions and the number of subject matter expert responses.

- **Tasks:** What kinds of tasks do you expect participants will want to complete when working in the community? Will they want to post questions in a virtual environment, share resources, and search for research materials? Or will they be meeting face-to-face to share knowledge about a particular technology? The tasks the community will want to complete will inform other aspects of your design.

- **Communication:**[35] How will community members communicate? Will they meet face-to-face? Or will most of their communication be online? Is it important that they get together at least once a month? Once every six months? Once a year? Or will the global nature of the community make face-to-face meetings difficult?

- **Technology:** What kind of technology, if any, will your community require in order to communicate and collaborate? Engage with IT to determine what systems are already in place and compare those with the features that the community will need, said McNulty. "Be sure that any community technology will allow users to access data they are accustomed to getting, as opposed to making them do everything in a new way," he said.

- **Activities:**[36] What kinds of activities will generate buzz within the community? For example, NexGen planned an annual conference that brought its members together to meet, network, and hear from professionals outside the community. This generated tremendous excitement and enthusiasm. When the economy soured, preventing many members from attending the conference, the group held a get-together using an Open Space format.[37] While they could not come together as they had originally hoped, the group decided it was critical to meet in some way, in some form. Essentially, the yearly conference complemented the group's regular meetings. Bringing everyone together for an event each year energized new and old members.

Etienne Wenger cautions people interested in communities from confusing their self-governing nature for the absence of internal structure. Learning activities can range from informal to very formal,[38] he wrote in *A Social Discipline of Learning*. "Some activities require almost no facilitation or organization, such as requests for just-in-time information or spontaneous conversations," Wenger wrote. "Some activities are quite formal, requiring facilitation, organization, and even protocols, such as training sessions, practice-development

---

35 Cambridge, Darren, Kaplan, Soren, and Suter, Vicki. Community of Practice Design Guide. 2005. p. 4.

36 2005. p. 4.

37 An Open Space format is a conference style where attendees decide what the group will cover and then proceed to create the agenda.

38 This work was in progress at this writing.

projects, or the setting of standards." Another activity Wenger suggested is inviting guests or experts as a way to incorporate broader, outside knowledge into the group's practice. This helps the community keep an open mind, so to speak, and avoid becoming insular.

- ■ **Roles:** Generally speaking, communities of practice need a sponsor, members, and two coordinator roles. Keeping this in mind, take some time to define how individuals will contribute. Sponsors support the formation of the community by allocating resources and allowing members the appropriate amount of time before they are required to show results, McNulty said. Members contribute time to exchange ideas, insights, and best practices to improve the collective intelligence around the focus topic.

As for the coordinators, one of these roles facilitates the community and answers questions. However, McNulty recommends that the facilitator answer as few questions as possible and instead connect the person inquiring with someone who has the knowledge. This strengthens the network of the community. The second coordinator plays a more administrative role. For this role, look for a more junior professional who will keep content fresh and the taxonomy intact. McNulty also recommended making the main coordinator a part of what he calls "the discovery phase," which is when CoP organizers are defining priorities and the challenges to accomplishing them.

During the discovery phase, organizers are also documenting common questions and even the rumblings about new innovations, McNulty said. Figure 6.2 describes the roles in more detail. "The coordinator is right there when we are asking these questions and looking for common topics," he said. "During this phase, the coordinator is gathering information, but we are also propping up this person, as they are going to be the go-to resource." The visibility the coordinator gains during this period will serve that person over the life of the community.

Don't underestimate the importance of the administrative role in a community of practice, McNulty advised.

Staying Organized When You're Not Online

The real benefit of being in a community is having access to the information you need, said Jacob McNulty. That means even CoPs that meet in person need a taxonomy.

And just because it's called a taxonomy doesn't mean it needs to be complex or high-tech, he said. Taxonomy is really just a system of organization, so it could be a manila folder or even a simple spreadsheet.

Coordinator (Mid-Level Career Professionals)

Description	Help the community focus on developing and refining its domain of expertise, maintain relationships, and oversee, as well as facilitate, the network's activity roadmap
Objectives	• Identify important and common issues related to the community's area of expertise • Oversee and facilitate community events (i.e., conference calls, webinars, summits) • Informally link people with similar interests, challenges, questions, etc. • Help build the knowledge base with best practices, lessons learned, tools and methods • Assess the health of the community and evaluate its value to members
Sample Activities	• Develop agenda for and facilitate community conference calls • Communicate with junior coordinators to gather information regarding member questions • Network with members to maintain a "finger on the pulse" of community interest • Interface with business team to direct support activities
Benefits	• Gain exposure to wide professional network of expertise both within and outside the organization • Unique developmental opportunity due to oversight and compilation of best practices and lessons learned • Maintain global purview across all activities within their technical discipline

Junior Coordinators (Early Career Professionals)

Description	Appointed personnel who are responsible for interfacing with other junior coordinators and coordinators to help facilitate the transfer of knowledge from on-site experts back to the broader community
Objectives	• Identify and transfer on-site knowledge back to broader community • Assist on-site experts with transferring tacit knowledge
Sample Activities	• Videotaping processes from dispersed sites, according to relevant topics and questions from other participants • Interviewing local experts regarding topics relevant to broader network • Helping local network members use updated collaboration system
Benefits	• Gain exposure to wide professional network of expertise both within and outside the organization • Unique developmental opportunity due to interaction with cross-functional local experts

Figure 6.2   *This chart describes the Coordinator and Junior Coordinator roles Jacob McNulty recommended in this section.* Source: Jacob McNulty, Orbital RPM

Some organizations provide specialized training to community leaders, managers, and facilitators. For example, Fluor's KM leadership, which includes community leaders and knowledge managers, undergo personal training as part of their responsibilities. The knowledge manager goes through a one-week formal training process with the central KM team. The vice president of knowledge management also holds community leader training, usually on a one-on-one basis. This training targets the specific needs of the business the community leader is in charge of, and it is tailored to the individuals' needs and prior experiences. Fluor also holds a biannual summit for all knowledge leaders, which gives everyone a chance to meet, network, and learn about knowledge sharing efforts across the organization.

Pilot

Piloting your community of practice before you announce it to a larger group is a great way to test it, and, if necessary, tweak it. To do this, select a small group of participants who are representative of the larger group. Initiate activities and ask the community to collaborate with other members.[39] Watch for issues with the technology, resources, collaboration, and communication. Also pay attention to how various roles interact.

Once the pilot is complete, ask pilot participants for feedback. How can the community better support their goals? Take note and make any necessary changes to technology requirements, purpose statement, and other documentation. The pilot also provides you with an opportunity to measure[40] early success and report on the results to executives and sponsors.

Go-Live

The goal of go-live is to formally launch the community, grab some attention for the group, and deliver some quick wins. Accomplishing a few quick wins will help people get excited and help you gain momentum. An example of a quick win is placing an article about the new community in an organization-wide newsletter with plenty of visibility. This will help you garner interest and attract new members.

During go-live, communications move into high gear, Passion said. Your goal for communication changes from simply building awareness to building understanding and creating a call to action. Use newsletters, emails, posters, even voice mail invitations to get the word out and recruit members into the community. Also create step-by-step guides or handouts that provide potential members with instructions on how to join. While this may be a very simple, short communication, new members will appreciate some step-by-step guidance. During go-live, urge executives and sponsors to talk about the community, its goals, and its relevance to the organization's overall goals. Executive promotion of the community will drive interest and curiosity, bringing more people to the table to participate and ultimately to capture and transfer knowledge.

---

39 This concept represented here: Cambridge, Darren, Kaplan, Soren, and Suter, Vicki. Community of Practice Design Guide. 2005. p. 5.

40 This concept represented here: Cambridge, Darren, Kaplan, Soren, and Suter, Vicki. Community of Practice Design Guide. 2005. p. 5.

Expand and Sustain

Go-live isn't the end of the road for communities of practice. Organizations must expand and sustain communities to keep them viable and energized.

To some degree, the community will be self-sustaining. Remember John McQuary's story about the new employee who tapped into the community to answer a client's question just months after being hired? Once community members and the organization become aware of how they can benefit from the community, they will return to it again and again. Here are some inspiring statistics: Fluor, which launched its knowledge management strategy and communities of practice in 1999, reported in 2009 that more than 27,000 members download 400 knowledge objects[41] daily. They submit 350 new or updated knowledge objects each week, and they post 300 questions and answers to the communities each week. Talk about self-sustaining!

This kind of following doesn't happen overnight, nor is it without effort. There are ways that organizations can help expand and sustain their communities of practice, which will help them achieve the goal of capturing and transferring Boomer knowledge. Here are a few ideas:

■ Share stories of individual and community successes with the rest of the organization.[42] Letting others know what the community is accomplishing reinforces the value of the community, creates excitement, and promotes a knowledge sharing culture.

■ Create a recognition program that highlights the knowledge sharing taking place within the community of practice. For example, the community leader could nominate individuals who collaborated to find a solution to a pressing issue each quarter. Executives or prominent sponsors could judge the solutions and present an award to the winner. Recognition and rewards don't need to be costly. If the budget is available to give the winners a gift card or bonus, fine. If not, mention the winners in staff meetings or internal communications. Remember, when recognizing or rewarding any effort, sincerity, timeliness, and personalization are key.

■ Bring community members together face-to-face whenever possible. This promotes a connection among the group and helps sustain virtual communities, McNulty said.

---

41 Knowledge objects can be documents containing data, information, and knowledge.

42 Cambridge, Darren, Kaplan, Soren, and Suter, Vicki. Community of Practice Design Guide. 2005. p. 6.

Don't skimp on your efforts to drive interest and participation in the community of practice. Lessons learned from Fluor's long history with communities sends this message home: Critical mass is required before substantial work process improvements are possible.

Top Tips for Maintaining Productive Communities of Practice

1. *Align objectives with organizational strategy.*

2. *Share knowledge across the organization by allowing people outside the community to post questions and get answers.*

3. *Take extra time to define the community's leadership roles, because this leadership can have a direct impact on the strength and success of the community.*

4. *Adjust roles as necessary.*

Source: Adapted from Fluor internal document.

Storytelling

If you've ever participated in a community, a social network, or even a mentoring program, you know that stories make up a big part of what is shared during our interactions. As humans, storytelling is a big part of our life—it's what we do, even when we don't realize we're doing it. We love to hear about other people's experiences, and we enjoy sharing our own just as much.

So can storytelling be used as a way to transfer knowledge from those experienced employees in the workplace? Absolutely. Storytelling is an excellent way to transfer complex, tacit knowledge. For example, in Chapter 1, we discussed the methods a small consulting firm used to capture the knowledge of Meryl Natchez, their CEO who was planning to retire. One method they used was to interview her at length about specific clients that she had worked with during the early days of the business. Salespeople hoped to make inroads with those clients again, but wanted to hear Natchez's stories about what the client's needs had been and whom she had worked with to make the engagements a success. During these interviews, the CEO gave an overview of the projects she had completed for the clients, but also told specific stories about how various phases of the projects had been carried out. Her stories also captured the culture of the organization, which is important for salespeople to be able to communicate during the sales process.

During the interviews with Natchez, salespeople brought along a new hire, a writer who would later help them develop proposals and other marketing content. They also tape recorded each of the interviews. An administrator transcribed the interviews and gave them to the proposal writer to store on the server. When questions came up about previous work discussed during the interviews, the proposal writer recalled the stories Natchez had told. If there were lapses in her memory regarding the details, she referred to the transcribed documents on the company server.

Storytelling can also be used to supplement clear-cut, already captured explicit knowledge. For example, a new employee working in a television newsroom receives a list of agencies and phone numbers she must call at the beginning of each shift. The purpose of these calls is to check what's going on in the coverage area and transmit any news to editors. The list is simple and straightforward, and the new hire could easily call each one without much instruction. However, the person training her has years of experience making these calls, and also insightful stories about how she has received more complete information from one agency versus another or from individuals who weren't even on the list. Although the new employee is working on a routine task, stories from others who are more experienced than she is will help her gain context that will help her do her job better.

While sharing stories can be an effective way to transfer knowledge, many organizations have historically placed a higher value on information that can be classified, calculated, and analyzed.[43] However, organizations are brimming with knowledge and insights that can't be calculated and categorized; stories can help experts convey this information. In addition, stories can help organizations make very dry information more interesting and accessible.

Stories work in organizations because they are implicit, not explicit, said Terrence Gargiulo of MakingStories.net, an author, speaker, and organizational development consultant who specializes in the use of stories.

"Information is structured to leave as little as possible to people's imagination," Gargiulo said. "Whereas stories are meant to trigger other stories and help people generate more of their own meaning."

What Is a Story?

Because telling stories is such a big part of the human experience, we tend to think we know exactly what stories are. But do we? Some experts say we have a lot to learn.

---

43 This concept represented here: Piktialis, Diane and Greenes, Kent. The Conference Board. Bridging the Gaps: How to Transfer Knowledge in Today's Multigenerational Workplace. 2008. p. 57.

"The greatest issue I bump up against in organizations is that many people don't know what a story really is," said Karen Dietz, owner of Polaris Associates Consulting, Inc., who works with leaders and executive teams to assemble and cultivate their most compelling stories. "We are so trained in left-brained methods of communicating that in fact we do very little telling of stories in presentations. We do a lot of telling about things."

Dietz provides a definition for us: A story is a packet of information that combines sensory language with an emotional arc that listeners can internalize and create meaning from. There is a big difference between a story and other kinds of documentation that organizations create. For example, a business report, which is typically free of emotional arcs, might say something like, "Our third quarter was marked by decreasing sales and increased transportation costs." On the other hand, a story might convey the information this way: "By the end of September, we were sweating bullets. Sales were free-falling, yet the cost of gas for our delivery trucks was skyrocketing."

A story can be a recollection of personal experiences; it can be an anecdote or a vignette. Stories are rich with detail and generally linked to a project, issue, or topic, Dietz said. Figure 6.3 provides more examples of forms of stories and story triggers.

The Multi-Faceted Art of Storytelling

There are three key elements to using stories in organizations:

- Story capture

- Story telling

- Story sharing

Often, when people hear or read the word "storytelling," they imagine someone standing and speaking to a group of listeners. But telling the story is just one piece of the program. To get the most out of stories, organizations must first decide what knowledge they want to transfer; this will help them decide the best stories to capture and document.

As you can see from Figure 6.3, organizational stories come in many forms. Because of these varying formats, organizations can convey stories in many different ways. They can be told in person, in a video, as an audio clip, or in writing. Whatever format you use, remember the goal is to engage your audience and get them thinking on their own. If your audience is passive, the story—and the storyteller—isn't accomplishing organizational goals. The audience needs to build their own meaning for stories to be effective.

Forms of Stories

Story: An act of communication providing people with packets of sensory material and an emotional arc, allowing them to quickly and easily internalize the material, comprehend it, and create meaning from it.

Story Form	Comments
Full story	The listener experiences emotions, characters, voices, plot, drama, contrast, problem, resolution, core message, story arc.
Anecdote	A short personal account (your personal take on a situation); a condensed personal story.
Case study	An analysis of a particular case or situation used as a basis for drawing conclusions in similar situations; a record of somebody's problems and how they were dealt with. The story is usually presented in sections: Situation, Solution, Result, Analysis.
Example	A particular single item, fact, incident or aspect that serves to illustrate an opinion, theory, principle, rule, guideline, or concept. Often used when talking *about* a story instead of telling one. *Usually not a story, although often mistakenly identified as one.*
News	A report of recent events or developments. This is an inverted pyramid structure that telegraphs the end of the story at the very beginning. The who, what, when, where, how, and why are usually in the first sentence or paragraph, with additional details coming later.
Profile	A concise biographical sketch. *Sometimes mistaken for a story.*
Scenario	An imagined sequence of possible events.
Testimonial	A favorable report or statement of qualities or virtues of somebody or something; an expression of appreciation; a statement testifying to benefits; a character reference or letter of recommendation. *Sometimes mistaken for a story.*
Vignette	A brief incident or scene as in a play or movie; a short elegant story.

Story Devices	Comments
Analogy	A comparison between two things that are similar in some respects; often used to explain something or make it easier to understand.
Aphorism	A concise statement of a principle; a terse formulation of a truth or sentiment.
Metaphor	A figure of speech in which a word or phrase literally denoting one kind of object or idea is used in place of another to suggest a likeness between them (the ship plows the sea).
Tag line	A phrase repeatedly used in connection with a person, organization, or product, especially in publicity. *Sometimes mistakenly identified as a story.*
Trigger	A word or series of words to initiate, actuate, or set off a story.

Figure 6.3   *A story by another name, just may be…a story!*

Dietz explained: "If I tell you a well-crafted story, your imagination is immediately engaged, your analytical mind is engaged, and if I give you sensory material for your five senses, your whole body becomes engaged."

As the audience absorbs the story, it often sparks memories of similar situations, and individuals come up with their own stories to share, Dietz said. With story programs, leaders should always ask for stories in return, whether they are in writing, face-to-face, or in other formats. The act of individuals creating their own meaning from stories and responding with their own stories makes story programs a very effective way to transfer knowledge.

In those stories being shared, groups and teams learn from each other and develop relationships and trust, Dietz said.

Keep Your Audience Engaged

The best way to tell a story is to relive the experience for the audience by sharing emotions and describing sights, sounds, tastes, and tactile impressions, said Dietz. When storytellers do this, they find they automatically and effortlessly feed vivid images and sensory material to the audience in ways that keep them engaged.

Practical Use of Stories

So how do you craft stories and use them to transfer Boomer knowledge, or, better yet, create a culture of knowledge sharing in the workplace? Dietz provides an example. Say you are crafting stories about a particular project to illustrate the importance of building a strong team. As we all know, there are many elements to working on a team, and storytelling could be used to create meaning around topics that include the following:

- How the team built its identity
- How the team defined its values
- How the team worked together
- What worked for the team and what didn't
- How the team avoided problems and got around stumbling blocks
- How the team brought the project to successful completion

Do you see how a more experienced team member could use this opportunity to share knowledge about the team and the project? To make a similar storytelling experience even more inclusive, consider inviting team members with less experience to share their stories of the team building experience and the project.

Keep in mind, though, that sharing stories is less about control and more about influence and creating meaning.

"With storytelling, you tell the story and then you have to let it go," she said. "You can predict a lot about how a story is going to be received and influence behavior. But 100 percent control of the results is difficult to guarantee. We are at the beginning stages of measuring results with story programs. You don't know what ultimately is going to happen."

On the other hand, Dietz said that organizations often get more than they expect from storytelling because the audience creates meanings in ways they may not have anticipated.

"Some parts of the story may stay latent until the person internalizes it and makes sense of it," Dietz said. "Because storytelling is so rich, values are conveyed in a dynamic way, and you may find yourself telling a story for a specific purpose that is rich in other messages as well. Your audience may get more out of it than what you set out to convey."

When leaders want to control a certain message, storytelling may not be the best fit. For example, say a leader wants to tell a story with a message that stealing from the company is bad, Dietz said. He wants to make sure that everyone internalizes the message in the same way, but with stories, you can only influence people, not dictate to them. Not everyone will internalize a story about stealing from the company in the same way. In this case, the leader may want to make a declarative statement about the company's policy on stealing in addition to telling a story.

Tell the First Story in Person

Storytelling is an intimate connection between two people—the storyteller and the listener, said BZ Smith, the professional storyteller we covered in the mentoring section of this chapter. Smith suggests that if an organization is using storytelling for the first time, face-to-face delivery is best. If this is not possible, the next best way to tell a story would be through the written word. Audio and video could also be effective methods, but these may work better once the organization is already steeped in a storytelling tradition.

Audio and video may also work well if the storyteller is too shy to get up in front of a group, Smith said. In this situation, the interviewer is just as important as the storyteller; the interviewer must be able to conduct a friendly, comfortable interview that gives the expert an opportunity to share information, institutional knowledge, and insights.

Storytelling Structure

Stories help people retain information and knowledge; an employee may not remember data points, but they will likely remember a good story and how it applies to the data. Stories may be less structured than other forms of information, but organizations can create a framework that makes storytelling an effective method for knowledge sharing.[44] There are many ways to approach storytelling. Here are a few to consider and adapt for your purpose and audience.

Method 1: Assess, Craft, and Deliver

Start by reviewing your assessment of your workforce. Who has knowledge that could be shared in a story format? Who needs this knowledge? What is the most appropriate level of detail?

Next, think about your objective for wanting to tell your story. Perhaps your objective is to tell a story that will help employees understand the importance of prequalifying a client during the sales process. Now look at your audience. Who are they?

"If your audience is Gen X, don't pull out a story about Jack Benny or someone they haven't heard of," said Meryl Natchez. "I've seen this happen a million times where someone bases their story on someone or something the audience isn't familiar with. The story falls flat."

If you don't have a good story, look around you, suggested Passion. There may be someone in the organization who can relate to the audience and the objective you are trying to meet. Ask them for a story.

Next, decide how you will deliver the story. Will you deliver it at an in-person meeting? Will the story be videotaped and kept in a knowledge library? Will you deliver it during a conference, or during a one-on-one meeting with your subordinate?

Method 2: Ask Your Audience for Material

Starting from your workforce assessment, think about what kinds of stories would resonate with your audience. Then talk to your potential audience and gather stories from them, Natchez suggested. Here are some questions to get them talking:

- Have you ever had an experience where you couldn't figure out how to complete a task?
- What did you do?

---

44 This concept represented here: South Carolina Office of Human Resources. Knowledge Transfer Strategies. www.ohr.sc.gov/OHR/wfplan/wfplan-development.htm. Retrieved 10/09.

- What was frustrating about this experience?
- Who did you ask for help?

"People will be thrilled to talk about their experiences," Natchez said. "The phrase 'tell me about…' is the key to eliciting stories from others."

Once you have a story you want to share with the group, ask the person who shared it with you for permission. Then use it to launch a conversation with the larger group about how to solve a problem or address an issue.

Don't make up stories, Natchez warned. A true story, or even one that is heard and repeated, will be well-received simply because it is authentic and real. And don't always try to give stories a happy ending. Sometimes, stories with unhappy, even disastrous endings can be more meaningful. That is, if they're true.

Method 3: Reconnecting Your Audience to the Topic

Introduce a story when people are paying the least amount of attention. For trainers and presenters of all kinds, a lull and lack of energy typically follows the lunch hour, Natchez said.

Stories will reconnect them to the material at hand. You may also use a story to illustrate a point and then give the audience an activity or task that connects them to the story. Do not tell a story in place of doing an activity; adults learn by doing. Rather, use the story to get them interested in the activity that will engage them and help them learn.

Keeping Stories Accessible

Storytellers, whether they are managers, experienced workers, or experts, design their stories for their audiences. This means keeping in mind a certain level of detail and length.

Keep stories short, sweet, and to the point. Kathleen Robinson, an organizational consultant and executive coach, offered advice that could apply to knowledge transfer in general, but especially to storytelling:

"We tend to think everything we do is important and critical to the organization or that it's the best way to do something," Robinson said. "We need to take a good hard look at exactly what information and knowledge is essential to the recipient's success. When sharing our wisdom and experience, it's good to consider whether it is both true and useful to someone else. Let's not be so attached to the way we have always done things. Let's look at our organizations with fresh eyes and ask ourselves, 'What's really needed here as we move forward?'"

Drawing in Your Audience

Meryl Natchez knows how to get a group to participate, and she shared her method in a story:

"My whole family came home for the holidays this year. And, as is common among adults, there are some simmering animosities. I was a little worried about this, actually. So, before the big day, I sent out an email to everyone saying that we were going to play a little game when they arrived. The game was to think of a piece of trivia about you that nobody in your family knows that would also be difficult for anyone to guess.

When the family arrived, each wrote a single line about this piece of trivia on a slip of paper. It could be something like, 'With my first paycheck, I bought a pair of red leather boots,' or 'I'm certified to sail a small watercraft.' You get the idea. They placed each of their slips of paper in a hat and a moderator drew them one by one. We all had to guess who belonged to each slip of paper. Once they were figured out, we each told our story about this little piece of trivia. This activity put everyone in a great mood, and the whole evening just flowed.

That's what a story should do. It should engage your audience and get things started."

Managers could adapt this method for use in the workplace. A little goes a long way, Natchez said.

"Stories humanize information. And you don't have to come off like you're real folksy. The objective is to get people to participate, buy-in, and break down the wall between the speaker and the audience."

Storytelling can be particularly valuable when sharing knowledge about relationships the organization has built with clients, vendors, and others. Client success stories are a good example, Robinson said. Draw these details out by asking the following questions:

- How did you meet the client or vendor?
- How did you work together to address a need?
- What happened as a result of your partnership?
- What did you learn from the relationship?
- What sustains the relationship?

Robinson makes a point that relationships must be built between individuals —they cannot simply be transferred. People can be assigned to a new reporting relationship or account relationship, but trust must be earned with each new relationship. Providing context through stories can help guide new relationships to success.

Take Time to Craft Your Story

Before you stand up in front of an audience, get familiar with whom you're talking to and the organization, department, or group they represent. Once you have done this, ask yourself what it is you want to convey. What is the strong thread that you want to carry through the story from beginning to end? This thought process is called story crafting, and it is a critical part of the storytelling process. When you take the time to craft your story, you are more likely to hold the audience's attention and less likely to get overly instructive, said BZ Smith.

"When you get didactic with your story, essentially, you are lecturing," Smith said. "It is critical to avoid this."

After Action Reviews

Storytelling can be a small or large part of many different knowledge transfer approaches. They may even have a place in After Action Reviews (AARs), also known as *lessons learned* or *sunset reviews*, which many organizations use to share and transfer knowledge immediately after an event.

Developed by the U.S. Army, AARs provide a way for organizations to learn from their successes and failures. Faced with losing valuable team members, organizations may opt to use AARs as a way to gain expert insight and promote feedback to improve processes and performance. Ideally, organizations make AARs a regular part of their work processes, encouraging regular review of events and programs and ongoing knowledge sharing.

While developed by and for the military, any organization can use the AAR process. AARs are defined by the U.S. Agency on International Development (USAID) as a discussion of an event that focuses on performance standards and enables individuals with shared interests to discover what happened, why it happened, and how to sustain strengths and improve on weaknesses.[45]

---

45 USAID. After Action Review Technical Guidance. www.usaid.gov. February, 2006. p. 1. Retrieved 1/9/2010.

A Different Perspective on AARs

Ainsley Nies, a Northern California-based leadership and learning consultant, has adopted a different process for AARs called "retrospectives" for a number of reasons. First, Nies said, retrospectives are structured to create an appreciative environment where personal perspectives are as significant as project statistics. Also, the term AAR suggests these reviews only happen at the end of a project. For a short project with little-to-no complexity, holding a review at the end may be appropriate, but for longer projects, Nies recommends her clients reflect on their progress over the course of the effort using the same collaborative processes inherent in an AAR, or retrospective. This way, individuals are given more opportunities to learn from each other and course corrections can be identified earlier when they provide the most value, she said.

Another reason Nies uses the term *retrospectives* is because some organizational leaders bristle at the term AAR because it connotes a regimented, somewhat militaristic process that doesn't jibe with their culture.

An AAR is not a critique; rather, it is an opportunity for individuals and teams to actively reflect on a project or event and learn from each other.

AARs are based around four questions:[46]

- What was expected to happen?
- What actually occurred?
- What went well and why?
- What can be improved and how?

Likewise, the AAR process consists of four steps:

1. Planning the AAR
2. Preparing for the AAR
3. Conducting the AAR
4. Following up using AAR results

Let's go through the four steps and provide some details[47] to help you conduct your own AARs.

---

46 USAID. After Action Review Technical Guidance. www.usaid.gov. February, 2006. p.12. Retrieved 1/9/2010.

47 Some details adapted from content covered here: USAID. After Action Review Technical Guidance. www.usaid.gov. February, 2006. pp. 1-41. Retrieved 1/9/2010.

Planning

First, identify the event, activity, or process that your team needs to discuss.

"This is a very specific kind of meeting," Nies said. "Just like every project, every retrospective is unique. It's important that you define the purpose from the beginning because it sets the context for many of the planning decisions that follow, such as who you invite and what you include in the agenda."

Nies also emphasized that organizers should include the purpose of the meeting on the agenda. This information is important for participants to have ahead of the meeting, so they can begin to think about their experiences and what questions they may want to raise.

Generally, an organizer, or someone who has a vested interest in completing the review, oversees the entire AAR process. Ideally, the organizer should select a note-taker, which ensures that a report is prepared following the review. The organizer should also select a facilitator and take responsibility for any next steps identified by the report.

Team leaders specify who should attend the AAR. Remember, the more participants that attend, the more complete the feedback will be. More complete feedback provides better opportunities for team learning and growth, so it's important to be sure that the group is well represented.

Schedule the AAR as soon as possible after the event, to help ensure participants' memories are fresh. If possible, bring participants together in one location; global organizations may need to make arrangements for conference calls or other virtual arrangements.

While some sources say organizers should keep AARs to 90 minutes, Nies said that the length of the meeting depended on the complexity of the project. As a rule of thumb, organizers should schedule enough time to elicit the feedback they need to promote knowledge sharing and create a report.

Finally, confirm who will support the AAR.[48] One of the goals of this kind of meeting is to give managers and project team members an opportunity to discuss what went well and what needs to be changed down the road. You should enlist leadership support early in the planning phase.

Preparing

When considering the use of AARs, some professionals may recall attending similar meetings where participants soft-pedaled everything to avoid offending anyone. When this happens, the group is unable to capture an authentic

---

48 USAID. After Action Review Technical Guidance. www.usaid.gov. February, 2006. p. 8. Retrieved 1/9/2010.

picture of what happened, and no one really benefits. As organizers prepare for the meeting, it's important to remember that successful AARs start with a strong facilitator. Select accordingly.

Facilitators may be an objective outsider or someone who knows the activity or topic—it's up to the individual organizing the AAR whom they want to use in this critical role. However, unless participants perceive the facilitator to be neutral, the meeting environment will not be a safe one, Nies said.

Preparing for the AAR also consists of inviting attendees and communicating to them how important their participation will be to the review. When you create your invitations, encourage attendees to arrive ready to participate and to speak openly about their unique experience.

Don't Let Technology Derail Your Meeting

Before a virtual meeting that uses technology, consider conducting a dry run. At the very least, take a few minutes before attendees arrive to prepare for the technological aspect. Attendees will appreciate a seamless meeting free from technology glitches.

Conducting

With everyone together, it's time to get started. The facilitator may want to consider kicking off the meeting with an anecdote or story that captures the group's attention and then move forward to explain the ground rules.[49] The AAR is not a critique, and it is not, as USAID notes, "a complaint session." No one has all the answers—this is a critical point to make. And it is not a full-scale evaluation, but rather an opportunity to learn from the experiences of the team.

The facilitator must set the stage from the beginning and ensure participants that they have entered a safe environment, Nies said. In order for the group to carry out an effective review, participants need to be comfortable sharing their truth about an event without fear of repercussions.

"I tell groups that every work effort is 'a social event' because it's the people not the planning documents that get the job done," Nies said. "That means every person made a contribution and will have a point of view. Without the perspectives of every person on the team, you have an incomplete picture of what really happened."

---

49 This concept represented here: USAID, After Action Review Technical Guidance, February, 2006. www.usaid.gov. p.11. Retrieved 1/9/2010.

Nies also suggested that facilitators build into the agenda a discussion on project successes. This discussion should happen early. It's easy to get bogged down in the negative, and Nies said that "starting on a positive note helps set the right tone for what follows." Additionally, the facilitator will get more mileage from specific answers than they will from generalizations, and skilled facilitators will listen for opportunities to dig deeper. The facilitator will also pay attention to who is not interacting and look for opportunities to get them engaged in the meeting, Nies commented. Throughout the process, the scribe or note-taker should be gathering thorough notes, preferably on flip charts so that participants can refer back to comments or themes throughout the meeting.

Make Your Introductions

Face-to-face meetings give attendees the opportunity to greet each other; virtual meetings do not. Facilitators should take a few minutes before the meeting starts to introduce everyone involved in the meeting. Give each person's full name if possible and briefly discuss their role in the meeting or project.

Following-Up

Once the AAR is complete, the note-taker or report writer creates a document with the group's responses to the four main questions. The organization can use this report as a reference in the future—it is a valuable tool that benefits the team if it is easily accessible. (For an example of making the results of the AAR available to the organization, see the AnswerLab case study at the end of this chapter.)

The focus of the AAR should be to promote discussion, learning and knowledge transfer, and to improve performance. At the end of the AAR, participants should be able to clearly identify what worked well and why, what did not go well, and where the team can make improvements. At this stage, leaders determine action items and who is responsible for carrying out tasks and activities. For example, organizations that use AARs as part of their knowledge transfer program may discover during the process that mentoring or reverse mentoring could benefit members of the group. In these cases, part of the follow-up plan could include pairing members and creating goals and objectives for them to work toward.

It's important that the AAR not end in a list of future best practices; organizations will benefit more when they make actual changes to documented policies and procedures. Otherwise, if people don't refer back to the report—or new team members join—the lessons will be lost.

Merging AARs, Wikis to Create Knowledge Base

After every project, AnswerLab staff come together to talk about what went well—and what went wrong. Amy Buckner, a founder of AnswerLab calls these get-togethers, which often occur in the office conference room, *project recap meetings*. She and her team have been conducting these meetings since AnswerLab's earliest days, and they remain a primary method of knowledge sharing and transfer.

During the recap meeting, team members discuss what went well, the clients' response to their work, and what the team might change going forward. Team members then draft a lessons-learned document and keep it in an online knowledge library for others to access when starting a similar project or working with the same client.

For the recap meeting and the knowledge library to have the greatest effect, team members must support two company tenets:

- All team members keep knowledge in a central place for others to access.

- All team members consult the knowledge library before starting a project.

Buckner said that while there is always room for improvement, she is generally pleased with the collaborative environment at AnswerLab. In addition to the knowledge library, the company uses an internal wiki for processes and procedures. The endless supply of wiki pages gives staff and contract researchers step-by-step information on everything from installing and configuring various software to conducting research studies at longtime client sites.

"We even have a page that recommends where to go to lunch if you're at a client site in San Jose," Buckner said.

Like the recap meetings, the company's information repository has been in place since the early days of the company. Buckner credits the company's first administrative assistant—a very organized Gen Xer who developed Web sites on the side—with creating what would eventually become the company's go-to sites.

"He was very organized, and he always used to say that we needed to keep critical information in one spot," Buckner said. "We still use that model today. It's good because we have our staff, but we also have contractors who interact with our clients. We want them to present the same brand standards as our staff members do, so we give them access to the wikis. It's our base camp."

> So, how does Buckner ensure that lessons learned result in improvements to operations? Basically, this comes down to knowledge sharing and communication among the team post-project and keeping lessons learned in a central place. Team members must also be disciplined about reviewing wikis and getting advice from co-workers before starting projects.

The Design Document

In many organizations, managers seek buy-in from executives and leaders at every stage of the planning process. A formal Design Document can help you secure the buy-in you need, and provide you—and your successors—with documentation of your program efforts. As with your Business Case and Project Charter, let your audience be your guide in regards to how detailed you make your Design Document.

Here are the basics:

Section 1. Business Problem

In this section, describe the primary business needs you want to address with your knowledge transfer program. Define your objectives and then move on to discuss the expected benefits to the program audience.

Section 2. Audience

Now describe who will participate in your knowledge retention program and who will benefit. If necessary, break the audience down and describe their different experience levels.

Section 3. Program Parameters

This section describes your proposed breakdown of the program and methods for delivery. Some details may change as you move toward development, but at the very least, try to specify how the organization will share knowledge. For example, if you're designing a mentoring program, provide information on meeting places, duration, and what you expect pairs to cover during their meetings.

Section 4. Scope, Prerequisites, Technical Requirements

Here, discuss what the program will cover, as well as items that fall outside the scope. Define any prerequisites that participants need to meet before joining the program. For example, if you are designing a storytelling program, consider how much experience a participant may need to get the most out of each session. This is also the time to define any technical requirements, such as necessary server space and Web tools.

Finish this section by drafting an outline of the program. The outline will be a quick reference document that will include an overview of the program with objectives and start dates.

Once you have documented your design plans and have received the buy-in you need, you are ready to begin developing your program. Your knowledge sharing program is within reach!

Section 5. Anticipated deliverables

In this section, discuss the deliverables you anticipate you will create for your knowledge transfer program. Table 6.2 provides some ideas to help you and your team brainstorm what you may need.

Table 6.2   Sample Deliverables

Method	Possible Deliverable
Mentor program	Mentee development plan templates
	Mentee agenda templates
	Best practices and tips for productive mentor-mentee meetings
	Training materials for mentors and mentees
	Web site content and events calendar
	Contact information for administrators and others who oversee the program
Communities of practice	List that provides contact information for members, administrators
	Web site that can serve as an online warehouse for resource documents, white papers, and other research
Social networks	Web site with access to forums, microblogs, and other social media tools
Story programs	Outline of knowledge and insights the organization wants to convey
	List of potential events and meetings where telling stories would be especially effective
After Action Reviews	Documented ground rules
	Facilitator instructions
	Agenda templates
	Email templates (for inviting attendees)
	Sign-in sheets
	Maps to location (if meeting off-site)

7

Ready, Set, Develop!

B y now you've analyzed your workforce, developed your goals and objectives, and even narrowed your focus to one or two knowledge transfer methods you'd like to develop. The design phase is all about using your data to create a blueprint. Now, in the development phase, you and your team will use that blueprint to create the deliverables for your knowledge transfer program based on a host of factors, including the complexity of your business problem, your objectives, your technology requirements, and your audience.

In every phase, it's important to gather feedback from stakeholders (and sign-off from sponsors). Keep this momentum going during the development phase. Don't forget to continue to communicate to stakeholders and sponsors so they are aware of the upcoming program. By involving a wide range of stakeholders in your development effort, you'll find that stakeholders are open to participating once you go live because they have a sense of ownership. This is a good thing!

If your solution has a technology component, now is the time to purchase or build the software you will need. Make sure that you test it during the pilot, before you go live. You will also need to test it again after the pilot is complete. Keep in mind, off-the-shelf products may not need the same level of testing as a homegrown system, but it's important to be prepared to test as needed. Make sure that you resolve technical issues before you go live because releasing a faulty tool may cause you to lose your audience before you even get started.

Finding a Representative Testing Audience

When selecting your testing audience, it's a good idea to recruit a cross-functional, diverse team of testers: a technical user, a technophobe, a casual user, and so on.

The Value of the Pilot

Ideally, a big part of the development process involves launching a pilot. While it's tempting to roll out programs without one (many organizations do), we encourage leaders to consider the value of piloting their programs during the development stage. Pilots give you the ability to gather feedback on your vision and help ensure that you are going down the right path. They also give you the opportunity to tweak elements of your program while it's still early, which increases the chance that your program will be received positively by your audience.

"When you don't pilot, you go through a huge effort to create your program, and you go live, running the risk of missing your target or being off base," said instructional designer Vic Passion. "Pilots allow you to define and tweak, and perhaps make substantial changes before you implement your program. It's an important step."

Pilots also let you start small. By starting small, you can test the logistics of your solution. Standing at the finish line of the design phase, you really don't have a sense of exactly what you will need in regards to time and resources. You have an idea, but without a pilot, you can't really say for sure how the program will impact you or anyone else on your team.

Pilots also allow you to test whether or not the materials and approach are what you intended them to be, Passion said. Imagine how disappointed you'd be if you built a program and launched it and some major element didn't work!

"Sometimes, we incorrectly estimate the problem and have to go back and make changes," Passion said. "Without a pilot, there are some very important, concrete things that you wouldn't know about until after you go live."

For example, imagine that a global company is looking for a way to bring its far-flung employees in closer contact to enable knowledge sharing. The IT director is excited about a new social networking package, so he makes plans to implement it. Six months after go-live, he finds that only 21 percent of the employees are using the social-networking suite of tools. He surveys the employees, only to find that what they really want is more face time with other employees. They spend their workdays communicating electronically and want more opportunities for personal contact. The IT director goes back to the drawing board, this time committed to doing a stronger analysis, design, and pilot before going live with his solution.

Fluor provides another example of the value of pilots. In 1999, the engineering, procurement, construction, maintenance, and project management company launched two pilot communities, said John McQuary, vice president of Knowledge Management and Technology Strategies. One pilot community represented a functional group, the other a business client account. By the end of 2000, the company had launched 32 global communities.

"From the pilots, we learned that our technology worked, and that our community deployment work process was sound," McQuary said. "Our focus then in 2000 was to deploy communities. At that time, most of our metrics were statistical. We really started to emphasize performance of the communities in 2001 and began to add qualitative and value creation-type metrics in addition to the quantitative and statistical ones."

The Unexpected Audience

Sometimes, you get this far and a colleague stops by and suggests you include an audience in your program that you didn't look at during the assessment phase. Rather than pull out your hair and throw up your hands, consider sending out a simple feedback form to get this new audience's reaction to the program you are developing.

For example, if you're piloting a mentoring program, send out a feedback form that asks potential mentees for their thoughts on the value of mentoring. You may hear an overwhelming, "Wow! That's great news!" Or you may receive only lukewarm comments. Taking time, even during the development stage, to check in with this new, potential audience will give you a sense of how well-received your whole program might be.

Develop a Pilot

There are a handful of steps to creating your pilot. Start by identifying participants who could test your program effectively. These are your guinea pigs, so to speak. Look for a representative sample, but keep it small. For example, if you anticipate your mentoring program will be made up of 100 mentees, select five or so for your pilot. Then decide how long you would like your pilot to be.

Social network expert Jacob McNulty, who often works with large, global organizations, has a different take on pilots and how large they should be.

"Start small and grow from there," McNulty said. "But put an asterisk next to 'small.' When you're piloting communities, you can't just have 10 people, because out of every population, there is going to be a percentage that is going to contribute and have a high level of activity. Then there will be the lurkers—people who check in and get some value but don't really participate. Basically, a small pilot still needs to have critical mass to deliver success."

Once you have selected your participants, spend some time helping them to understand the program and their role in the pilot. Then build an evaluation tool. For example, if you are designing a formal mentoring program, you might have a questionnaire that helps you understand the participant better. The questionnaire could ask questions such as:

- What are your perceptions of mentoring?
- Have you ever received mentoring?
- If you have received mentoring, describe the experience.
- What kinds of tasks or processes do you generally need help with?
- Do you find that you seek out help on a daily basis? Weekly basis? Monthly basis?

Selecting the Right Pilot Participants

When choosing pilot participants, be careful with resistors, or people who take a negative view of your program. You want people who are open to the possibilities of the program. You might find that, by involving participants who are slightly resistant to your method or on the fence, you can get great feedback and also convince them of the value by having them participate in the pilot. This approach will also help with buy-in when others see that your pilot program was inclusive. However, Passion suggests screening out participants with a very negative view because their input will be too biased.

After you have screened your participants and made your final selections, start testing every element of the pilot you have created. Whether it's a sign-in sheet, or an evaluation form, or a Web site where participants enroll, test, test, and test some more.

The pilot is a great time to confirm what works. But during this testing period, you'll also learn, for example, if the paperwork is too lengthy, or the Web site has glitches, or the evaluation instructions are too difficult to understand. For storytelling pilots, you may learn that the approach you have taken works well, but your storyteller needs some coaching.

If you are testing the use of AARs, you may find process issues. Here's an example: Say your pilot shows your team is not taking time to review write-ups of AARs on the Intranet, and as a result, few are acting on the findings. You could consider changing the process and opt instead to discuss the team's findings at the next departmental meeting (with some stories, of course).

During the pilot, you may also learn that certain aspects of your knowledge transfer program don't address the needs of your audience. Now is the time to tweak those areas so the program will achieve your objectives once you go-live. Feedback on the tactical and logistical elements will let you know what specific items you need to fix.

Communications and Development

During the development stage, you will be working to raise awareness for the program you are working on, and tailoring your message to your audience. Let's assume at this stage that you will have two audience groups: One represents your pilot, and the other represents those outside this group.

Your communications push for pilot participants will likely start with sending a message that you need recruits. Look at your organization and your program and decide how large the pilot group needs to be. What's the best way to recruit pilot participants? Will you use a friendly email? Leave individual voice mails? Perhaps drop a note in their box? There are many ways to find pilot participants.

"I've seen initiatives where leaders go out and hand-pick pilot participants," Passion said. "The benefit of this approach is you have more control over who participates at this level."

Once you have your pilot group, your communications will likely need to become more targeted. For example, you might need to provide pilot participants with instructions or guidelines. Ideally, your communications should encourage a two-way street between program leaders and pilot members; creating an open-door feeling will encourage participants to provide the feedback you need to fine-tune your program.

Stick with It

Once the decision is made to move forward, stakeholders and executives need to be committed to the pilot, said Veronica Zaman at Scripps Health. In 2003, the five-hospital health care system piloted its nurse-mentoring program in one hospital; soon after, other hospitals in the Scripps system adopted similar practices. By the end of 2004, each of the Scripps' hospitals had a nursing mentor program in place.

"We started in one hospital, and it worked," Buzachero said. "Then it was adopted by all the other hospitals. We didn't try to spread it everywhere at once."

For Scripps, creating clear roles before piloting was critical.

"Before we rolled out the pilot, we were very clear about roles," Buzachero said. "We negotiated the roles of everyone on the unit, including the physicians. When you have a new player on the unit, you have to be clear about what everyone is doing so that when the pilot starts, everyone understands and it clicks."

Of course, there were adjustments, but Buzachero and the rest of the team expected this. Adjustments included tweaking some aspects of the budget and looking at how the nurse mentor fit into the hospital's care model.

"The beauty of the pilot is that people have a chance to influence the program before it becomes final," Buzachero said.

For the rest of the group, your communications may be very different. You may want to simply pique their interest about the pilot. As responses begin to trickle in from pilot participants, consider sharing this feedback with the rest of the group, keeping interest high. These communications could be delivered in an email or newsletter, or an executive or group leader could discuss them during a meeting or company gathering. With this communication, you will let everyone know about the pilot and that the program is moving into the next phase.

Some organizations take a very different approach to communications during the pilot phase. For example, when Cerner Corp., a company that offers healthcare IT services, piloted its uCern social media platform in 2009, they started by selecting about 600 of its 7,500 employees for the pilot. Then they turned on access to everyone in the company, but didn't announce the new platform.

Soon, the 600 or so pilot participants started reaching out to others in the organization, many of whom were not involved in the pilot.

"People were getting emails that said they were now connected to so-and-so, and they had no idea what was going on," Robert Campbell, CLO, said.

The buzz around uCern grew. Soon, it was viral, with users connecting and trying it out, and in some cases, feeling like mavericks because they had "snuck in" to the pilot. It was all part of the master plan, Campbell said.

"We wanted to take advantage of people we knew would be early adopters, so we deliberately planted the seeds before we did any kind of formal announcement," he said. "It was a very different kind of rollout."

Six weeks after the initial pilot when Cerner finally made a formal announcement to the organization about uCern, there were already 2,500 active users.

"Within a very short time, everyone was on," Campbell said.

Your Thoughts, Please

One of the main goals that organizations set when they launch a pilot is to gather feedback. When it starts coming in, roll up your sleeves and get ready to gather even more. Say your pilot is 90 days long. Passion suggests sending out an online or paper-based evaluation form at 30 days and at 60 days. At 90 days, she suggests inviting some or all of the pilot participants in for an interview, rather than sending them an online or paper-based evaluation form. The number of participants you invite will depend on how large the group is.

"Surveys are good, because they provide quantitative data—you can crunch the numbers," Passion said. "But you're not going to get very deep feedback if you use paper-based or online evaluations. On the form you'll read, 'yes, it went great,' and then a little bit more. But if you sit down with someone, you are much more likely to elicit the rich feedback that will help you really finetune your program."

Another approach is to conduct interviews at 30 days. That way, you'll know early on if your program is missing the boat.

Here are some tips for creating surveys that draw out helpful insights:

- Keep the survey as short as possible. Many participants will not respond if the survey takes longer than five to ten minutes to complete.

- If relevant, reassure participants that survey results are anonymous and treat the responses as such. On the other hand, let respondents provide their names and contact information if they'd like someone to contact them.

■ If the audience is comfortable with technology, deliver your survey using an online survey tool, which makes it easier for participants to respond and for you to collate the results.

When drafting your survey, include a mix of question types. You'll most likely want to include questions about participants' attitudes and opinions using the Likert scale, such as "On a scale from one (Completely Disagree) to ten (Completely Agree), indicate if you feel you will be able to apply what you learned from the storyteller in your position." Be careful, however, to ensure that the questions are all structured similarly so that participants who are skimming the questions don't accidentally give you the opposite response.

Also, include free-form questions so that you can capture unanticipated feedback, such as, "Please provide any other feedback." You might also want to include a Likert-scale question and follow it with a free-form question, such as, "If you disagreed with the last question, tell us why."

Let Yourself Be Surprised

As you move from design to development, remember to keep an open mind. By this time, you've predicted where your organization will suffer shortfalls, documented your goals and objectives, and assembled your sponsors and stakeholders. Depending on your process and needs, you may have analyzed the data so deeply that you can see exactly where the program could go right—and where it could go wrong.

Remember, though, you are working with knowledge, a complex, dynamic, and undeniably fascinating mix of experiences, values, and insights. As carefully as you plan, your knowledge transfer program will take on a life of its own. Be prepared, but give yourself permission to be surprised.

Consider this: When Erik Johnson and his team at Sabre Holdings developed SabreTown, they started with a social network with a small amount of structure. SabreTown had a general framework, but in the interest of keeping it from becoming a top-down, hierarchical corporate communications vehicle, they kept it simple. They had a council in place that talked about the new social network in their various departments, but they weren't overbearing, Johnson said.

"We had some FAQs for people who were using SabreTown for the first time, and some methods users could follow," Johnson said. "After two, four, six months, more of the organization was using it, and soon, people were finding ways to use SabreTown that we hadn't even planned for! They were finding ways to create links and graphic files."

Surprise!

8

Rolling Out Your Knowledge Transfer Program

As you can see from the organizations we've covered, managers and leaders do not simply launch their program and then walk away. Rather, they remain engaged and interested, watching their audience in action and listening for feedback. When they receive feedback that warrants changes, they adjust the program accordingly, and then go back to observing the program in action. Such is the nature of the implementation phase, which is often punctuated by audience feedback and subsequent tweaks and changes.

We are confident that any changes you may make during the implementation stage will be manageable and doable. Why? Because throughout this book, we have followed a systems approach[1] to creating a knowledge transfer program. That means we have described processes for gathering information and data, creating a charter, and designing and developing a program with clear objectives and metrics. If you follow this approach, you will gather significant information to support your program; you'll know it inside and out. You will also have information about alternatives waiting on the back burner, just in case.

"If you pilot your solution, you will implement it on a smaller scale, so the actual implementation should be easier and more efficient," said Vic Passion, an instructional designer and project manager.

---

1 American Society for Training and Development. Basics of Instructional Systems Development. March, 1988.

On the other hand, if you don't pilot, it's as if you're the lead actor in a Broadway play on opening night, and you've never done a dress rehearsal. You'll need to build the infrastructure of a program that is completely new to your audience, and in some ways, to you and your team.

Our experience has shown us that somewhere between rollout, feedback, and some adjustments, many programs achieve momentum. It's almost as if they begin to run themselves. But don't fool yourself—programs need sponsors, advocates, and managers to keep them fresh, relevant, and effective. They also need stakeholders and users who are curious about how the program works and enthusiastic about giving it a try. To remain viable, your knowledge transfer program must meet your audiences' needs, and those needs change from time to time.

Linking the Program to Staff Goals

David Austin, president of Contextware, a knowledge management solutions company, compared the implementation process to pruning a bush. There are stages over the life of the program when someone must take ownership, make adjustments to some areas, and leave other areas alone to grow. Organizations must decide for themselves what these intervals should be, based on a host of factors, including the complexity of the program, the audience, and changing business goals and objectives. To ensure that the program gets a regular check-up and the nurturing it needs to flourish, Austin recommends linking general program upkeep and participation to staff goals and performance reviews.

Karen Dietz, owner of Polaris Associates Consulting, Inc., who works with leaders and executive teams to find and craft their most compelling stories, also said that linking organizational and program objectives to individual performance is an effective way to keep a program viable. While Dietz focuses on stories, this concept can be applied to any knowledge transfer program.

For story programs, leaders must first be clear about what the organization's goals and objectives are and then develop the stories that will become a vehicle for achieving them. These stories could answer questions such as the following:

- Who are our customers and clients? What are they like?
- What are the organization's vital processes and procedures, and how do we get work done around here?
- What is our corporate culture? What is our vision? What are we most proud of as an organization?
- Who are the organizational heroes and villains?

Once leaders know what stories they want to share, they must add structure to the program in the form of performance evaluations. This way, story-telling activities, such as collecting and crafting stories and measuring their effectiveness, become part of someone's job description.

"When you put the structure in, storytelling becomes an established system within the organization," Dietz said. "This is really what keeps the program humming along after it's off the ground."

Dietz provided an example of a hospital she discussed in *Wake Me Up When the Data Is Over*, a book she co-wrote with Lori Silverman.[2] The hospital was in the red and needed to create targets, goals, and metrics to help turn its finances around. Leaders decided one way to bring the hospital into the black was to reduce the amount of waste the hospital generated, Dietz said. They approached their cleaning staff and asked them to report to their supervisors any methods they discovered to help them meet their waste goals. Cleaning staff obliged, and began reporting the methods they discovered. Supervisors measured the results of these efforts against established metrics and picked the greatest cost-savers. Then supervisors held events and invited cleaning staff to stand up and tell the group stories about the methods discovered to reduce waste. Supervisors also captured these stories and used the hospital newsletter to spread them across the organization.

"There was so much momentum, many people across the organization began to focus on ways to cut costs, and within record time the hospital was in the black," Dietz said.

We'll talk more about how managers can use various performance measures to improve and build on their knowledge transfer program in Chapter 9, "A Long View of Evaluation." For now, let's talk about another key aspect of successful program implementation and maintenance: project management.

Keeping a Watchful Eye

A strong project manager can make the difference between a knowledge transfer program that meets organizational goals and one that veers woefully off course. Project managers serve as the go-to person for the program and are responsible for keeping the program on-budget, on-schedule, and within scope. They are in charge of communicating the status of the program to relevant parties and delegating tasks as necessary. Project management tools,

---

2 Karen Dietz discussed this example during interviews. For more information see: Silverman, Lori. *Wake Me Up When the Data Is Over*. Jossey-Bass. 2006. pp. 78-92.

such as project schedules (see Figure 8.1) and templates for catching action items (see Figure 8.2) can help project managers and their team members do their jobs more efficiently.

Depending on your program's complexity and size, project management responsibilities may be folded into other roles. But, a rose is a rose is a rose—leaders should make project management a priority whether or not an individual's title reflects this responsibility.

"You always need someone who wears the hat of the project manager even if they are wearing other hats as well," Passion said. "That means that through every phase, you have a project manager on hand."

Keep in mind, every program requires more concentrated project management at different times. For example, if you are launching a community of practice, you will probably need more project management during design, development, and piloting than you will after you launch the program and after it has hit its stride. Regardless of the method used, once the program is in maintenance mode, managers must decide how much time and expertise are necessary to keep it going. For example, will they continue to monitor it, but less frequently? Or will they turn the program over to a project coordinator or administrator who may also be working on other tasks within the organization?

Mentoring Program Pilot Kickoff
Note: In addition to below, status conference calls will be held every Wednesday at 1pm

Owner	Process	Deliverable	Timeframe	Start Date	End Date
Denise	Kickoff meeting	Revise schedule if needed Receive list of invitees from Kurt	1 day	Wednesday, 9/24	Wednesday, 9/24
Denise	Develop invitation email	Invitation email List of invitees	3 days	Thursday, 9/25	Monday, 9/29
Kurt, Marie	Review invitation email and list of invitees	Consolidated Review Feedback	3 days	Tuesday, 9/30	Thursday, 10/2
Denise	Revisions to email and list	Final invitation email and list of invitees	1 day	Friday, 10/3	Friday, 10/3
Denise	Send emails to pilot invitees	Sent email	1 day	Monday, 10/6	Monday, 10/6
Denise	Plan pilot kickoff	Agenda	1 day	Tuesday, 10/7	Tuesday, 10/7
Kurt, Marie	Review Kickoff Agenda	Consolidated Review Feedback	3 days	Wednesday, 10/8	Friday, 10/10
Denise	Orient mentors and mentees	Send pilot package to interested mentors and mentees	1 day	Thursday, 10/9	Thursday, 10/9
Denise	Kick off pilot	Kickoff meeting with interested mentors and mentees Signed agreements	1 day	Monday, 10/13	Monday, 10/13

Figure 8.1   *This project schedule was created for a sample mentoring program, but the framework can be used for any kind of knowledge transfer program.* Source: TechProse

A.I. No.	Source	Description	Action taken	Responsible	Date opened	Date due	Date completed	Status
1	E-mail							
2	E-mail							
3	V-mail							
4	J. Doe							
5								
6								
7								
8								
9								
10								
11								
12								

Figure 8.2   *This template provides a format for documenting action items.*

Vic's Tips for a Seamless Go-Live

1. *Fight the urge to agree to an unreasonable project schedule. Instead, create a schedule that allows time for resolving problems, should they come up.*

2. *Try to anticipate risks so they don't come as a surprise.*

3. *Have the right people lined up to address issues as they come up during implementation. For example, if you're launching an online community of practice, be sure you know exactly who in your IT department can lend a hand if there are any technology glitches.*

4. *Create a list of names and contact information for everyone involved in the implementation phase. This way, if something goes wrong and you need to get in touch, you won't be scrambling through phone lists and emails to figure out the best contact.*

Managing Risk

The best project managers know how to clearly describe and plan for project success. They also know how to anticipate risk and recognize warning signs. When problems arise, as they inevitably will, the best project managers know what steps to take to resolve issues that could threaten the program.

Figure 8.3 provides a list of some typical risks and warning signs.

Problem	Action
Unrealistic expectations	Don't agree to what you know your team can't do. Negotiate what is possible.
Unclear expectations	Document your understanding, and don't commit until you get written agreement.
Changes to project schedule Changes to objectives Other changes to underlying factors that affect your ability to deliver	Assuming you have done your planning beforehand, you can demonstrate the effect of these changes on your schedule, deliverables, resources, and budget. Summarize the impact in a project change memorandum (or other formal project document) and get signoff from key sponsors.
Personnel changes	Have a checklist and supervise detailed project turnover, inform stakeholders, and adjust schedule if necessary.
Lack of executive support	This is a serious problem that you must escalate to the highest level to which you have access. Build strong cross-functional relationships, and cite research on failed projects and do your best to identify the highest level executive sponsor you can enlist. Develop an ongoing communication plan with relevant updates to keep the project at "top of mind" for the enterprise.
Lack of IT support	IT requirements should be addressed in your initial plan and agreements. If problem persists, meet with key stakeholders and negotiate agreements with least impact on IT and greatest benefit to your team. Lack of adequate support affects project schedule, deliverables, resources, and budget. Summarize the impact in a project change memorandum (or other formal project document) and get signoff from key sponsors.
Absence of standards & metrics	Starting with defined criteria for success is essential to a well-managed project. Meet with key stakeholders, show samples, recommend standards, and agree on metrics for success.

Poor communication
  • No review comments or signoffs on deliverables
  • Key people missing meetings
  • Not being included in communication loop
  • Hearing information from second-hand sources (rumor mill)
  • Conflicting directives (lack of focus)
	Provide written, weekly status of potential and existing problems and suggested actions. Don't let unresolved action items or areas of concern persist week after week. Meet with the stakeholders responsible for these areas. If you are in the same geographic location, arrange a lunch meeting, bring donuts, or use other incentives to get stakeholders to meet and discuss issues. If necessary, meet one-on-one with stakeholders to determine reasons behind lack of communication. Address the root cause.

Inability to adhere to review cycles	Potential for this should be addressed in your initial agreements, if problem persists, meet with key stakeholders and explain impact on project. Come to agreement on how to manage this.
Conflicting demands of multiple projects	Map demands, determine what you can delegate, and inform stakeholders when conflicts have direct impact on delivery.

Unanticipated demands on time	In your initial planning, anticipate at least one-day per week for unanticipated demands on your time and team-members' time. Schedule your deliverables to allow for this. Should demands exceed this estimate, document and submit impact to stakeholders.

Figure 8.3   *When in doubt, look to this table for ideas on how to address risks and problems.*   Source: Meryl Natchez

You are also likely to uncover program-specific risks. Consider documenting these items and creating a "Problem/Action" checklist like the one in Figure 8.3. The list and remedies may come in handy if you need to hand off the program to a coordinator or another team member.

Managing Momentum

For many managers, the fun part of launching a program is seeing it thrive and, of course, benefit the organization.

Motorola's knowledge communities provide a good example of a sustainable method that has demonstrated substantial benefits to the business. The company's knowledge community method has done more than hit its stride—it has evolved beyond what leaders and organizers originally envisioned. Here are two examples.

Motorola used a knowledge community to deploy a new set of practices for Agile software development. Engineering leaders had made previous attempts to implement the new processes, but conventional methods, such as conference calls and email attachments, simply did not engage practitioners. A community was proposed as an alternative. A few months after practitioners regrouped in the new community and abandoned conventional methods of communicating, the new Agile software methods were implemented throughout Motorola, worldwide.

So why did the energized knowledge community work when conventional methods had not? First, community leaders said it offered asynchronous[3] access and collaboration.

Second, practitioners found support in the community that they hadn't experienced when communicating via email and conference calls. Basically, everything practitioners needed to learn the new software development process

---

3 This means "not at the same time." Asynchronous participation could include the use of discussion boards or wikis, which enable interaction even if participants are not online at the same time.

was on the home page of the community. It was a one-stop resource. The community used a blog (also accessible from the home page) that described implementation stories and tips. Practitioners resolved many of their process problems by reading the blog. If the blog didn't have the answer, it redirected users to training and support links. Other features, such as forums and personal invitations to contribute drove rapid adoption and participation, reducing learning time and increasing productivity. Today, Motorola attributes an 8x productivity improvement to the use of a knowledge community supporting Agile software methods deployment (see Figure 8.4).

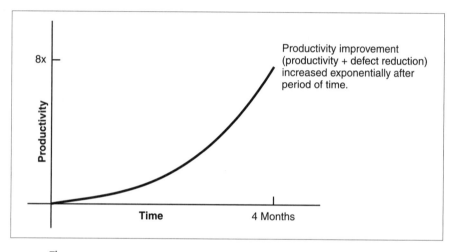

Figure 8.4   *This chart illustrates the jump in productivity that Motorola realized after the launch of its Agile software community.*

Motorola also uses its communities to host the company's annual global engineering symposium, a 30-year tradition that brings hundreds of people together to exchange the latest techniques, methods, and tools around a theme. Traditionally a face-to-face event held in hotels and other meeting places, in 2009 Motorola cancelled the event during the economic downturn. In response, Motorola's Knowledge Community Resource Officer proposed to continue the symposium using communities as the meeting place instead of hotel rooms. Hosting the event in this way would allow speakers to create their presentations in their respective countries using a standard webinar tool and record them for later playback. Leaders accepted the proposal, and the planning team got to work setting up 224 presentations, from nine global locations in twelve communities, one for each topic area.

Motorola had never held a symposium in its communities before—for 30 years prior to that, the event had been held in hotels. They performed three dry runs with session hosts globally, and in September 2009 kicked off the first virtual symposium. The theme was engineering productivity.

Motorola recorded each presentation with audio, and copied them into the community that supported that session or topic—an ideal arrangement for participants in other time zones. When people had time, they visited the community to view presentations, slides, and questions and answers.

Response to the community-hosted symposium was overwhelming, Art Paton, senior learning consultant at Motorola said. According to Motorola, the symposium set new records for global presenters and attendance. Even more surprising was the number of people who went back to the communities for each topic in the months following the symposium. In the 120 days following the symposium, more people visited the communities to check out symposium topics than ever attended the live presentations. The communities continue to draw attention and enable ongoing collaboration on engineering topics, which is quite a change from the symposium binder that sits on the bookcase collecting dust, Paton said.

Next Steps for Knowledge Transfer

Motorola didn't implement its knowledge communities and ensuing activities specifically to prepare for Boomers stepping away. Still, organizations facing changing workforce demographics can learn a lot from the way the company has prepared itself for the future.

First, these tools take a very long step toward leveling the playing field in regards to age, gender, and skill level, according to Paton. For example, it's a lot easier to post a question in a blog than it is to walk up to the vice president and ask a question, especially if you are 20 years old.

Additionally, communities serve as repositories, because what you put in, stays in. That means if a senior person or subject matter expert contributes his or her knowledge to the community, it remains there for others to explore and use. However, for the knowledge to have value, the community must capture it in the form of stories that give context and illustrate how the knowledge was applied, Paton said.

In addition, many of the tools that make internal communities a reality also allow organizations to invite others outside the company to join the community. These extranets can have many different uses. One function could be to connect retired staff, often called "alumni," to the organization and invite them to continue to share their knowledge after they leave. Organizations could work out the details, which could include consulting contracts for alumni.

Cerner, a health care IT company, is another example of an organization that has continued to add functions to uCern, its enterprise social media system post-implementation. After the eight-week pilot, the organization continued to tweak the system to make it even more usable. For example, Cerner was very aware that individuals had preferences about the way they managed their social networks. Some preferred to receive notifications about posts and messages via RSS feeds; others wanted to manage all their groups and contacts through their company email inbox. Cerner obliged, and added functions to allow users to manage their uCern posts and activities in a variety of ways.

"The biggest lesson for us was that the system has to be extremely usable and easy," said Robert Campbell, Chief Learning Officer. "To make it sustainable, and get beyond the initial surge, you have to get it embedded into the way people work. It has to add value."

Asking Your Audience What They Need

Programs evolve over time. This is especially true when a dedicated project manager keeps a finger on the pulse of the organization *and* the program's audience. Often, these managers request feedback on a regular basis, and when they notice the audience needs are changing, they step in and adapt the program.

Dr. Rachel Permuth-Levine, the wellness director for the National Heart, Lung and Blood Institute (NHLBI) is a good example. In her role as wellness director, and as director of the mentoring program, Dr. Permuth-Levine often heard that institute staff members were hungering for more networking opportunities. Often, mentees used the mentoring program as a way to land new positions, she discovered. Dr. Permuth-Levine, who describes herself as someone who doesn't believe in career limitations, obliged, and she tweaked the program to include meetings where people could network and learn more about each other.

In the second year of the program, Dr. Permuth-Levine began to allow mentees to have more than one mentor. She also began to promote the opportunity for mentees to seek mentors who worked for the National Institutes of Health, the federal agency that houses the NHLBI. These changes to the program gave mentees additional options and were the result of Dr. Permuth-Levine being sensitive to her audience's needs.

Listening to your audience after implementation is crucial, especially when working with Gen Y, a group that is generally known for its outspoken views of the world and work. Intuit, a Mountain View, California-based software company, learned this immediately after launching its Rotational Development Program (RDP) in 2004.

Developed by the Small Business Group to help ensure a growing talent pool in product management, Intuit's two-year program recruited undergraduates who excelled in school, exuded leadership qualities, and were involved in internships and business societies in their free time. "RDPers," as they were called, were guided through four six-month rotations that gave them broad exposure to the business, as well as exposure to varying levels of leaders and managers. RDPers were also encouraged to network with Intuit's leaders, who often imparted soft skills and other business expertise learned over their careers. Nancy Smithline, program leader, one of the program's developers, said that a lot of thought went into which leaders would guide RDPers on their journey through Intuit. The team had also carefully designed the curriculum so that participants gained a deep understanding of Intuit's products and customers.

Initially, Intuit sent its RDPers to Tucson, Arizona, for several weeks where they could sit in on phone calls at the company's call center to learn more about the diverse customer base. The group also spent some time in classroom-style lectures. It wasn't long before participants were making suggestions on how Intuit could customize these aspects of the program to their own specific learning style.

"We heard from them that this was not how they learned," Smithline recalled. "They told us they wanted to be able to read some of the content from the lectures on their own time, and that they wanted a more hands-on approach. This generation is very social, and they learn through interaction and collaboration. They felt that part of the program was too passive, and they didn't feel they were making a difference."

Smithline and her team listened to the feedback, which included requests to work directly with customers in the San Francisco Bay Area, rather than sitting in on phone calls others were making in Tucson. Eventually, the RDP development team tweaked the curriculum a bit, using the ideas that previous groups had provided.

John Mastrorilli, a program leader who oversees Intuit's Financial Rotational Development Program, said that he and Smithline welcomed the feedback they received about their respective programs. After all, Intuit created these programs as a first step toward grooming future leaders of the organization. Participants with innovative ideas and a desire to make a difference were exactly what the organization had in mind.

Gen Y participants were not shy about telling program leaders what they wanted, Mastrorilli said. And they were very encouraged by the fact that they had the ability to influence the direction and shape of the program.

Communications and Implementation

While it may be tempting, perhaps even typical, to create a communications plan that takes you through implementation and beyond, stop and think about Tammy Erickson's comments in Chapter 1, "When Boomer Brains Walk."

"I generally think the model that says Boomers are going to package their wisdom and bestow it on younger generations is doomed out of the gate," she said. "On the other hand, I've done some research that shows Gen Ys, in particular, are thrilled if they can tap Boomer expertise around problems that are important to them. So, it's not a situation where the Boomer lays down the law and says, 'here's how a job needs to be done.' Instead, younger workers can go to Boomers if they run into problems and need help."

The essence of this advice is to approach knowledge transfer in a way that creates a two-way street among Boomers and the next generation of workers and leaders. Keeping this in mind, you should develop a message that carries with it the spirit of openness and knowledge sharing, rather than an image of Boomers standing on a mountaintop handing down tablets of knowledge.

When creating your communications plan, consider building in an element of fluidity, suggested Carolyn Murphy, a communications consultant and writer. And don't assume it's going to be fully baked, or that the plan you set in motion in January is going to look the same at the end of the year.

Murphy suggested using media that appealed to Gen X and Y, such as blogs, wikis, or tweets, and simple videos rather than scripted, highly produced ones. Keeping communications media flexible also allows managers to make quick changes as needed.

"Anything that looks like it's old school isn't going to appeal to the new school," said Murphy. However, Murphy is quick to say that managers must choose communication vehicles based on their assessment *and* their audiences, which could include Boomers, Gen X, and Gen Y. Look to your assessment first and then decide what technology you'll use and how you'll communicate with each group.

Other examples of keeping your plan fluid could include inviting your audience to co-develop some communication deliverables, Murphy suggested. Also, consider setting up opportunities for Gen X and Y workers to talk about what they want from an ongoing program, which will help increase their interest in the program. Murphy also suggested that leaders give Gen X and Y workers plenty of opportunities to provide feedback as the program progressed. By keeping this group engaged, leaders will avoid making them feel as if they are merely passive recipients of someone else's knowledge. And they are more likely to contribute their own valuable knowledge to the organization.

Whatever you do, don't stop communicating once the program is successful, said Meryl Natchez, a longtime technical communicator and project manager.

"You need to keep people informed," Natchez said. "Whether it's via a Web site or a wiki or a note on the bulletin board in the break room, if people don't know what's happening they think nothing is happening. If you stop communicating at least once a month, you've lost your program."

Some managers make reminders and check-ins part of their larger program and communication plans.

"Once I book all the rooms, confirm the speakers, and the meetings are on people's calendars, the program runs itself," Dr. Permuth-Levine said. "But you really have to remind people about what's coming up; you can't just let it go because that's how programs die. I also check in with everyone mid-course just to see how everyone is doing."

Managers must also keep sponsors engaged, and one way to do that is through praise. Take time to recognize people who are supporting the program, doing the work, and participating. Send this praise up and down the chain of command. Be sincere, open, and honest about how the program is progressing, in order to build credibility and trust. And don't forget to have the occasional party or cake and coffee to celebrate success.

What's the Goal of Your Communications?

Consider these questions when you're creating communications for your knowledge transfer program:

1. *Who is your audience? Boomers? Gen X and Y?*

2. *What have they told you they want to learn from your communications? What do you want them to learn from your communications?*

3. *What do you want them to do with the information?*

After you answer these questions, you'll have a better idea of what the best communication method might be and how frequently you need to communicate with your audience.

Most importantly, if you hit a snag after implementation, let people know. For example, if a key subject matter expert on the program team leaves abruptly, don't attempt to tell the group that everything is on track. Corporate lies are immediately detectable, and if your audience perceives you are being anything less than honest, your program loses credibility. Instead, tell the group you've experienced a setback and invite them to make suggestions on how to re-create the curriculum.

Create a Transition Plan

It's a good idea to create a transition plan as you move from one phase of your program to the next. To do this, document changes in key players and the different skill sets that are required at each stage. While we recommend creating a transition plan at the beginning of the program, the need for this kind of documentation is more critical at the end of the implementation phase. With a transition plan in place, your staff can pick up and carry on if you need to turn your attention elsewhere after the program is off the ground.

Overcoming Challenges

Talking about successful programs is very satisfying, but we all know that success is just one part of any story. Every manager must overcome challenges—whether it's gaining buy-in, reaching stakeholders, making time… the list goes on. The good news is, there are many ways to stare down a challenge. One place to start is in someone else's shoes. Here are some common challenges to implementing a knowledge transfer program, and the solutions that managers found to overcome them:

Challenge: Gaining sponsor and stakeholder buy-in.
Gaining sponsor and stakeholder buy-in can be tough. Many managers can tell stories about launching programs only to have people drag their feet about jumping on board.

Solution: Share success stories and praise early adopters.
Sharing success stories and praising outstanding individual effort is a great way to draw attention and interest to any program. This works with sponsors and stakeholders.

Using Webinars to Energize Your Program

It's no secret that every program loses steam after a while. When this happens, consider using a webinar to give your program a shot in the arm and rally the group.

Webinars are a great way to promote informal learning,[4] collaboration, and knowledge transfer, said Pierre Khawand, a training expert who hosts regular, noontime events, or "lunch-and-learns" through his company, People-onthego.com. And there is no end to the topics you can cover in a webinar format. For example, you could hold a webinar that celebrates the first 100 mentor-mentee relationships in the organization and provides information on how others could get involved. Or you could use it to share social network success stories and demonstrate for lurkers how the network could help them connect to others in the organization when they have questions.

Of course, a webinar is only as good as its content—and its presenter. Here are a few simple steps[5] to follow when planning a webinar:

- Determine the topic, target audience, and presenter, and a date that works for the presenter and your audience.

- Schedule time with your IT department to determine the best process for presenting the webinar and any technical challenges.

- Send out an invitation to the webinar a few weeks before the event.

- Schedule a trial run and invite a few attendees who can provide meaningful feedback. Conduct the trial run and gather feedback on content and for the presenter. How can you make the webinar better?

- Revise the presentation and coach the presenter as needed.

- Conduct the webinar on designated date.

- If appropriate, send out a questionnaire following the webinar that provides attendees with additional information or feedback forms.

---

4 In an August, 2009 story in ASTD's magazine, *Training & Development*, Tony Bingham reported that "rough estimates indicate 80 percent of learning is informal and 20 percent is formal."

5 Based on TechProse's Webinar Planning Checklist. September 3, 2009.

Sometimes, managers have trouble getting buy-in from sponsors, which can impact funding and support for the program. One way to get around this is by starting small with a pilot that shows sponsors what success looks like.

Challenge: Participants don't have the time.

Often, business and personal priorities overshadow programs intended to spark knowledge transfer and professional development. Regardless of the type of program, there are always participants who find it difficult to make time for activities, events, meetings, and follow-up.

Solution: Don't ask for more than is possible.

For mentoring programs, consider the amount of time that participants need to get the most out of the program; then plan their normal duties accordingly. This approach can be applied to other knowledge transfer programs as well.

If their normal duties prevent them from participating in the program, consider pushing other, more flexible deadlines to accommodate scheduled mentor-mentee meetings. If necessary, scale back the program, especially if participants consistently complain about not having the time.

Sometimes, you may just need to let participants out of the program, according to Dr. Permuth-Levine.

"We track attendance at the seminars, and if we see people aren't going, we send them a really nice message that gives them an easy way to opt out," she said. "We don't want to spend the money and time on people who aren't going to be able to complete the program. And some people may have simply determined that the program isn't what they expected or work-related duties prevent their continuation in the program."

Challenge: Program manager becomes overwhelmed.

Most of us wear many hats. In fact, few of us have the luxury of giving one project all our attention. Managers who oversee knowledge transfer programs can become overwhelmed, and when this happens, they neglect elements of the program.

Solution: Delegate some tasks.

Chances are you will spend less time on the program once it is up and running than you did during other phases. If you're feeling anxious once it's off the ground, consider handing over tasks to other members on the team.

You may want to do this even if you aren't feeling overwhelmed, simply to give more junior staff members or others on your team experience with managing a program.

If you go this route, select someone whom people trust and enjoy working with, someone who can continue to secure buy-in for the program, Natchez said. It's also important to remind the person who's coordinating the program to ask for help if they also become overwhelmed.

Managers may also consider making tasks they delegate a part of the coordinator's performance objectives. This will increase the likelihood that they view the new tasks as part of their job and career development.

Spread the Work and Opportunities Around

As your knowledge transfer program progresses and evolves, remember that others in the organization may want to join you in your work. Don't ignore these requests to help; rather, welcome them as a way to improve and expand your program's reach.

Angela Mark, who works as co-lead in administrating Dr. Permuth-Levine's NHLBI mentoring program, is a good example of how a co-lead can help a program flourish. Mark helps Dr. Permuth-Levine with some of the planning details, but she also helps mentors and mentees with logistics and questions. In the end, Mark also benefits greatly from the experience and gains visibility in the Institute.

"I learn so much that I otherwise would not have had the opportunity to learn," Mark said. "There is also a great deal of gratification with helping individuals find their match, especially when knowledge is transferred, and you see that person move up the ranks in the institution. Then we know we have done our job well."

9

A Long View of Evaluation

When you evaluate a knowledge transfer program, you step back and look at it from all sides, during every phase over the life of the program. Because evaluation is an iterative process, you will take a slightly different approach each time you evaluate a program. For example, during the analysis phase, you developed a baseline and metrics. You also looked for workforce data and other information about your audience. You analyzed the type of workforce you would need in the future, looked at data on existing staff, and then compared your findings to reveal the gaps. You may have also supplemented your data with surveys and other audience reports.

During the design phase, but mostly during development and piloting, you asked your audience for feedback on the Web site, community functionality, mentor-mentee evaluation forms, and other program deliverables.

Now that you've launched your program, you need data that will help you go beyond what people say and think about the program. You need to go deeper and look at the program as a whole. We call this *program performance evaluation*, and while many managers dread this deep dive into a program, the data they find can be the ticket to additional funding and executive buy-in down the road.

"Program evaluation can take a long time," said Dr. Rachel Permuth-Levine, who designed, piloted, and launched a mentoring program at the National Heart, Lung and Blood Institute (NHLBI) in 2007. "If people like the program, it's easy to say, 'okay, people are happy with it, so why do I have to evaluate it?' But if the program costs money, and if you want the program to continue, you're going to need to do that evaluation."

Reasons Why Organizations Don't Evaluate

There are a few trends that experts see with evaluation. First, many organizations don't perform a thorough analysis during the planning stage or document their baseline. Without a baseline, they have nothing to reflect on after implementation, and measuring the program's progress and value is all guesswork. In other words, they don't see the before and after—they only see the after. On the other hand, managers who arm themselves with a baseline and performance-based objectives before designing the program can evaluate their programs more easily after launch and present metrics that demonstrate value.

Then there are organizations that avoid performing a thorough analysis during the planning stage and a program performance evaluation after the program is launched. Abandoning these tasks leaves gaping holes in a program. Managers that take this route risk spending a great deal of time on design, development, and implementation, only to have their programs cut because they can't prove their value to the organization.

It's easy to understand why organizations skip the evaluation step. After all, evaluation takes time, and organizations don't always have time to spare. Additionally, organizations often make a big push to design a program, pilot it, and launch it, said Vic Passion, an instructional designer and project manager. If they performed an analysis at the beginning, they might forgo evaluating whether their program lined up with the metrics, goals, and objectives they set in the early stages.

"Once organizations get through the implementation phase, the excitement around the program dies off a bit, and leaders stop tracking it as closely," Passion said. "Everyone swivels their focus to other tasks or projects, or they work really hard to get the program into maintenance mode so they can move on to other things."

Dr. Permuth-Levine has another theory for why evaluation gets left behind.

"It's not fun," she said. "And depending on the program, you may need someone who is dedicated to evaluating the program. This is really hard to do when you're short-staffed."

Making Program Performance Evaluation Fun!

If you're working with Gen X, and especially Gen Y, you know how important *fun* is to the workday. Here are some ideas for how to make program performance evaluations more pleasant for individuals and teams.

First, if you are linking individual performance to the execution of the program evaluation, consider downplaying this for now. Establish high standards, yes, but remember that holding individual performance metrics over someone's head can throw a wet blanket on the whole concept of having fun to get through an arduous task. Then do the unexpected—let the team set the rules, suggested Angela Palmier of Resource ETC, LLC, a Chicago, Illinois-based consulting firm.

"When you have hired people for their expertise and then you hand them a bunch of constraints, it doesn't work, and they aren't engaged," Palmier said. "You have to get out of the way."

Palmier suggested that managers get the team together and give them a short amount of time, say three hours, to brainstorm and come up with a plan. Gen Xers will love this, she said, as this group tends to want to mobilize and get the job done. Tell the group that at the end of the three-hour period, you want their top three solutions for getting through the program performance evaluation. Provide some guidelines, if necessary, and then get out of the way.

Dr. Barbara Moquin, senior public health advisor at NHLBI also has some tips for how to make program evaluations fun. A longtime public health and employee wellness leader with a background in nursing, psychiatry, and mental health, Dr. Moquin takes a comprehensive approach to motivating groups. That means encouraging interaction among team members, managers, and facilitators and finding ways to make the work intellectually stimulating and meaningful. Or, as Dr. Moquin said, "Making the ordinary extraordinary."

So how do you make the ordinary extraordinary for a group that has just made a big push to implement a program and now wants to move on to something new? Dr. Moquin suggests that the group pause to reflect on their efforts and focus more on the journey than the destination.

Reflecting on the effort in this way sets the scene for a fun and productive process to evaluate the program. Throughout the effort, Dr. Moquin also gives teams opportunities to stretch, exercise, meditate, and laugh.

Laughing your way through an evaluation may seem odd to some, but Dr. Moquin cites strong research that has found humor therapy could be an effective technique to use in groups. She has been known to start meetings and presentations by asking everyone in the group to stretch their facial muscles, bob up and down, and laugh. While this technique certainly breaks the ice at meetings, Dr. Moquin said you can use it in many different group settings.

"It's an immediate release," Dr. Moquin said. "I've used this exercise with all kinds of audiences for years. I've used it with White House staff, with admirals and generals, and everyone just loves it. Everyone forgets themselves for just a few minutes and acts really relaxed."

Dr. Moquin also suggests that managers use techniques that involve the senses. For example, Dr. Moquin plays music that is lively and energizing, preferring tunes that are scientifically developed to alter brain waves and relax listeners. She also uses peppermint oil, known for its invigorating properties, to scent the environment where teams are working. And, instead of serving cookies and sugary drinks during breaks, she suggests offering water, fruit, and raw vegetables to help keep everyone's energy up.

Incentives May Be the Ticket to Getting the Job Done

Sometimes, a little incentive can go a long way. If you think you're going to need more than just a fun environment to motivate your team, consider these incentive ideas by Dr. Moquin.

- *Most people will jump at the chance to save time and money. Raffle some prime staff parking spots, housecleaning services, grocery shopping delivery, or babysitting services.*

- *Offer a one-time monetary incentive for completing the program evaluation, or let the team go home a half-hour early when all the work is done.*

- *Offer coupons for free coffee, movies, or gym visits.*

Make Metrics a Priority

So now that you know how to make a program evaluation a fun endeavor, let's roll up our sleeves and get to work. We will try not to harp on this too much, but it's critical that organizations invest the time and resources at the beginning of the program to analyze their organization, establish a baseline, and create some detailed metrics. (Also see Chapter 5, "Boarding the Knowledge Train," for more information.) Managers who have these elements in place before they design and pilot their program will have the first half of the tools they need to thoroughly evaluate their program after launch. It's that simple.

The best program performance evaluations use detailed metrics, as well as subjective observations from participants and others in the organization. Many organizations depend solely on subjective participant evaluations of the program. Also known as "smile sheets," these evaluations provide valuable information, but they don't show to what extent the program has helped people perform their jobs better.

Depending on your organization, data exists in a variety of places. Sometimes, it's difficult to get to, but ideally, that's not the case. Generally speaking, here are some sources of data in an organization:

- Supervisors
- Human resources
- Finance department
- Support logs
- Customer service department

Passion suggested that managers give themselves time to get to the bottom of what can become a data scavenger hunt.

"In some cases, it will not be an easy thing to do," Passion said about accessing relevant data. "You have to ask yourself what data you really need and who is going to give it to you. In some cases, the data you need doesn't even exist. In those cases, it's easier to connect with someone who is measuring something similar to what you need to measure."

In large organizations, it can be helpful to appeal to the IT department. Business intelligence resources might be accountable for creating reports that have just the data you need, or they might be able to refer you to the right person or department who does.

Dr. Permuth-Levine also suggested using individual employees as a source of data. For example, when she evaluated her institute's program, she contacted individuals and asked them if they had been promoted or if they had changed jobs as a result of her mentoring program. She also asked if they had been given additional responsibilities.

"We have already seen as a result of our programs that people move to other areas in the organization, which is great," Dr. Permuth-Levine said. "This way, the knowledge is retained in the institute, but people are happier because they are in a content area that they enjoy."

Look at Your Program from Many Directions

To perform an effective evaluation, it's critical that organizations gather as much data as possible on numerous aspects of the program. For example, gather qualitative and quantitative data; look at data related to staff, supervisors, managers, and executives; look at data related to customer satisfaction, support, and health and safety; and look for internal indicators of the performance of your program, as well as external indicators (such as media reports). This will give managers a broad view of what's working, what isn't, and what's changing in the organization as a result of the program. Even though you won't be able to attribute every change to your program, a broader evaluation will help you, and your sponsor, see all the possible ways that your program has made a difference.

Use Data to Evaluate Success

There are many types of data that will help you perform a more in-depth program evaluation. Some of this data are quantitative; others are qualitative. Again, managers benefit tremendously if they gather this data before they begin designing their program.

Here are some examples of qualitative data:

- **Knowledge transfer:** In Chapter 5, we covered the steps Meryl Natchez took to create metrics for knowledge transfer. Each metric built on the next and followed an employee's progress from basic to more advanced tasks. Now that you have launched your knowledge transfer program, it's time to reflect on the knowledge transfer metrics you collected during analysis and look at the progress employees have made. Can you pinpoint the areas where knowledge transfer has occurred?

■ **Customer comments:** We all know that customers are much more likely to let you know when something goes wrong than when it goes right. If you use customer comments to evaluate your program, you are going to need to know it all—good and bad. Your customers are a valuable source of data and can provide insight that will help you evaluate your program accurately. You can find customer data in suggestion boxes, questionnaires, and even online. You can also get good qualitative data by picking up the phone and talking to your most valued customers and asking them if they've noticed any changes in the services or products they receive.

Here are some examples of quantitative data:

■ **Attrition data:** This data shows numbers of people leaving, and depending on the organization, why people are leaving. One way to use this data during program performance evaluation is to look at your audiences' attrition rates before and after the program was launched. For example, what were the attrition rates for Gen X and Y employees before you launched your knowledge transfer program? What were the rates after you launched the program? Why were members of these groups leaving? What are their reasons for staying? Cross your fingers that the data is comprehensive because this data can help prove that your program is valuable enough to keep your audience from moving on to other opportunities.

■ **Employee performance data:** Organizations collect this kind of data in many different ways. It can be qualitative, describing an employee's work style and methods, or quantitative, with hard numbers showing how much the individual produces. Some organizations collect both qualitative and quantitative measures. This is ideal, as it will provide managers with even more information about how an employee performed before program launch and after. Subjective data, gathered during an informal chat with an employee's supervisor, can also build a case for how much an employee has progressed over time.

■ **Accident, error, and defect data:** Like attrition data, accident, error, and defect reports can help you paint a compelling picture of your knowledge transfer program. Managers can use this data in many ways. First, they can analyze before-and-after data to understand how the program has changed or improved the way employees do their jobs. Managers can also create charts that illustrate the data and compare participants' safety and error records for individuals who are not participating in the program.

Managers who crunch these numbers may want to make these reports available to others in the organization who may be considering similar programs for their groups. Program evaluations that report a reduction in accidents, errors, and defects can be effective tools for gaining executive buy-in and expanding a program's reach.

- **Attendance rates**: Since 1999, Pratt & Whitney Rocketdyne has used attendance rates to measure its success of knowledge transfer events, such as its Knowledge Management Share Fair. In 1999, 200 employees attended the Share Fair; by 2008, attendance had doubled to 400 employees.

  "If people find the events are valuable, they will come back," said Chief Knowledge Officer Kiho Sohn. "Each year, attendance has grown—and not by a small amount."

- **Adoption measures:** These are among the metrics Cerner, a health care IT company, uses to evaluate its enterprise social media system, uCern. Several of the adoption measures include the total number of groups and members, percentage of groups and members that are active, and frequency and quality of contribution.

Looking Outside Your Organization for Evaluation Help

Dr. Rachel Permuth-Levine suggested that organizations look outside for help with program evaluations if no one on-staff can dedicate some time to this task. There are plenty of places to look, she said. Start with your local college or university department of statistics or survey research. Faculty or graduate students may be also looking for projects and may complete an evaluation at low or no cost.

Dr. Permuth-Levine also suggested bringing on a qualified intern to help with this work. The key word here is "qualified." An intern must have a high level of knowledge in statistics and survey research to effectively evaluate a large-scale program.

If You Skip a Step…

Earlier in this chapter, we talked about a common evaluation trend, which is the tendency of many organizations to forgo performing an analysis before the design phase. Organizations so frequently forge ahead without a baseline or metrics that we thought we should spend some time on the reality of the situation. While we believe documenting a baseline and creating metrics at the beginning is prudent, all is not lost when organizations skip this step.

Designing a Customer Questionnaire

Questionnaires are a great way to measure if your organization and customers are benefitting from your knowledge transfer efforts. However, a questionnaire is only as good as the questions it presents. For this purpose, you will ask questions that address customers' satisfaction with products or services. You will also attempt to learn if customers have noticed a difference in the level of knowledge among staff members.

Consider starting your survey with a brief introduction that shares the reason you are reaching out. In a few sentences, tell your customers you have implemented a knowledge transfer program in an effort to improve your products or services, and that you would appreciate their feedback as you evaluate the effectiveness of the program. You may even want to describe the program briefly. For example, you could share that your mentoring program has paired more experienced workers with new hires, or that your community of practice brings people across the organization together to learn and collaborate. Keep your introduction brief, but do provide your customers some context for why you are asking them to take time and complete the survey.

When drafting your survey, vary the kinds of questions you ask. For example, write some questions in a multiple choice style, others that use a Likert scale (1 to 5), and a few that allow customers to describe their experience.

Here are some questions to get you started:

- How would you rate the service you generally receive?

- On a scale of 1 to 5, how knowledgeable do you find our staff to be when you call with questions?

- Are staff members generally able to directly answer your questions? Or do they often need to get back in touch with you after consulting another staff member?

- What kind of information would you like our staff to be more prepared to assist you with?

Remember, keep your survey short; customers should be able to complete it in five to ten minutes.

"You can definitely get by without a baseline and metrics," Passion said. "You'll only be able to share the data you collect after program launch, but some of this data can be very compelling. For example, you can use qualitative data from evaluation forms or gather anecdotal data from participants. You may even be able to share participants' stories and hear how much the program has helped them."

It's Never Too Late to Evaluate

If you didn't gather metrics at the beginning, start now and create an evaluation schedule that will give you what you need in the future. You may want to check in on the program at 30, 60, and 90 days, or at three months, six months, and one year. Do what makes sense, but keep in mind that trends can be difficult to see when you only look at two data points.

And, if there is time, consider using face-to-face interviews to gather data, Passion said.

"It's very helpful to have an evaluation that is not just data-driven," Passion said. "Try to hold interviews with a cross-section of participants if you can. Also talk to hiring managers, the ones who have worked with newly hired staff who are participating in the program. Ask them how much impact the program has had on these new hires. Has it improved the organization's ability to up-skill new hires?"

Managers may also ask participants to self-assess and describe how they have grown in their careers or improved their practice since the launch of the program. Managers who take this approach should make these questions as quantitative as possible by linking them to a scale, Passion said. By doing this, managers can tie their efforts to business results and crunch the numbers that executive leaders need to see to continue their support of the program.

Specific Evaluation Methods

Now let's look at some specific methods that organizations and experts have used to evaluate their knowledge transfer programs. Let's start with Dr. Permuth-Levine, who provided a real-world example of a project manager who must evaluate her program to ensure that it stays relevant and funded. While Dr. Permuth-Levine did not collect a baseline before she designed, piloted, and launched the NHLBI's mentoring program, she developed quantitative and qualitative measures to help her evaluate her program as it progressed. Although Dr. Permuth-Levine's evaluation form was designed specifically for her mentoring program, her approach could be applied to other methods as well.

Dr. Permuth-Levine's program is one-year long, so she checks in with mentors and mentees mid-course and again at the end of the course. During these evaluations, Dr. Permuth-Levine focuses on individual measures. She asks the same set of questions mid-course and at the end of the year, but adds a few questions to the end-of-the-year evaluation that provide her with data on program performance. These questions are the following:

■ Would you return to the program next year?

■ Would you recommend the program to another employee?

Dr. Permuth-Levine gathers quantitative data by asking mentors to answer some questions using a scale from 1 (strongly disagree) to 3 (neutral) to 5 (strongly agree). She maps the questions to the program's objectives, which include creating more networking opportunities and promoting knowledge transfer.

Dr. Permuth-Levine also asks mentors and mentees to answer a series of qualitative questions. The questions are similar for both audiences. Here are a few sample questions from her toolkit:

■ Have your original goals as a mentor/mentee been met? Please discuss.

■ How satisfied are you with your mentor/mentee match?

■ What has been the most valuable aspect of participating in the program? The least valuable aspect?

■ Describe how useful the Web site, emails, and other communications have been.

■ How easy or difficult was it to meet the time commitment for the program?

So what would Dr. Permuth-Levine change about her evaluation method?

"I would want to do much more qualitative work," she said. "I would want to gather some really specific case studies of mentor/mentee outcomes. I've heard some really great stories, but right now, these kinds of responses don't come through with the questions we ask in the survey. To get these kinds of case studies, we would need to do more one-on-one interviews to elicit that kind of information."

The Value of Numbers, Stories, and Graphics

As you can see, organizations frequently seek quantitative *and* qualitative data when evaluating programs. In fact, when it comes to knowledge transfer, we believe this is the best way to give executives, sponsors, and others in the organization a really clear picture of the benefits of the program.

Keep Questions Parallel...or Not

There are at least two schools of thought on phrasing survey questions. Some experts suggest keeping questions parallel. That means questions are either worded in a negative way or a positive way. Here's an example of a negative statement: "My mentee doesn't arrive with an agenda." On the other hand, positive phrasing looks like this: "My mentee is always on time for our meetings."

When writers keep questions parallel, this helps ensure that skimmers won't interpret them incorrectly and make a mistake.

However, other experts, such as Dr. Permuth-Levine, say it's important to mix negative and positive questions. This helps ensure survey takers read and think about each question.

"We switch the structure throughout the survey," Dr. Permuth-Levine says. "We want to make sure people aren't answering the questions on auto pilot."

Jacob McNulty of Orbital RPM also mixes hard data with softer, more qualitative data when evaluating communities of practice and enterprise social media. He focuses on three elements:

- **Social Network Analysis:** McNulty's team performs this before he designs the community or network, and after the program is launched. The SNA he performs before the program is launched serves as a baseline.

- **Case Studies:** After the program is launched, McNulty gathers stories about how collaboration has helped community members, and he assigns values to the time saved.

- **Activity Data:** McNulty uses a collaboration platform to analyze the data from the activity occurring in the social network.

When you look at a sociogram that results from social network analysis, you're looking for the ideal amount of density, or connections, between people, McNulty said. During the initial social network analysis, McNulty often saw very low density numbers in the sociogram. When his team performed the post-implementation analysis, nine to twelve months later, they wanted to see that connections had increased, but not by a tremendous amount.

"In an organization of 20,000 people, you don't want everyone to be connected to everyone else because it would be chaos," McNulty said. "We want to see a higher density in connections, but we really try to strike a balance.

We're looking for ideal patterns of interaction that will support knowledge transfer and information flow, but minimize an over-abundance of communication ties and confusion."

Communicating Your Results

After you've completed your program evaluation, take some time to think about how you will communicate the results of your knowledge transfer program to the group. This is a crucial step that many leaders don't think about, even if they have asked the group to fill out evaluation forms or provide other feedback, said Dr. Moquin.

"The results of program evaluations rarely get mentioned," said Dr. Moquin. "I've heard people say, 'I was asked to fill out some forms, but I never heard anything.' People like to know their opinion is valued."

Sometimes, people assume program results were negative if they don't receive an update. Or, even worse, they assume that managers are hiding the results because they are negative.

With this in mind, create a plan for how you will communicate the results of the evaluation to the rest of the team. Consider discussing the data results during an all-hands meeting or other get-together, and allow team members to share their individual experiences with the program to balance out the numbers.

Angela Palmier encourages organizations to ask team members to talk about "the good, the bad, the ugly, and the beautiful lessons learned." Sharing in this way works best if the lessons learned are communicated across various departments, giving others an opportunity to hear about successes and failures. Combining the data with sharing and storytelling can be especially meaningful to Gen X and Y, Palmier said.

"It's funny because our Boomer parents who became teachers all told us to share, share, share," she said. "We grew up sharing in school, but then we get into the business world, and that all stops. Companies need to talk about what they're doing and share across departments."

Sharing can do more than just provide team members with an opportunity to educate others; it can also spark innovation and creativity and provide the team with the tools to develop future programs.

Palmier also suggested that organizations share their experiences with knowledge capture and transfer with media organizations. Get the word out and outshine your competition.

Sociograms showing the connections across a global organization before and after implementation provide a vivid backdrop for other elements of McNulty's evaluation. Activity data pulled from social business software provides additional quantitative data on who talks to whom and what actions take place within the organization.

Of course, case studies are more low-tech than sociograms and activity data analysis, but they can pack quite a punch. McNulty looks for the human element when collecting case studies, and he starts by asking the audience how the new system or community helps them do their jobs. With these questions, he's looking for an increase in collaboration and a decrease in the amount of time staff needs to complete tasks. From there, he uses staff members' hourly rates—or salaries—to calculate ROI. While McNulty and his team are very conservative with their ROI calculations, he said it's often easy to pinpoint the savings to an organization. This is especially the case when an organization captures procedures in the community or network that others can access anytime, anywhere.

McNulty uses the example of senior mechanics who may be retiring. Junior mechanics will be taking their place, and will undoubtedly run into some of the same questions the senior mechanics did during their careers. With collaboration tools, when you capture someone's fix, it's there forever, McNulty said. However, coordinators (similar to the ones we discussed in Chapter 6) need to be responsible for making information accessible to community members or the larger staff. These activities need to be part of their daily work flow and performance objectives if the organization wants to make knowledge capture and transfer a priority.

Since We're Talking ROI...

Return on investment, like program evaluation, doesn't stir a great deal of excitement in many managers' hearts. There's good reason for the lack of interest in the subject—calculating ROI is slippery and very subjective. However, executives speak and understand its language, so it behooves you to become somewhat fluent. Fundamentally, your objective with calculating return on investment is to show the benefits of the program and how it pays for itself—and more. The simple formula used in Chapter 5 is Benefit − Cost/Cost = ROI.[1] Here are some additional details.

1. **Start by looking at the metrics you are using to evaluate your program.** For example, say you are using attrition data and customer comment data as metrics. Assign a price to the cost of attrition.

1 Source: Kenneth H. Silber, PhD. Calculating Return on Investment, Version 4.0. www.silberperformance.com. April 3, 2002.

How much does it cost to lose an employee at your organization? Remember, keep your calculations simple and conservative. Then assign a price to the cost of each customer complaint. How much does it cost each time you must address customer complaints?

2. **Attach a price to each of the expenses you invest in creating and running your program.** Include the time required by staff, equipment, materials, and everything you can think of. Again, try to keep your calculation simple and conservative.

3. **Compare the cost of your program to the cost of attrition and customer complaints.** Then divide the cost by the sum of these two figures, and you have found the ROI for your program. Executives and sponsors find case studies and success stories so much more compelling when managers frame them with some strong ROI numbers.

When preparing to discuss return on investment with others, consider creating a table (see Table 9.1) to illustrate the benefit easily. Theoretically, if managers of the mentoring program for a 5,000-employee company (illustrated in Table 9.1) claimed that they lowered attrition by 1 percent, that's the equivalent of losing 50 fewer employees per year. We can assume the following conservative costs related to attrition: Costs to find 50 new employees ($50*40*100=\$20,000$) plus costs to orient new employees ($50*40*100=20,000$). Using this calculation, we realized a benefit over the development costs entered in the table.

Table 9.1   Return on Investment for Mentoring Program

Investment	Cost**	Benefit	Cost**
Time to analyze workforce	$4,000*	Decreased attrition**	$40,000
Time to design mentoring program	$6,000	Fewer customer complaints	
Time to develop and pilot mentoring program	$10,000		
Time to implement (through end of first year)	$8,000		
Software costs to support program	$1,000		

*This chart uses a $100 hourly rate.
**All numbers are for illustration only and do not reflect potential costs or benefits.
***This table is based on a 6 percent attrition rate.

Think About Your Audience

When it comes to planning a program evaluation effort, one size does not fit all, said Dr. Moquin. Just as you did with your business case, project charter, and other planning documents, think about who you will present your data to and plan accordingly.

"You need to know where your audience is coming from so you can give them the information they need. Ask yourself how you will deliver your message so it is relevant to them." she said.

Keep in mind, ROI has its caveats, which is why managers should err on the side of caution with their calculations and temper their excitement, Passion said. For example, say you measure the payoff of your knowledge transfer program and you notice that attrition rates have dropped since implementation. Before you attempt to take sole credit, remember that other factors beyond your control may be partly responsible for your program's success. Those factors could include changes in the economy that are keeping staff from leaving the organization for other jobs.

"There are also going to be some metrics from which you can't extract value," Passion said. "That's why it's a good idea to use more than one data point when calculating ROI."

Denise Lee finds that return on investment in the case of knowledge sharing is largely anecdotal. However, when it is based on the evaluation strategy that gives managers and leaders a way to view actions against objectives and performance against goals, these anecdotes can be used to support ROI.

Lee described a global consulting firm that had long had a knowledge sharing program that not only captured tacit knowledge of the senior partner but also transferred it to those who followed. The primary ROI determinant was how seamless the transition from senior partner to successor was in the eyes of the client. Could ROI be much better than a happy client?

Robert Campbell is among the organizational leaders who said that there are no absolutes when calculating a payoff. This is especially true when the organization has implemented a variety of programs with similar or parallel goals.

So just what is the payoff?

With uCern, a social media platform that connects associates and clients via discussion groups, blogs, and user-generated video, Campbell said the biggest payoff was the transparency between Cerner, its staff, and its clients. The system, which Cerner rolled out to clients eight weeks after its internal pilot, broke away from traditional barriers that often existed in organizations.

Campbell recalled speaking to a colleague who mentioned he had posted a highly technical question to uCern and received an answer from the president of the organization, who also provided context and background. Campbell's colleague was thrilled.

"Before uCern, he would never have thought of approaching this executive with a question," Campbell said. "Now, with uCern, he received a very complete answer and 50 or 60 other people can also benefit. And the answer is captured in the system and available to others who may need it in the future."

While Campbell's response referred to a high-tech solution, the essence of his comment could apply to any knowledge transfer program. Whether it's mentoring or storytelling, CoPs, social networks, or AARs, organizations can benefit from collaborative environments where individuals readily share what they know. And while many organizations may be interested in Boomers sharing what they know, other generations have knowledge that is also valuable. In fact, Cerner is a perfect example. The organization is fairly young, and does not feel the pinch of Boomers leaving as acutely as others, Campbell said. But, in many ways, uCern is the answer to knowledge loss issues that may still be many years away.

"We do see uCern as a part of the answer for capturing knowledge," Campbell said. "What's important is that this is not a one-time knowledge capture event. It is dynamic. Whenever new knowledge becomes available, it replaces the old, and the entire organization has access to it. The process is organic and continuous."

10

Nurturing a Knowledge Culture

With your knowledge transfer program, you have prepared your organization for the departure of some of the most valuable members of your workforce. But you've done much more—you've set the foundation for a knowledge culture, a sustainable approach that many business leaders consider a best business practice.

So, what exactly is a knowledge culture? And why is it considered a best business practice? There are many theories, but we believe that a knowledge culture is one where every member of the team freely contributes knowledge they think will benefit their colleagues and the organization as a whole. The benefit of building a knowledge culture is that you create the business processes necessary to make constant knowledge capture simply a part of doing business. If you do it right, your employees see the value and document their knowledge every day, as opposed to your launching big, fancy (and sometimes expensive) knowledge capture programs.

For some organizations, nurturing a knowledge culture will come easily, whether or not they have a knowledge transfer program in place. For others, it will be a tremendous challenge.

Larry Prusak, a knowledge expert, consultant and co-author of *Working Knowledge: How Organizations Manage What They Know*, said the organizations that will struggle the most to adopt a knowledge culture are those where leaders make all the major decisions. Organizations like these don't last, and if they do, they are very dysfunctional.

Prusak draws a parallel between decision-making and pay, and cites a statistic that some CEOs earn more than 400 times what their employees earn. Organizations that compensate individuals who make all the major decisions at a higher rate than the rest of the team will also struggle to shift to a culture where everyone's knowledge is valued, he said. Such huge disparities in compensation send a not-so-covert message to employees that what they know is worth much less than what the CEO knows, according to Prusak. It also emphasizes how little value is placed on employee knowledge.

Even organizations that aren't plagued by organizational burdens may need guidance when building a knowledge culture. Here are a few ways to instill the spirit of knowledge sharing in your organization:

- Shift from a hierarchical management style to one that is more inclusive —from command and control to collaborative.

- Cultivate a customer-centric view of knowledge. Invite your staff to consider who can use what they know.

- Consider generational learning styles and the role they play in a knowledge culture.

New Management Style Eases the Shift

More organizations are moving away from the hierarchical structure where longtime workers are perceived as having all the knowledge, said Deborah Osgood of the Knowledge Institute, a New Hampshire firm that specializes in entrepreneurial education, development, and marketing communications. There are many reasons for this shift, experts say. First, Generation X and especially Millennials tend to have little regard for hierarchies and often prefer to go straight to the source for the knowledge they seek, regardless of traditional communication channels. So what if they have to text the CEO to get what they need? And, Osgood says, these groups must be free to innovate and make constructive contributions in the workplace if a business is going to compete effectively. In response to these unstoppable workforce and generational trends, a manager must become a go-to-as-needed resource, rather than an all-knowing leader who enforces a power position across the organization. This means adopting what Osgood calls a *facilitative management* style.

For Osgood, a more conscious and in-tune management style is the key to creating a knowledge culture in an organization. Osgood has honed this management style on the job, through trial and error. A longtime business leader who ran a manufacturing business before co-founding the Knowledge Institute,

Osgood has been managing people and businesses since the mid-1980s. In manufacturing, the business model was essentially "show up, produce, get paid," she said. If a worker wasn't there, they didn't perform the task, the company couldn't ship the product, and no one got paid. This business called for a Theory X[1] management style. Here, work was highly structured and routine, and complying with production standards took precedence over creativity.

Osgood sold the business in 1996 and co-founded the Knowledge Institute, which initially created an online directory of government and non-profit small business assistance programs. Osgood went from a production-based manufacturing business to a knowledge-based service one. Employees at the Knowledge Institute needed to make self-directed decisions about where to find information, how to organize it, and what type of Web site to create that would add value to the entrepreneurial development process.

Osgood immediately knew that managing employees at this new venture required a completely different management style than the one she had used in her previous business.

"I sincerely welcomed it," she said. "Theory X can be a real downer for both manager and employee."

Osgood shifted to a Theory Y management style, opting for a more inclusive and democratic approach to managing her staff. The shift was not without challenges. Older employees were accustomed to being told what to do and reacted with suspicion when asked to contribute their ideas, Osgood said. On the other hand, younger employees were much more comfortable presenting their ideas and saw the invitation as an opportunity.

In an effort to get everyone on board and comfortable with her new management style, Osgood began to model the knowledge behavior she wanted to see in the organization. To do this, she facilitated sessions where all employees shared their ideas on a given topic. For example, one week the company met to discuss ways they could better serve their customers. A Gen X staff member spoke up and suggested using social media. Osgood documented the idea on yellow sticky notes and posted it on the wall for the team to consider. Another staff member spoke up and said that social media was not a professional method of communication. Osgood wrote this viewpoint on a sticky note and put it up on the wall. Then she asked the group to consider what social media offers. More ideas went up on the board.

---

1 In his book *The Human Side of Enterprise* (McGraw-Hill, 1960), Douglas McGregor introduced the concept of Theory X and Y management styles. Theory X assumes the average person dislikes work and therefore needs to be controlled and directed to get them to deliver. On the other hand, Theory Y assumes the opposite and is based on the idea that people will self-motivate if given the opportunity.

After some discussion, the group decided to try using social media for a week and return with recommendations on how the company should proceed. Eventually, older workers learned to trust the process, and Osgood's knowledge culture took off.

Creating an environment where people felt safe having ideas that differed from managements' was critical to the company's knowledge culture. The yellow sticky notes are among the tools she swears by.

"Whenever ideas are exchanged, use the yellow sticky notes so everyone's ideas go up," she said. "After a while, the pecking order goes away."

Over the years, Osgood has also added a common parenting technique to her facilitative management method. Instead of asking the team to come up with two solutions—which can be perceived as good and bad, right or wrong—she always seeks three. This removes the urge to vote one or the other idea down, and keeps the group thinking and collaborating. It's how Osgood cultivates what she calls "organizational citizenship," and creates an environment where each person participates and brings value to the larger group.

"By the time we get to the third choice, people are very engaged," Osgood said. "There is no good answer or bad answer. With three, you keep things very nonjudgmental."

Mind Your Seat

Something as simple as where leaders sit during meetings can have a profound effect on an organization's burgeoning knowledge culture. In many organizations, the leader always sits at the head of the table, and while they may not realize it, they are reinforcing a power position that may intimidate others. Osgood believes that hierarchies can destroy a knowledge culture, so she suggests everyone on the team—including the leader—sit in a different place around the table at every meeting.

Who's the Customer?

For Kent Greenes, knowledge cultures boil down to the simple premise that every person has knowledge, and that knowledge has many different "customers." For example, a Boomer subject matter expert has several knowledge customers, which could include management, peers, practitioners, and novices. Each of these customers needs something different from the Boomer subject matter expert, and each has a different opinion regarding what aspect of the expert's knowledge is most valuable.

Then there is the Boomer himself. He has his own opinion about what aspects of his knowledge are most important. (We cover knowledge self-capture later in this chapter.)

Once we understand that knowledge has different customers and that we have our own ideas about what is important to others, we can begin to think about who could benefit from what we know. When we routinely consider what knowledge others need, we begin to forge a knowledge culture, Greenes said.

"In organizations with very formal processes, managers can build in key decision points that say, 'go tap the database to find out what information is out there,'" Greenes said. "I don't think this is sustainable, though, because you won't get the informal sharing that is so effective; you'll only get what's planned. You'll only get what you pay for."

Rewriting the Job Description

Greenes asserts that in a knowledge culture, people go beyond their job descriptions to facilitate the flow of knowledge. Eric Kowalchyk, a Gen Y product manager for Intuit, may just prove Greenes' theory. In 2004, Intuit recruited Kowalchyk into its Rotational Development Program, a two-year program that gives high-achieving undergrads broad exposure to the business. Kowalchyk, who was 24 when Intuit recruited him, recalls how he and his fellow "RDPers" leveraged networks and shared knowledge across the organization. For example, if Kowalchyk was working with a Boomer manager who shared knowledge on various topics, he and others would pass it on to others in the group who weren't in attendance. This became a common, often informal practice, he said.

"We would share knowledge over lunch, over email...sometimes, we would post things we learned on shared sites we collaborated on," he said.

Kowalchyk said he has encountered Boomers who prefer to keep what they know to themselves, almost as a power play. This is a difficult mindset for Gen X and Millenials to accept because they have become so accustomed to creating networks across organizations and freely sharing what they know.

"The way I see it, why not share your knowledge so we all have it?" Kowalchyk said.

When managers consider the trends that define the various generations, Millenials could just be the future of knowledge cultures. Growing up with Web 2.0 tools at their fingertips, this group wants to approach work collaboratively. Other generations have also embraced these tools, and they use them as a way to express themselves and connect friends, colleagues, even strangers.

This is not to say that only managers who implement Web 2.0 tools can nurture a knowledge culture. There are many other ways to do this; however, the key is to make learning, sharing, and knowledge transfer routine and easy.

Greenes advises that organizations use After Action Reviews to help transform their culture, whether they implement a formal knowledge transfer program or not. If used routinely, AARs, with their simple structure and four basic questions, make knowledge sharing a regular part of an organization's learning structure. Managers can implement AAR's simple structure in one area of the business and spread the word about the results. They can also train their peers in other areas of the business on how to implement them.

Once knowledge sharing is woven into the organizational tapestry, losing Boomers—or any key worker—becomes less of a reason for panic and concern. When learning becomes explicit, knowledge cultures are much easier to sustain.

However, leaders can't simply say that knowledge sharing is everybody's job and expect the whole team to jump on board. Sure, there will be individuals who readily adopt the responsibilities of a knowledge culture, but others will assume someone else is already doing it and choose not to act. In other words, knowledge cultures don't just happen.

"It takes leadership," Larry Prusak said of creating a knowledge culture. "Leaders need to drive it and communicate to the group that this is how we make money—this is how we do our work. People need to understand it. And they will through communications, incentives, and enforcement."

Dual-Purpose Questions

Keep in mind that the free-form questions highlighted in the knowledge self-capture sidebar can also be helpful in creating stories to share with the organization. Consider documenting your knowledge through self-capture and taking it a step further by creating stories to share with others who could benefit from what you know.

The Generational Factor

Nearly every organization today has a multigenerational workforce. That means generational learning styles will play a role in the development of a knowledge culture.

Many organizations have made an effort to understand how different generations want to acquire knowledge. In fact, Greenes said that interest in generational learning styles reminds him of managers' use of Myers-Briggs personality type indicators during the 1980s.[2] The trend continues to this day.

With Myers-Briggs, or MBTI, employees answer a series of questions about how they view the world and make decisions. An MBTI facilitator then scores their responses and provides a detailed narrative about the individual's personality type. Whether employees believe the MBTI scores are accurate or not, filling out the questionnaire and discussing preferences and personality type gives everyone an opportunity to look inward.

"Many companies got into Myers-Briggs and learned there were no right or wrong personalities," Greenes said. "They learned that people had a better chance of working effectively with one another if they understood where people were coming from."

For Greenes, understanding generational learning differences is just as important as understanding personality types. But just as with MBTI, managers should use what they know about generational learning styles as guidelines, not hard-and-fast rules.

"It can be confusing because some generations have preferences that are typical of other generations," Greenes said. "For example, I am a Boomer, but I prefer to learn like a Millennial. I want to tap many different sources until I find what I need. Now that I can do this easily using the Internet and other tools, that's the way I prefer to work."

Every person is different, regardless of age. But some general rules exist that can help managers zero in on the best way to build a knowledge culture in their organization based on their staff's various learning styles. Osgood has built her organizations' knowledge culture on the premise that every person has strengths and weaknesses. In her view, a good facilitative manager builds on the strengths, making the weaknesses less relevant. Osgood does this by encouraging participation, creativity, and innovation across the organization and paying attention to how her staff responds. She also has some general ideas about people, honed over nearly three decades in management, that she relies on when getting to know individuals from varying generations.

---

2 Mother-daughter team Katharine Cook Briggs and Isabel Briggs Myers developed the Myers-Briggs assessment in 1943. In 1975, CPP became the exclusive publisher of the Myers-Briggs instrument. In 2008, CPP reported that more than 3.5 million questionnaires were completed worldwide every year. www.cpp.com, www.opp.eu.com.

Generally speaking, Osgood finds that Boomers expect a more structured, hierarchical, authoritative environment because this is what they are accustomed to finding in the workplace. Younger workers want the exact opposite environment, she said.

"Many of these young people did not have a lot of structure when they were growing up and so they find too much structure in the workplace oppressive," Osgood said. "Instead, what they often seek is constructive guidance."

Older workers want managers to tell them what to do, and they will do it. Younger workers want to be given space to try new things, but they want to be reassured often that what they are doing has value. Osgood takes time to accommodate these generational nuances and has even come to discover some trends on her own along the way.

For example, being a Boomer herself, she recalls how Boomers went through school and basically received a diploma twice: once when they graduated from high school, and again when they graduated from college. On the other hand, the younger generations likely started receiving diplomas in kindergarten, and frequently received awards and other formal recognition throughout their educational career for academics, sports, membership in community organizations, the list goes on. Younger generations became accustomed to receiving praise just for showing up; Boomers did not have this experience, Osgood said.

After years of working with younger individuals, Osgood said she thinks that by the time they get to the workplace, they tend not to trust the manager who doles out praise for every little thing. This generation has received so much recognition over their lifetime that it is not a motivator in the same way that it has been for Boomers.

"Younger workers are looking for something real," Osgood said. "They want to make a difference. As a facilitative manager, you have to find out what this is and within the framework of the organization's mission, collaborate in creating a work environment where they can prove to themselves that they can do it, and then reward them accordingly when they do. They really respond to this kind of management."

Of course, being dialed into individuals' needs and differences to this degree takes time and energy. But it's worth it.

"If you are a conscious manager, that means you are living in the moment," Osgood said. "When you come into a meeting, you can't be thinking about your spouse or other to-do items on your schedule that day. You have to be there in that moment and totally attuned with your team to facilitate a knowledge culture."

Capturing Your Own Knowledge

We may think we know what we need from colleagues, but the truth is, they probably know better than we do. When it's time to tap someone's knowledge, don't simply ask for what you think you need, let them tell you what they believe will be helpful. Personal insights are important, and can yield information and knowledge that's previously been hidden.

Knowledge self-capture[3] accomplishes two objectives. First, it creates a hard and soft copy trail of information and knowledge for others to refer to. And second, it gives readers, who could include managers, mentees, peers, and others, an opportunity to ask additional questions for the record.

There are many ways to approach knowledge self-capture.

One method requires individuals to reflect on major projects or initiatives they contributed to during their career.[4] Once they have singled out some projects, they begin to document their role and the approach they used. Piktialis and Greenes provide some questions to help individuals draw out valuable knowledge. Those questions include the following:

- How did the outcome meet your expectations? How did it fail?
- What surprised you most? What frustrated you most?
- If you were starting the project tomorrow, what would you do differently and why?

Another method for capturing this kind of knowledge is to pinpoint a few recent projects that you want to ask the individual about. Then ask a cross-section of your team to provide a handful of questions they would like to ask the individual. By doing this, you'll receive a variety of questions from different levels of the organization. Select the most specific questions and organize them in a document. Present the individual with the list before they begin the knowledge self-capture process. Having a list of questions from the team will help focus the individual, and may also spark memories of topics they may not have planned to discuss.

If time and resources permit, consider asking a note-taker to meet with the individual one day a week to help them document their knowledge. Having another person to interact with can also spark ideas and help the individual focus.

---

3 Diane Piktialis and Kent Greenes discussed knowledge self-capture in The Conference Board report, Bridging the Gaps: How to Transfer Knowledge in Today's Multigenerational Workplace.

4 Ibid. 2008. p. 43.

Recruiting in a Knowledge Culture

Every person is not going to embrace the idea of freely sharing knowledge. In fact, Deborah Osgood has noted that people who prefer to be the center of attention tend not to feel comfortable in such an open, democratic environment. Here are some questions that Osgood uses during interviews to learn more about how a candidate might fit into her organization's culture:

1. *Give me an example of work you recently performed in a team environment. What did you like about the experience? What didn't you like?*

2. *What have you learned about yourself? Osgood said she is often surprised by how people respond to this question. When they ask for clarification, Osgood lobs the question back, gently insisting they answer the question the way they want to interpret it.*

Making the Change

Creating a knowledge transfer program and instilling behaviors that nurture a knowledge culture require research, resolve, action, and soul-searching. As you can see, there are many moving parts to these initiatives. And, as with any large effort, leaders benefit from using strategies that help the organization embrace new programs and ideals. These strategies, also called *change enablers*,[5] include:

- Senior leadership support
- Communications and recognition
- Training
- Measurement

These strategies aren't new. You've used and relied on them in different ways throughout the process, from analysis to evaluation. Now let's look at them from the perspective of leaders who are working to sustain a knowledge transfer program and build a knowledge culture.

---

5 The American Productivity and Quality Center. Retaining Today's Knowledge for Tomorrow's Work Force: Strategies and Tactics for Knowledge Retention and Transfer. Consortium Benchmarking Study. www.apqc.org. 2007. p. 58.

Senior Leadership Support

To keep a knowledge culture alive, managers must communicate its value to the team. They can't do this important work alone. Executives, while perhaps not directly involved with day-to-day knowledge activities, must support the organizational effort in a visible, enthusiastic way. Essentially, staff must be aware that executives and other leaders believe in sharing knowledge and cultivating an environment where every individual has something valuable to offer.

Senior leadership support is so important that some organizations include knowledge-sharing goals in performance appraisals.[6] Fluor, an engineering, procurement, construction, maintenance, and project management company whose knowledge communities we discussed in Chapter 6, is one such organization.

At Fluor, leaders at all levels show their support for knowledge retention efforts in very visible ways, the APQC reported in Retaining Today's Knowledge for Tomorrow's Work Force. Executive-level representatives for each of the industry groups review Fluor's knowledge management activities, and other leaders guide the organization's various knowledge communities.

Knowledge management projects are often viewed as belonging either to IT or Human Resources. But Fluor's emphasis on deploying communities across the organization and communicating results led to a feeling of ownership across all business units.[7] Without executive support, this far-reaching change would not have been possible.

In some organizations, senior executive support may mean a top-down mandate to use the system that supports the knowledge culture.

Communications and Recognition

There are many ways to share the news that comes out of a knowledge culture. Some organizations the APQC, a best practices and benchmarking research firm, has studied routinely distribute messages about knowledge sharing through communities of practice, employee networks, and newsletters. Others use lunch-and-learn sessions and bring the group together in a more personal way to discuss the flow of knowledge in the organizations.

Fluor, which launched its first knowledge community in 2000, communicates often about knowledge sharing across the global organization. However, they are careful not to spam their audiences with needless email. Instead, they

---

6 American Productivity and Quality Center. Retaining Today's Knowledge for Tomorrow's Work Force: Strategies and Tactics for Knowledge Retention and Transfer. Consortium Benchmarking Study. 2007. p. 60.

7 Fluor internal document.

change the content on the home page of their knowledge management site twice a week. Communications might include stories related to knowledge management and communities, and images to draw audiences. Changing the home page on a regular basis keeps the content fresh, and reminds staff that their knowledge management system is always changing.

Communications Director Tara Keithley said that Fluor keeps these home page communications short, simple, and provocative. For example, Keithley once heard from a colleague that individuals were emailing each other looking for pieces of information instead of going into the knowledge management system, where questions—and their answers—would be captured for others to view. Keithley took the email request and posted it to the home page with the question, "Does this look familiar?" The goal was to remind Fluor staff to go to the knowledge management system first. This way, knowledge and answers to questions wouldn't be hidden in individual emails scattered across the organization.

Fluor also celebrates its knowledge communities during its annual Knowvember campaign. During the campaign, the Fluor knowledge management team urges its global staff to send in success stories around their use of knowledge communities. Then the contest is on, with executives serving as judges. Because the stories are always about people collaborating to find solutions, Fluor decided to invite winners to name a charity of their choice, and the company makes a generous donation. The winning stories are featured on the knowledge management site home page, along with the charity the winner chose.

Knowvember does more than just get people talking about how they share knowledge, it gives the organizations new stories to communicate, internally and externally, said John McQuary, vice president of Knowledge Management and Technology Strategies. Posting the story and congratulating the winners in a very public way also serves as a form of recognition.

Training

Training gives individuals the skills, knowledge, and attributes they need to function effectively in a knowledge culture. Training could be a simple lunch-and-learn about how to use the new wiki. Or it could be a course on facilitating a community of practice, or the best ways to interact and work with a mentor or mentee.

Managers may also want to blend training methods. For example, for a storytelling program, prospective storytellers may benefit from coaching and computer-based training. This approach would allow individuals to receive face-to-face feedback while also providing some basic content in a training module they could use anytime. AAR facilitators may also benefit from some coaching and instruction on how to lead these meetings effectively.

Measurement

"You can't improve what you don't measure."[8] Remember this common adage as you sustain your knowledge culture. Tracking metrics for the life of the effort will help you stay informed about what's going well and what needs to change. You may continue to use the same metrics that you created during the analysis phase. These will be among the most meaningful because they will provide an accurate picture of how the program and culture have evolved over time.

You may decide to add other metrics as time goes on. Whereas in the beginning you may have used attrition and customer surveys as data points, now you may be more interested in success stories and trends. Remember, when you change your data points, you must allow yourself some time to become familiar with what looks good. Adding metrics can be helpful, but it also means you must wait a while before you have anything solid to report. Every time you add metrics, you go back to the drawing board.

A Sound Investment

As many leaders know, going back to the drawing board isn't always a bad thing. In fact, leaders may learn their organizations are at risk of losing Boomer knowledge during regular reviews of operations and productivity.

Each leader will face the challenge of preserving knowledge in a different way. Some will choose to prepare, or make up for lost time. Some will wait, citing data that shows Boomers staying in the workforce longer. Others, who may not employ many Boomers, if any, will keep running the business as they always have. Regardless of the route they choose to take, leaders should build their plans for the future on solid workforce and audience analyses. And, whether or not managers implement programs designed to transfer Boomer knowledge to incoming generations, they would be wise to focus on their people and instill an interest in sharing knowledge across the organization.

Deborah Osgood, reflecting on her years in manufacturing, said that as more companies move routine production work overseas, American companies must foster innovation and creativity in their workforce if they want to

---

8 American Productivity and Quality Center. Retaining Today's Knowledge for Tomorrow's Work Force: Strategies and Tactics for Knowledge Retention and Transfer. Consortium Benchmarking Study. 2007. p. 63.

remain competitive. One of the most effective ways to do this is to encourage individual talents and build a collaborative culture where knowledge flows from person to person, regardless of age.

Initiatives such as mentoring and storytelling programs, communities, and regular After Action Reviews are an excellent place to start. Once you've launched the program, keep going.

"If you have invested the time and efforts to design a program to capture and transfer knowledge, take the extra step and make it part of the way you run your organization," said Vic Passion. "If you build the mechanism and limit it to a single program, you aren't getting the most bang for your buck."

In other words, if you develop a mentoring program or a community in response to Boomers leaving, consider whether you want to build another one. If your answer is yes, leverage the program somewhere else in your organization. Make it viral. Look for ways to make knowledge sharing so easy that it becomes second nature.

Of course, preparing for knowledge loss and forging a knowledge culture takes hard work and time. But hanging on to knowledge and energizing your organization are attainable goals—all you need is a plan.

"You have to help people understand why you're doing this, and the value it can bring to the organization," Passion said. "Then you have to answer the question, 'what's in it for me?'"

Bibliography

Books

Beazley, Hamilton, Jeremiah Boenisch, and David Harden. *Continuity Management*. Wiley. 2002.

Coupland, Douglas. *Generation X: Tales for an Accelerated Culture*. St. Martin's Press. 1991.

Croker, Richard. *The Boomer Century, 1946-2046: How America's Most Influential Generation Changed Everything*. Springboard Press. 2007.

Cross, Robert L. and Andrew Parker. *The Hidden Power of Social Networks: Understanding How Work Really Gets Done in Organizations*. Harvard Business Press. 2004.

Davenport, Thomas H. and Laurence Prusak. *Working Knowledge: How Organizations Manage What They Know*. Harvard Business School Press. 1998.

DeLong, David W. *Lost Knowledge: Confronting the Threat of an Aging Workforce*. Oxford University Press. 2004.

Dychtwald, Ken. *Age Power: How the 21st Century Will Be Ruled by the New Old*. Tarcher. 2000.

Dychtwald, Ken, Tamara J. Erickson, and Robert Morison. *Workforce Crisis: How to Beat the Coming Shortage of Skills and Talent*. Harvard Business Press. 2006.

English, Michael J. and William H. Baker. *Winning the Knowledge Transfer Race.* McGraw-Hill. 2005.

Freedman Marc. *Prime Time: How Baby Boomers Will Revolutionize Retirement and Transform America.* Public Affairs. 2002.

Koulopoulos, Thomas M. and Carl Frappaolo. *Smart Things to Know About, Knowledge Management.* Capstone. 2001.

Lancaster, Lynne C. and David Stillman. *When Generations Collide: Who They Are. Why They Clash. How to Solve the Generational Puzzle at Work.* Harper Paperbacks. 2003.

Leonard, Dorothy and Walter C. Swap. *Deep Smarts: How to Cultivate and Transfer Enduring Business Wisdom.* Harvard Business Press. 2005.

Liebowitz, Jay. *Making Cents Out of Knowledge Management.* The Scarecrow Press. 2008.

Murray, Margo. *Beyond the Myths and Magic of Mentoring: How to Facilitate an Effective Mentoring Process.* Jossey-Bass. 2001.

O'Dell, Carla and C. Jackson Grayson. *If Only We Knew What We Know: The Transfer of Internal Knowledge and Best Practice.* Free Press. 1998.

Polanyi, Michael. *The Tacit Dimension.* Doubleday & Company, Inc., Garden City, New York, 1966.

Sadler, William. *The Third Age: Six Principles for Personal Growth and Rejuvenation after Forty.* Da Capo Press. 2001.

Strauss, William and Neil Howe. *Generations: The History of America's Future 1584 to 2069.* William Morrow & Company. 1991.

Sujansky, Joanne and Jan Ferri-Reed. *Keeping the Millennials: Why Companies Are Losing Billions in Turnover to This Generation—and What to Do About It.* Wiley. 2009.

White, Jan V. *Graphic Design for the Electronic Age.* Watson-Guptill Publications, New York. 1988.

Williams, Robin. *The Non-Designer's Design Book.* Second Edition. Peachpit Press. 2004.

Zachary, Lois. *The Organization's Guide: Creating a Mentoring Culture.* Jossey-Bass. 2005.

Selected Reports, Articles, and Other Documents

AARP (Report prepared by Towers Perrin). "The Business Case for Workers Age 50+: Planning for Tomorrow's Talent Needs in Today's Competitive Environment." 2005.

AARP and Roper Starch Worldwide Inc. "Baby Boomers Envision Their Retirement, an AARP Segmentation Analysis." 1999.

AARP, Cummins, Rachelle. "Putting Aging Workforce on Employment Planning Radar: Results from an AARP/Florida Trend Survey." October, 2005.

American Society of Training and Development. *Training and Development* (various issues).

Cambridge, Darren, Soren Kaplan and Vicki Suter. Community of Practice Design Guide. 2005.

Cappelli, Peter. "Will There Really Be a Labor Shortage?" *Organizational Dynamics*, Vol. 32, No. 3. 2003.

Coile, Courtney C. and Phillip B. Levine. "The Market Crash and Mass Layoffs: How the Current Economic Crisis May Affect Retirement." June, 2009.

County of Fairfax, Virginia, Department of Human Resources. Strategic Workforce Planning. August, 2003.

The Coyne Partnership, Inc. (Media Overview). "Smaller Than You Thought: Estimates of the Future Size and Growth Rate of the Retirement Market in the United States." May, 2008.

Dohm, Arlene. "Gauging the labor force effects of retiring baby-boomers." Bureau of Labor Statistics. *Monthly Labor Review*. July, 2000.

Fullerton, Howard N. Jr. *"Labor Force Participation: 75 years of change, 1950-98 and 1998-2025."* Monthly Labor Review. December, 1999.

Gotsill, Gina. "Cultural Consideration." *The Hospitalist*. December, 2008.

MetLife Mature Market Institute. "Boomer Bookends: Insights into the Oldest and Youngest Boomers." February, 2009.

Oblinger, Diane G. and James L. Oblinger. Editors. Educating the Net Generation. Educause e-book. 2005.

Toossi, Mitra. "Labor Force Projections to 2016: More workers in their golden years." Bureau of Labor Statistics. *Monthly Labor Review*. November, 2007.

USAID. After Action Review Technical Guidance. www.usaid.gov. February, 2006.

Wootton, Barbara H. "Gender differences in occupational employment." Bureau of Labor Statistics. *Monthly Labor Review*. April, 1997.

"Women at Work: A Visual Essay." Bureau of Labor Statistics, *Monthly Labor Review*. October, 2003.

Index